GOD *and* EMPIRE

GOD
and
EMPIRE

Jesus Against Rome,
Then and Now

JOHN DOMINIC CROSSAN

HarperOne
An Imprint of HarperCollinsPublishers

HarperOne

HarperCollins books may be purchased for educational, business, or sales promotional use. For information please write: Special Markets Department, HarperCollins Publishers, 10 East 53rd Street, New York, NY 10022.

HarperCollins Web site: http://www.harpercollins.com
HarperCollins®, 📖®, and HarperOne™ are
trademarks of HarperCollins Publishers.

FIRST HARPERCOLLINS PAPERBACK EDITION PUBLISHED IN 2008
Designed by Joseph Rutt

Library of Congress Cataloging-in-Publication Data is available.

ISBN: 978-0-06-085831-5

08 09 10 11 12 RRD(H) 10 9 8 7 6 5 4 3 2 1

for Sarah
on
our twentieth wedding anniversary

CONTENTS

GOD *and* EMPIRE

PROLOGUE

> From the first chipped stone to the first smelted iron took
> nearly three million years; from the first iron to the hydro-
> gen bomb took only 3,000 years.
>
> —RONALD WRIGHT,
> *A Short History of Progress* (2004)

For a very long time I have been pondering the texts and wandering the ruins of the Roman Empire. Initially, I did so as a biblical
scholar doing research for books I was writing on the historical
reconstruction of earliest Christianity: *The Historical Jesus* in 1991,
The Birth of Christianity in 1998, and *In Search of Paul,* co-authored
with the archaeologist Jonathan Reed of the University of La-
Verne, in 2004. I presume those three books as prelude and preparation for this book on *God and Empire*.

I have always thought of the historical Jesus as a homeland Jew
within Judaism within the Roman Empire. I have always thought
of the historical Paul as a diaspora Jew within Judaism within the
Roman Empire. For me, then, *within Judaism within the Roman
Empire* has always been the absolutely necessary *matrix* rather than
the annoyingly unnecessary *background* for any discussion of earliest Christianity. You can see that three-layer matrix, for example,
in the subtitles to the first and last books just named. For the historical Jesus, *The Life of a Mediterranean Jewish Peasant* emphasizes
Rome, Judaism, and Jew. For the historical Paul, *How Jesus's Apostle
Opposed Rome's Empire with God's Kingdom* emphasizes Jew, Rome,

and Judaism. Whether you start or end with the Roman Empire, the Roman Empire is always there.

But there is now a new reason for studying the textual and archaeological history of the Roman Empire. I have been hearing recently two rather insistent claims from across the spectrum of our religio-political life. The first one claims that America is now—and may always have been—an empire and that, in fact, the virus of imperialism came—like so many others—on those first ships from Europe. The second and subsidiary claim is that America is Nova Roma, the New Roman Empire, Rome on the Potomac.

Both of these claims are at least 150 years old. In the *New York Times* for June 27, 1860, Walt Whitman published a poem entitled "The Errand-Bearers" that triumphantly proclaimed America's imperial destiny:

> I chant the new empire, grander than any before—As in a
>   vision it comes to me;
> I chant America, the Mistress—I chant a greater supremacy....
> And you, Libertad of the world!
> You shall sit in the middle, well-pois'd, thousands of years....
> The sign is reversing, the orb is enclosed,
> The ring is circled, the journey is done.

That poem was later included as "A Broadway Pageant" in his epic *Leaves of Grass* of 1871.

Indeed, the American Empire had already been described elsewhere as the reborn Roman Empire by that same date. In his 1858 work *The Autocrat of the Breakfast-Table,* Oliver Wendell Holmes—father of the same-named associate justice of the U.S. Supreme Court—announced that "we are the Romans of the modern world—the great assimilating people. Conflicts and conquests are of course necessary accidents with us, as with our prototypes."

Within a few years of those triumphal claims, America dissolved into civil war, with one side defending the evil of *slavery*—the in-

justice of class over class—and the other side the (greater?) evil of
empire—the injustice of nation over nation. Still, even a terrible
civil war could be seen in parallel to Rome's story, and so as con-
firmation of our Roman destiny.

There is indeed a certain parallelism between the march of the
Roman Empire from Italy, around the Mediterranean, and out to
what they called "the earth" and our own advance from continen-
tal, through hemispheric, and on to global American Empire. But
it is the modern voices that assert the Romano-American Empire
that moved the creation of this book. That parallelism is repeated
again and again today—sometimes proudly, sometimes sadly,
sometimes with approval, sometimes with disapproval.

In the past year, I have read about a dozen books on this
topic—mostly on the sad and disapproving side of it. Here is but
one example, from Chalmers Johnson's 2004 book *The Sorrows of
Empire:*

> Americans like to say that the world changed as a result of
> the September 11, 2001, terrorist attacks on the World Trade
> Center and the Pentagon. It would be more accurate to say
> that the attacks produced a dangerous change in the thinking
> of some of our leaders, who began to see our republic as a
> genuine empire, a new Rome, the greatest colossus in history,
> no longer bound by international law, the concern of allies,
> or any constraints on its use of military force. (p. 3)

Furthermore, his chapter 3 is entitled "Toward the New Rome."
He emphasizes that America is "not an empire of colonies but an
empire of bases" (p. 23), but that we are still "the second coming of
the Roman Empire" (p. 284).

In a magnificently parabolic scene in John's gospel, Pilate confronts Jesus (or does Jesus confront Pilate?) about the kingdom he
proclaims. "My kingdom," says Jesus in the King James Version of
the incident, "is not of this world: if my kingdom were of this
world, then would my servants fight, that I should not be delivered

to the Jews: but now is my kingdom not from hence" (18:36). I take five foundational points from that brief interchange.

First, Jesus opposes the Kingdom of God to the kingdoms of "this world." What "this world" means is discussed throughout this book, but especially in chapter 1, whose title, "Empire and the Barbarism of Civilization," is my own translation of the "this world" of Jesus.

Second, Jesus is condemned to death by Roman Pilate, in Roman Judea, in the eastern reaches of the Roman Empire. But he never mentions Rome as such, and he never addresses Pilate by name.

Third, had Jesus stopped after saying that "my kingdom is not of this world," as we so often do in quoting him, that "of" would be utterly ambiguous. "Not of this world" could mean: never on earth, but always in heaven; or not now in present time, but off in the imminent or distant future; or not a matter of the exterior world, but of the interior life alone. Jesus spoils all of these possible misinterpretations by continuing with this: "if my kingdom were of this world, then would my servants fight, that I should not be delivered" up to execution. Your soldiers hold me, Pilate, but my companions will not attack you even to save me from death. Your Roman Empire, Pilate, is based on the injustice of violence, but my divine kingdom is based on the justice of nonviolence.

Fourth, the crucial difference—and the only one mentioned—between the Kingdom of God and the Kingdom of Rome is Jesus's nonviolence and Pilate's violence. The violence of Roman imperialism, however, was but one incarnation at that first-century time and in that Mediterranean place of "this world"—that is, of the violent normalcy of civilization itself (see my first point).

Fifth, the most important interpreter of Jesus in the entire New Testament is Pilate. He clearly recognizes the difference between Barabbas and Jesus. Barabbas is a violent revolutionary who "was in prison with the rebels who had committed murder during the insurrection" (Mark 15:7). Pilate arrested Barabbas along with those of his followers he could capture. But Jesus is a nonviolent revolutionary, so Pilate has made no attempt to round up his companions. Both Barabbas and Jesus oppose Roman injustice in the Jewish homeland, but Pilate knows exactly and correctly how to calibrate their divergent oppositions.

I emphasize that contrast between Pilate's Kingdom of Rome as violent repression and Jesus's Kingdom of God as nonviolent resistance because that juxtaposition is the heart of this book, which is an attempt to rethink God, the Bible, and empire, Jesus, Christianity, and Rome. Jesus could have told Pilate that Rome's rule was unjust and God's rule was just. That would have been true, but it would have avoided the issue of whether God's just rule was to be established by human or divine violence. So, beneath the problem of empire is the problem of justice, but beneath the problem of justice is the problem of violence.

From all of that, I raise three questions in this book for American Christians—or better, for Christian Americans. Since the Old Roman Empire crucified our Lord Jesus Christ, how can we be his faithful followers in America as the New Roman Empire? As we move through the book, a second question arises. Is our Christian Bible violent or nonviolent—is it actually for or against Jesus's nonviolent resistance to "this world"? By the time we get to the end of the book, and especially in its final chapter, a third question will have appeared. Is Bible-fed Christian violence supporting or even instigating our imperial violence as the New Roman Empire?

Monday, May 8, 2006
Hiroshima, Japan

EMPIRE AND THE BARBARISM OF CIVILIZATION

There is no document of civilization which is not at the
same time a document of barbarism.
—WALTER BENJAMIN,
On the Concept of History (1939)

Between 1945 and 1950, I spent my high school years at St. Eunan's
College in Letterkenny, Ireland. It was a central boarding school
for all those villages and towns in County Donegal too small to
have a secondary school of their own. I had a classical education
and every day for five years studied Greek and Latin, the original
languages of Homer and Cicero.

Even in that first generation of postcolonial Ireland, no teacher
ever mentioned that as we were learning to imitate the syntax of
Caesar's *Gallic Wars* we were ignoring the slaughter of our Celtic
ancestors. Moreover, no teacher ever emphasized twin facts that
now seem to me the two most important lessons of a classical education. Greece, having invented democratic rule, warns us that
we can have a *democracy* or an empire, but not both at the same
time—or at least not for long. Rome, having invented republican
rule, warns us that we can have a *republic* or an empire, but not
both at the same time—or not for long. Do we think those lessons

do not apply to a *democratic republic?* Or do we suspect that they may apply with doubled force?

ROME AND EMPIRE

I look at the Roman Empire neither to praise it nor to bury it, but to understand it as fairly and accurately as I can. Otherwise, I will not be able to understand where the Christian biblical tradition stands on Rome or any other empire (chapter 2) or why Rome crucified Jesus of Nazareth (chapter 3), executed Paul of Tarsus (chapter 4), and exiled John of Patmos (chapter 5).

First Among Equals—with All the Equals Dead

Rome invented an excellent solution to the danger of royal tyranny. There would be no dynastic kings, but two high aristocrats called consuls would rule together for one year. That way each could keep an eye on the other, and both would be out at the same time. That system was strong enough to withstand Rome's first great external threat, the attack of Hannibal from Carthage on the other side of the Mediterranean.

The consular system prevented royal tyranny for a while but eventually engendered civil war. Consular aristocrats became imperial warlords, and why then would they cooperate with each other? Too much, far too much, was now at stake. It looked as if the Roman system would self-destruct along the fault line created by that hyphen of republican-imperialism or imperial-republicanism, destroying the Mediterranean world as well in the process. The first round of that civil war set Julius Caesar against Pompey. It ended with both of these warlords assassinated, one in the Roman Senate, the other on an Egyptian beach. The second round set Antony and Octavian, Caesar's avengers, against Brutus and Cassius, Caesar's assassins. After two battles at Philippi near the eastern coast of Greece, the Caesarians were victorious, and the last hope for republican restoration died with the suicides of the defeated Brutus and Cassius. It was time for the third and final round.

Imagine San Francisco Bay as it opens westward to the Pacific Ocean with the twin promontories of that opening connected by the Golden Gate Bridge on a north-south axis. Imagine now another similar but smaller bay opening westward to the Ionian Sea between Greece and Italy. Its twin promontories extend and pass one another, and today they are connected by an underwater tunnel on an east-west axis. That is the Ambracian Gulf on the northwestern coast of Greece, and there by the summer of 31 BCE Antony and Cleopatra had gathered an army of one hundred thousand troops and a fleet of five hundred ships. But despite their superior numbers on both land and sea, they had two intensifying problems.

First, their fortified camp was on the marshy and mosquito-ridden flats of the bay's southern promontory, and malaria had decimated their forces during the summer of 31 BCE. Second, though their fleet was safely moored inside the gulf, it was also securely trapped behind that difficult opening, whose exit demanded a sharp turn first to port and then to starboard around the narrows of the southern Cape Actium. By September 2, their initial numerical superiority had been lost to disease, desertion, and despair. When their much-diminished fleet finally cleared the gulf that morning, it was possibly for fight, but probably for flight.

Antony's line of battle had three squadrons in formation to left, center, and right, with Cleopatra's flotilla immediately behind his center. Her flagship had taken on board both sails and pay-chest, so that escape seemed their primary purpose. Octavian had a similar triple formation waiting out in the Ionian Sea, with himself and Agrippa leading their left squadron to oppose Antony leading his own right. With the expected afternoon breezes, both of these northern fronts maneuvered to outflank one another, but Antony, after closing with the enemy, abandoned his own flagship to join Cleopatra on hers. That northward drift had opened up gaps in Octavian's line that allowed Antony, Cleopatra, and their escort ships to escape to Alexandria—not to fight another day but to die another day.

Antiquity's last great naval battle was over with around five thousand casualties. The Assisi-born contemporary poet Sextus Propertius gave Augustus this encomium in his *Elegies:*

> My songs are sung for Caesar's glory; while Caesar is being sung, do even you pray attend, Jupiter.... Where a bay lulls the roar of the Ionian Sea ... hither came to battle the forces of the world.... Apollo, leaving Delos ... stood over Augustus' ship.... Anon he spoke: "O savior of the world ... Augustus ... now conquer at sea: the land is already yours: my bow battles for you.".... Second only to his bow came [Julius] Caesar's spear.... But Father Caesar from the star of Venus looks marveling on: "I am a god; this victory is proof that you are of my blood." (4.6)

What sublime impertinence! Shut up, Jupiter, and listen, while I recount how the divine Apollo admires Octavian's cosmic salvation and the deified Julius admits Octavian's divine genealogy.

Octavian negotiated pay and peace with Antony and Cleopatra's abandoned legions and prepared to pursue them to Alexandria, where their deaths solved the inconvenience of displaying a Roman general and an Egyptian queen as condemned prisoners in Octavian's eventual triumphal procession. Better a double suicide far removed from Roman eyes. But Octavian immediately executed young Caesarion, son of Cleopatra and Julius Caesar, who was, after all, a *divi filius,* or "son of god" by birth, not adoption, like Octavian himself. Caesarion was a son of god too many. Octavian was *Princeps,* first among equals with all the equals dead, and he would soon be the "One-to-Be-Worshiped" (*Sebastos* in Greek), or the Divine One (*Augustus* in Latin).

It was finally over, definitively over, after twenty years of interlegionary fratricide that had devastated much of the Mediterranean world and threatened the very survival of the Roman

Empire itself. Imagine, therefore, a giant sigh of relief, as it were, from all around that Roman lake, because whatever one thought about imperial military control, imperial civil war was worse. That relief helps to explain Ramsay MacMullen's claim, in his 2003 book *Romanization in the Time of Augustus,* that

> Roman civilization eventually appeared everywhere, as one single thing, so far as it was ever achieved. The degree of achievement, however imperfect, remains a thing of wonder, familiar to everyone.... Never, however, was there greater progress made toward one single way of life, a thing to be fairly called "Roman civilization of the Empire," than in that lifetime of Augustus.... The natives would be taught, if it was not plain enough on its face, that they could better rise into the ranks of the master race by reforming themselves—by talking, dressing, looking, and in every way resembling Romans. They would and did respond as ambition directed. They pulled Roman civilization to them—to their homes, their families, their world. (pp. ix–x, 134)

Granted the immediacy and ubiquity of Roman domination, how was it maintained and expanded? What was the source of Roman imperial power?

The Hawser of Imperial Power

Any attempt to understand Rome or to compare it to other empires, past or present, requires some basis in historical, comparative, or macro-sociology. Otherwise, contrasts are undisciplined, and we can say whatever we want about similarities and dissimilarities.

Michael Mann, Professor of Sociology at the Berkeley campus of the University of California, is writing a four-volume study on *The Sources of Social Power;* the first two volumes were published in 1986 and 1993. In the first volume, *A History of Power from the Beginning to A.D. 1760,* Mann writes that:

the interest of Rome lies in its imperialism. It was one of the most successful conquering states in all history, but it was *the* most successful *retainer* of conquests. Rome institutionalized the rule of its legions more stably and over a longer period than any other society before or since.... This empire of domination eventually became a true *territorial* empire, or at least had about as high a level and intensity of territorial control as could be attained within the logistical constraints imposed on all agrarian societies.... What Rome acquired, Rome kept. (p. 250, emphasis in original)

A *territorial* empire keeps the army on the periphery and integrates everything within those guarded frontiers into one functioning whole. So how and why did Rome become the first territorial empire in the history of the world?

For Mann, social power is not so much a thing in itself as a combination of four types of power united together: *military* power, the monopoly or control of force and violence; *economic* power, the monopoly or control of labor and production; *political* power, the monopoly or control of organization and institution; and *ideological* power, the monopoly or control of interpretation and meaning. Following Mann, I think of social or imperial power as a giant hawser mooring ship to shore, a hawser that has four interwoven strands and whose overall strength comes both from those individual components and also from their tight combination and closed interaction.

Rome's *military* power was based on the legions, each with six thousand fighting engineers at full complement. They were stationed along the Rhine, the Danube, the Euphrates, and the North African frontiers. The twenty-eight (and then only twenty-five) legions built well-paved all-weather roads (no mud) and high-arched all-weather bridges (no flood); with this infrastructure, they could move with all their baggage and equipment at a guaranteed fifteen miles a day to crush any rebellion anywhere. It was not nation-building but province-building, and the idea that such was not the military's job would have seemed ludicrous to the legions.

Rome's *economic* power grew along and upon that same infrastructure. Built for military use, it was thereafter available for travel and trade, contact and commerce. Furthermore, the cash payments to the legions along the frontiers helped to monetize the periphery. After military conquest, the imperial program was Romanization by urbanization for commercialization. And of course, those who oppose your globalization, *then and now,* come violently or nonviolently against you along the global arteries you have created.

Rome's *political* power was established through a self-consciously Romanized aristocracy created across the entire empire that allowed some high local elites to be members of the Roman Senate. It was even eventually possible for a Romanized provincial to become emperor. "The Roman landholding elite," concludes Michael Mann, "was about as 'classlike' as any group in any known society, past or present" (p. 270). Local elites saw very clearly what they got in return for imperial loyalty.

Rome's *ideological* power was created by Roman imperial theology, and it is not possible to overestimate its importance. Military power certainly secured the empire's external frontiers, but ideological power sustained its internal relations. Do not think of it as propaganda enforced by believing elites upon unbelieving masses. Think of it as persuasive advertising accepted very swiftly by all sides. I return later to look at the content of that theology—in written text and on carved inscription—and at how it worked as the ideological glue that held the Roman world together.

I had read and been persuaded by Mann's fourfold analysis of social and imperial power before the terrorist attacks against our country on September 11, 2001, but that day confirmed it for me. Although thousands of Americans were tragically killed, that slaughter was not the primary purpose or logic of the combined attacks. Think, once again, of these four types of social power.

Our *military* power was symbolized globally by the Pentagon: it was struck by American Airlines flight 77 out of Washington's Dulles Airport. Our *economic* power was symbolized globally by the twin towers of the World Trade Center: they were struck by American Airlines flight 11 and United Airlines flight 175, both out of Boston's Logan Airport. Our *political* power was symbolized globally by the White House and the Capitol: United Airlines flight 93 was half an hour late out of Newark, and once the passengers learned by cell phone about the terrorists' aim to crash into one of those buildings, their courage brought down the plane in a rural field far from Washington. "With the sounds of the passenger counter-attack continuing," wrote *The 9/11 Commission Report,*

> the aircraft plowed into an empty field in Shanksville, Pennsylvania, at 580 miles per hour, about 20 minutes' flying time from Washington, D.C. [The terrorist-pilot] Jarrah's objective was to crash his airliner into symbols of the American Republic, the Capitol or the White House. He was defeated by the alerted, unarmed passengers of United 93. (1.1)

But what about that last and most crucial of all types of power—what about our *ideological* power? In this case, the purpose of that terrorist attack (and all terrorist attacks?) was not to destroy our ideological power directly. Indeed, the immediate global outpouring of sympathy only strengthened it. But the terrorist purpose was to damage and destroy our ideology indirectly, to *have us do it for them,* to tempt us and lure us into actions at home and abroad that would slowly but surely erode our ideological power both internally and externally.

Mann's fourfold analysis of social and imperial power is extremely helpful and convincing. But I have one fundamental disagreement with his analysis—not concerning the violent heart of civilization, nor those four *parts* of power, but concerning something even more basic: the two *modes* of power.

Since there is always a military component to power for Mann, he presumes a basis of force and violence—that is, of power-as-violent. He never considers nonviolent power—the power not of force and violence but of persuasion and attraction. I always find power ambiguous until it becomes clear whether we are dealing with the violent power of domination or the nonviolent power of persuasion. Throughout the rest of this book, I probe that second mode of power, and I want even at this point to emphasize its existence, since violent repression and nonviolent resistance are both modes of social power.

Roman Imperial Theology

I focus now on Roman imperial theology as the ideological power of the Roman Empire, deliberately avoiding such dismissive terms as "Roman mythology" or "Emperor cult." (I certainly would not describe the medieval European world as "Christian mythology" or "the Christ cult.") I have two reasons for this special emphasis on ideology within the fourfold structure of imperial power.

First, Rome spoke of itself in transcendental terms as an empire divinely mandated to rule without limits of time or place. It did not simply proclaim dominion around the Mediterranean Sea. It announced world conquest, global rule, and eternal sovereignty.

Second, when Jesus of Nazareth, Paul of Tarsus, and John of Patmos came against the Roman Empire, they did so not with military, economic, or political power but exclusively with ideological power. To understand them later in this book, we must first understand the details of that ideology because it necessarily dictated the terms and titles of their resistance and their rejection of Roman imperialism.

For my present purpose, I focus on only two sources of that ideological glue that held Roman imperialism together—poetic texts about Augustus and inscriptions from Augustus. For other sources, such as coins, images, and structures, I recommend—with, of course, complete impartiality—the book *In Search of Paul* mentioned in the prologue. Do not think of those sources as propaganda enforced from the top down on an unbelieving population. Think of Roman imperial theology as an immensely successful advertising campaign that inundated everyone, everywhere, from all sides and at all times. Think of it the way modern-day advertising proclaims to us not just that a particular product or service is superior to all others, but that trade, commerce, business, and profit rule our present and shape our future.

I begin with key texts from the Augustan poets, Virgil, Horace, and Ovid, and continue with the most important inscriptions dictated by Augustus himself. These texts and inscriptions were constitutive of Roman imperial theology from Augustus, through Augustus, and even after Augustus.

Virgil

In Christian terms, Rome's Old Testament was Homer's *Iliad* and *Odyssey,* texts about a land war that led to a sea voyage, and its New Testament was Virgil's *Aeneid,* about a sea voyage leading to a land war. Virgil's great epic celebrating Rome's manifest destiny was published after the poet's death in 19 BCE by decree of Caesar Augustus. Four aspects of that destiny are dramatized in the *Aeneid.*

First, *heavenly decree.* Rome began in heaven, according to Virgil's *Aeneid,* when the goddess Aphrodite-Venus reminded her father, the supreme god Zeus-Jupiter, of his promise that the Romans would descend from "my Aeneas" (the child of the divine Venus and the human Anchises) as "rulers to hold the sea and all lands beneath their sway" (1.231, 236). Zeus-Jupiter affirmed his promise: "For these I set no bounds in space or time; but have given empire without end.... The Romans, lords of the world, and the nation of the toga. Thus it is decreed" (1.278–83).

Second, *ancient lineage.* In the *Iliad,* the Trojan hero Hector is killed by the Greek hero Achilles, who cruelly and contemptuously drags Hector's body by its pierced heels behind his chariot to the beached ships of the Greek fleet. As Troy falls, Hector appears to Aeneas as a specter from Hades "showing the wounds, the many wounds, received outside his father's city walls" (2.278–79).

Forewarned of impending disaster, Aeneas flees the doomed city, carrying on one shoulder his aged father, Anchises, and holding by the other hand his young son, Ascanius-Julus. But above all else, Anchises carries on his lap their household gods. In other words, Rome's ancestry began with *piety* for both family values and ancestral gods as those proto-Romans followed their destiny and Venus's star westward to Italy.

Over a full millennium before the time of Julius Caesar, Ascanius-Julus, the alleged progenitor of the Julian line, moved the future of the Julio-Roman world from Troy to Rome and from East to West—by the promise of Zeus-Jupiter and by the protection of Aphrodite-Venus. Many of those who could neither read nor even hear the *words* of Virgil knew that story from *images* around the Roman world. "The Flight to Italy" was as recognizable to first-century Romans as "the Flight to Egypt" was to later-century Christians on the stone shafts of Ireland's high crosses or on the stained glass of Europe's Gothic cathedrals.

Third, *prophetic promise*. Rome's foundational epic continued with reiterated preparatory and prophetic confirmations about its future glory. And notice that its manifest destiny was never just about rule over Italy or the Mediterranean but about dominion over the whole world.

In Hades, Aeneas is reminded of his vocation while visiting his dead father, Anchises. "You, Roman," says Anchises, "be sure to rule the world (be these your arts), to crown peace with justice, to spare the vanquished and to crush the proud" (6.851–53). The "proud," of course, were all those who resisted the "peace" of Romanization.

In Italy, Latinus, king of Latium in west-central Italy, gave his daughter Lavinia as wife to Aeneas, thereby establishing peace between the native Latins and the immigrant Trojans. He had heard an oracle proclaim that "strangers shall come, to be your sons, whose blood shall exalt our name to the stars, and the children of whose race shall behold, where the circling sun looks on east and west, the whole world roll obediently beneath their feet" (7.98–101). Later he recognized that Aeneas "must be the offspring, glorious in valor, whose might is to master all the world" (7.257–58).

Fourth, *divine victory.* None of the preceding claims would have been credible or even possible without this fourth and final element—without, that is, Octavian's naval victory off Cape Actium. Virgil knew that, of course, so how could he link his *Aeneid*'s thousand-year-old Trojan beginning to its contemporary Actian consummation? In a minor stroke of genius, he had Vulcan, the smith-god consort of Venus, create a great shield for Aeneas on which Rome's predestined future was visually prophesized.

That shield would depict "the story of Italy and the triumphs of Rome" (8.626) across a thousand-plus years from Aeneas to Augustus. But in that summary-update of Roman history, everything before Actium got the same amount of space as Actium itself! And that battle was not portrayed as the civil war of one Roman warlord against another, but as the great contest of civilized Western deities against barbaric Eastern ones:

> On the one side, Augustus Caesar stands on the lofty stern, leading Italians to strife, with Senate and People, the Penates [official gods] of the state, and all the mighty gods; his auspicious brows shoot forth a double flame, and on his head dawns his father's star.... On the other side comes Antony with barbaric might and motley arms, victorious over the nations of the dawn and the ruddy sea [Indian Ocean], bringing in his train Egypt and the strength of the east and farthest Bactra [Afghanistan]; and there follows him (oh the shame of it!) his Egyptian wife.... Monstrous gods of every form and barking Anubis wield weapons against Neptune and Venus and against Minerva. (8.678–99)

At the heart of the *Aeneid* is a divinely detailed prophecy of September 2, 31 BCE, that fateful day when the future rule of the

Roman Empire and the future shape of the Western world hung in the balance for one long afternoon.

Horace

Since Rome had many gods and goddesses, there was always the danger that the divine Augustus might be seen as but one more god among the many—or worse still, that he might be seen as a rather belated divinity. Horace, Virgil's friend and contemporary, averted that danger with this encomium in his *Epistles:*

> Romulus, father Liber, Hercules, Pollux and Castor who, after mighty deeds, were welcomed into the temples of the gods, so long as they [lived among us], lamented that the goodwill hoped for matched not what they deserved. Upon you [Augustus], however, while still among us, we already bestow honors, set up altars to swear by in your name, and confess that nothing like you will arise after you or has arisen before you. (2.1)

Other human beings who had greatly benefited their fellows were divinized only after their death, but Caesar Augustus was unique in having achieved divine status while still alive. Nothing like him, therefore, had come before or would come after him.

Ovid

This younger contemporary of Virgil and Horace explains the meaning of the title "Augustus" in the *Fasti,* his never-completed poem on the Roman calendar:

> [Augustus's] name is shared by Jupiter Supreme. The Fathers call holy things "august," they call temples "august," duly or-dained by priestly hands. "Augury," too, derives from the

word's root, and all that Jupiter "augments" with his power. (1.608–612)

But in a later chapter he more or less turns Augustus into Jupiter incarnate—or better, into the Jupiter of earth:

> Holy Father of the fatherland, the *plebs* gave you this name, the senate gave it and we knights. History gave it first: you received your true names late. You have long been Father of the World. Jupiter's name in high heaven is yours on earth: You the father of men, he of the gods.... [Caesar Augustus's] leadership has Romanized the sun....All beneath high Jupiter is Caesar's. (2.127–38)

Despite all of that, Ovid was eventually exiled to the Black Sea's western coast for inadequate obedience to Augustus's moral rearmament of the Roman aristocracy. From there, in his *Tristia* (*Sorrows of an Exile*), he imagined himself restored to Rome, wandering with a guide around the Palatine Hill and seeing a magnificent palace:

> "Is this the home of Jove?" I asked. I thought so, auguring from the crown of oak above. Learning its owner [was Augustus], "I was right," I answered. "It's true this is the home of mighty Jove." (3.1)

Here Augustus *is* Jupiter, and no qualifications are added. Unfortunately, even that adulation did not obtain reprieve, and Ovid died at the back of the Roman beyond, three years after Augustus.

It is interesting, by the way, how little trouble these Augustan poets had with a *living* human person being at the same time a *living* divine being. Their logic was flawlessly simple. Gods run the world. Caesar runs the world. Therefore, Caesar is a god. For a fuller and more detailed outline of Roman imperial theology, I turn next to two inscriptions—one very short and the other very long—dictated by Augustus almost forty years apart. Watch for the consistency of their content.

Nicopolis in Greece

The "Victory City" of Nicopolis was built by Octavian to commemorate his Actian triumph, to Romanize the surrounding area, and to secure the legionary highway connection from the Via Appia southward in Italy to the Via Egnatia eastward in Greece. "To extend the fame of his victory at Actium and perpetuate its memory," wrote the Roman historian Suetonius in his early-second-century life of *The Deified Augustus,* "he founded a city called Nikopolis near Actium, and provided for the celebration of games there every four years; enlarged the ancient temple of Apollo; and consecrated the site of the camp that he had used to Neptune and Mars, after adorning it with naval spoils" (18:2).

Today signs from the Ministry of Culture are posted at the ruins of the city's large theater and small odeum, warning: APPROACHING IS PROHIBITED. DANGER OF MONUMENT PARTS' COLLAPSE. You can still enter the much better preserved and more safely secured stadium where Octavian established the quadrennial Actian Games, second only to the Olympic Games, as part of his new city's elevated status. But the ancient city's most important ruin is slightly farther to the north, near the small village of Smirtoúla, where Octavian pitched his command tent at the foot of the Mikhalitsi Hills, with the Bay of Gomares and his fleet to the west and the Gulf of Ambracia and the opposing fleet to the east.

There was nothing particularly unusual about Octavian establishing a new Victory City, and besides, he could hardly have placed a triumphal arch on the site of a naval battle out in the Ionian Sea. But in an astonishing act of advertisement both for Rome and for himself—or better, for Rome as now himself—he also turned his command tent into a sacred memorial. That shrine-monument made, as it were, this quite extraordinary theological statement: *From here I went forth under heavenly protection to complete my divine mission and to fulfill Rome's imperial destiny.*

The monument's elevated platform had porticoes along the left, right, and back, but only the foundation-ground is more or less extant today. On the front supporting wall, Octavian carefully embedded a single row of about thirty-five bronze attack-rams, a tithe from those on his opponents' captured ships. They are all long gone, of course, but the extant holes indicate their original size and power (the biggest weighed about two tons). Above them Octavian placed a long Latin inscription in capital letters over a foot high. Time, slope, and weather have broken that text to pieces, but enough survives to make the full content relatively certain.

The best guide to the monument is the 1989 book *Octavian's Campsite Memorial for the Actian War* by William M. Murray and Photios M. Petsas. Murray and Petsas proposed a complete textual reconstruction from the various chunks of the inscription that had been recorded earlier or were still scattered around the site. Some of the sections depicted in that book are now missing, presumably lost forever. In reply to my query about them, Professor Murray, Dean of the University of South Florida's Department of History, said in an e-mail on April 13, 2005, that

> Konstantinos Zachos (the current ephor) thinks this happened during WWII when blocks were removed from the site (by the Italians, I think) for various defensive constructions on the hill. Zachos hopes one or more of these blocks may reappear in the future, but frankly does not know where they might be. His fear is that they were chopped up for use in other constructions or burned for lime.

All the extant units are now gathered in their proper sequence at the top of the site's east side, with only a roof above them and weeds all around them. As just noted, fifteen letters seen before the war are no longer present in that lineup, but thirty-three new letters have been discovered and added to it. The new ones confirmed their proposed reconstruction, which I adapt slightly as follows:

> IMPERATOR CAESAR, SON OF GOD, FOLLOWING THE VICTORY IN THE WAR WHICH HE WAGED ON BEHALF OF THE REPUBLIC IN THIS REGION, WHEN HE WAS CONSUL FOR THE FIFTH TIME AND IMPERATOR FOR THE SEVENTH TIME, AFTER PEACE HAD BEEN SECURED ON LAND AND SEA, CONSECRATED TO MARS AND NEPTUNE THE CAMP FROM WHICH HE SET FORTH TO ATTACK THE ENEMY NOW ORNAMENTED WITH NAVAL SPOILS

It is hard to overemphasize four aspects of that monument: first, its meaning as the inaugural manifesto from the victorious Octavian; second, the significance of its immediate construction in 31–29 BCE; third, the importance of its location on Octavian's own tent site; fourth, and above all else, the value of its content as a succinct summary of Roman imperial theology. It indicates the practice of *religion,* worshiping the appropriate gods, to secure a blessing for a *war* that resulted in *victory* and secured *peace* on land and sea. And that gives us the sequential program of Rome's imperial theology: *religion, war, victory, peace*—or more briefly, *peace through victory.*

Ancyra in Turkey

The most complete commentary on that inaugural inscription is in this second one, by far the most important inscription in all of Roman antiquity. Before his death in 14 CE, Augustus wrote in Latin a 2,500-word eulogy of his accomplishments to be inscribed on bronze plaques at the entrance to his new family mausoleum in Rome's Campus Martius. That bronze was melted down long ago, but a relatively full and bilingual copy still exists in the Temple of Rome and Augustus at Ancyra, then capital of Roman Galatia, now Ankara, capital of modern Turkey.

The shrine-mosque of the fifteenth-century Sufi saint Haci
Bayram Veli stands on a plaza in Old Ankara poised serenely above
the swirling traffic in the streets below. It is a place for pigeons,
pedestrians, and parked cars. It is a haven for young mothers with
their children and old grandfathers with their tea. The north wall
of that Roman temple is attached at its west end to the mosque's
minaret and at its east end to the mosque's office. That position
may have helped keep the temple shell erect until it was recently,
but most belatedly, restored and preserved.

The Latin text appears on the inside of the foyer's north and
south walls, and the Greek translation is on the outside of the
long south wall. The appended overture of the Latin text announces in much larger letters than the rest that it is a copy of the
Res Gestae Divi Augusti (*The Acts of the Divine Augustus*), "by which
he brought the whole earth under the empire [*imperium*] of the
Roman people." Intertwined in that fascinating autobiographical
text are Roman imperial theology's four programmatic themes of
religion, war, victory, peace.

- *Religion:* The text includes lists of temples built or restored
  by Augustus; the gifts from booty made to many of those
  temples; "the eighty silver statues of me" melted down for
  offerings to Apollo; and the refunds made to the temples of
  Asia "despoiled by my late adversary"—the never-named
  Antony.
- *War:* In describing "those many civil and foreign wars by
  land and sea throughout the world," Augustus records that
  "at my command and under my auspices two armies were
  led almost at the same time into Ethiopia and Arabia Felix;
  vast enemy forces of both peoples were cut down in battle
  and many towns captured."
- *Victory:* "I added Egypt to the empire of the Roman people,"
  Augustus proclaims, and the long list of conquered peoples
  includes, for example, this account: "When an army of Da-

cians crossed the Danube, it was defeated and routed under my auspices, and later my army crossed the Danube and compelled the Dacian peoples to submit to the commands of the Roman people."

- *Peace:* The Senate decreed that "an altar of the Augustan Peace should be consecrated next to the Campus Martius" (an altar, you will notice, not of Roman but of Augustan peace). Augustus expounds: "I brought peace to the Gallic and Spanish provinces as well as to Germany, throughout the area bordering on the Ocean from Cadiz to the mouth of the Elbe. I secured the pacification of the Alps from the district nearest the Adriatic to the Tuscan sea, yet without waging an unjust war on any people."

Compare, in conclusion, these twin core-phrases from both of these Augustan inscriptions—the first one immediately after Octavian's victory at Actium, the second immediately before his death. At the start, in 31 BCE, Rome was about "victory ... [with] peace secured on land and sea" (*victoriam ... pace parta terra marique*), and at the end, in 14 CE, Rome was still about "peace secured by victories on land and sea" (*terra marique parta victoriis pax*). Religion, war, victory, and peace—this was the Roman imperial theology, easily summarized as "peace through victory."

A River Too Far

The emperor's divinity was the incarnate heart of Roman imperial theology and stayed as such long after Augustus was dead. I conclude by discussing one very important aspect of that transcendent claim: any empire must learn when enough is enough, even if it can never admit that its enough is already far too much.

The Roman Empire suffered two humiliating defeats during the lifetime of Octavian the Augustus. First, in the decade after Octavian's birth, in 53 BCE, Crassus lost his life and five legions to the Parthian armies when Rome pushed eastward beyond the Euphrates toward the Tigris. The loss of those sacred standards festered deeply in Roman imperial consciousness—but was it worth another eastern war?

In 1863 a statue of Augustus was discovered in the villa of Augustus's wife Livia at Prima Porta on the Via Flaminia. He is depicted as a general addressing his troops, but he is also divinely barefooted. His military cuirass tells what he did about those captured standards, but does so amid a succinct summary of Roman imperial theology.

At its top is heaven's protective canopy, and at its base is earth's peaceful fertility. Beneath heaven, a New Era dawns as the Sun's chariot drives away both Night with its torch and Dawn with its dew-vase. On either side of the center are conquered peoples and supportive divinities. All of that surrounds a triumphant center depicting Roman victory. It is, however, a triumph not of warfare but of diplomacy. Personified Parthia stands with knee unbent and head unbowed as it hands back to personified Rome the captured standards of those doomed legions. Augustus knew when diplomacy was wiser than war.

Another great humiliation occurred in the decade before Augustus's death: Varus lost his life and three legions to the Germanic tribes as Rome pushed eastward beyond the Rhine toward the Elbe. The German general, Arminius, having fought with Julius Caesar in Gaul, had learned the Roman order of battle and line of march and the legionary strategies, tactics, operations, and weapons. As Varus's heavily encumbered forces marched back westward to their winter quarters on the Rhine, Arminius lured them along a track that narrowed between bog and hill, waited for them behind a sod-wall and under forest cover, then attacked when they were both unprepared and stretched too thin. After that disaster, Roman legions still roved east of the Rhine—and did so immediately to give Varus's soldiers honorable burial—but Augustus knew that the Rhine was now to be his east-west boundary in the north. And that, of course, is why conquered France speaks a Latin language today and unconquered Germany does not.

Augustus knew the difference between war and diplomacy. He understood about a river too far. He settled for imperial boundaries on the Rhine, not the Elbe, and for imperial limits on the Euphrates, not the Tigris. He also learned another vital lesson, this one from Arminius: when you train and arm tribal forces to fight *for* you, they can use that knowledge to fight *against* you just as well.

In 1776 Edward Gibbon published the first of six volumes on *The Decline and Fall of the Roman Empire.* On the first pages of that magnificent work's first chapter, he notes an earlier awareness of imperial limits:

> The seven first centuries were filled with a rapid succession of triumphs; but it was reserved for Augustus to relinquish the ambitious design of subduing the whole earth, and to introduce a spirit of moderation into the public councils.... On the death of the emperor [Augustus], his testament was publicly read in the senate. He bequeathed, as a valuable legacy to his successors, the advice of confining the empire within those limits, which Nature seemed to have placed as its permanent bulwarks and boundaries; on the west the Atlantic ocean; the Rhine and Danube on the north; the Euphrates on the east; and towards the south, the sandy deserts of Arabia and Africa. (pp. 1–3)

In texts, inscriptions, images, and structures, Augustus never proclaimed rule over Rome, Italy, or the Mediterranean alone but always announced dominion over all of land and sea, east and west, world and earth. Nevertheless, he understood very well the difference between public rhetoric and foreign policy.

On the last pages of that same first chapter, Gibbon emphasizes what resulted later when that awareness of imperial limitation was lost:

This long enumeration of provinces, whose broken fragments have formed so many powerful kingdoms, might almost induce us to forgive the vanity or ignorance of the ancients. Dazzled with the extensive sway, the irresistible strength, and the real or affected moderation of the emperors, they permitted themselves to despise, and sometimes to forget, the outlying countries which had been left in the enjoyment of a barbarous independence; they gradually usurped the license of confounding the Roman monarchy with the globe of the earth. (pp. 24–25)

What Gibbon terms "the vanity or ignorance of the ancients" is simply the normal blinders of any country's lust for everlasting empire and every empire's delusion of everlasting rule. It is not accidental ignorance but essential arrogance that dooms empires to the dustbin of time and the graveyard of history. "Empires," according to Charles S. Maier's 2006 book *Among Empires: American Ascendancy and Its Predecessors,* "are epics of entropy" (p. 76).

In conclusion, imagine this question. There was a human being in the first century who was called "Divine," "Son of God," "God," and "God from God," whose titles were "Lord," "Redeemer," "Liberator," and "Savior of the World." Who was that person? Most people who know the Western tradition would probably answer, unless alerted by the question's too-obviousness, Jesus of Nazareth. And most Christians probably think that those titles were originally created and uniquely applied to Christ. But before Jesus ever existed, all those terms belonged to Caesar Augustus. To proclaim them of Jesus the Christ was thereby to deny them of Caesar the Augustus. Christians were not simply using ordinary titles applied to all sorts of people at that time, or even extraordinary titles applied to special people in the East. They were taking the identity of the Roman emperor and giving it to a Jewish peasant. Either that was a peculiar joke and a very low lampoon, or it was what the Romans called *majestas* and we call high treason.

Those titles were fully appropriate for one who had saved "the world" from war and established peace "on earth." The first Christians therefore had to present a positive counter-mantra and a positive counter-program to Roman imperial theology's sequence of religion, war, victory, and peace. Victory, by the way, does not bring peace but only a lull—whether short or long—and after each lull the violence required for the next victory escalates. Is there any possible alternative to "first victory, then peace," or "peace through victory"? Yes, it is this: "religion, nonviolence, justice, peace"—or more succinctly, "first justice, then peace," or "peace through justice." That counter-program is the subject of this book.

But that is to jump ahead. I need first to raise two other questions about imperial violence—if you will excuse that redundancy—and I take them up in the final two parts of this first chapter.

The first question concerns empire and civilization. Are all empires, past and present, but deeper manifestations of what we call "civilization"? Since its invention along the irrigated floodplains of great rivers like the Tigris and Euphrates, has civilization always been inherently imperial? Is escalatory violence but civilization's drug of choice, and is it an addiction we cannot overcome or even control?

The second question starts from the end of the first one. Is the normal imperialism of human civilization simply an inevitable manifestation of human nature? Is our addictive and escalatory violence not just something we made but something we are? Is the human race, in other words, as doomed as the saber-toothed tiger?

EMPIRE AND CIVILIZATION

It does not help us understand the Roman Empire, let alone America as the New Roman Empire, to think of it as the "evil empire" of the first century or the "axis of evil" in the Mediterranean. As the greatest pre-industrial and territorial empire—just as we are the greatest post-industrial and commercial empire—Rome was the expression, no more and no less, of the *normalcy of civilization's violence,* first-century style.

Usually we use the term "civilization" for everything that is good about our humanity—for example, poetry and drama, music and dance, art and architecture, image and narrative. Correspondingly, to call individuals or groups, places or actions, "uncivilized" is normally a calculated insult. So I need to explain very clearly what I mean in this book by the "brutal normalcy of civilization." The point I wish to emphasize is that imperialism is not just a here-and-there, now-and-then, sporadic event in human history, but that civilization itself, as I am using that term, has always been imperial—that is, empire *is* the normalcy of civilization's violence. It is, of course, always possible to oppose this empire in favor of that one, to oppose yours in favor of ours. But if you oppose empire-as-such, you are taking on what has been the normalcy of civilization's brutality for at least the last six thousand years.

My epigraph for this chapter was taken from Walter Benjamin's philosophical theses *On the Concept of History,* written in 1939 and published posthumously. As a Jewish cultural and social critic, Benjamin creatively combined the Marxist materialism of Bertolt Brecht and the Jewish mysticism of Gershom Scholem. He died somewhat mysteriously in September 1940 at Port Bou on the Franco-Spanish border as he and his group tried to escape from Nazi-occupied France. It is possible that he committed suicide when it seemed they would not be allowed to cross the border; if so, his desperation may have facilitated the group's successful crossing the next day. His aphorism at the head of this chapter is a first and fundamental reminder of the dark underside and all-too-often brutal basis of civilization itself.

Here are two more preliminary examples. First, in his 1998 book *Plagues and Peoples,* William H. McNeill compares and speaks repeatedly of "the microparasitism of infectious disease and the macroparasitism of military operations" (p. 72). He also speaks of "the macroparasitic basis of civilization" (p. 25), and even of "the fulminating sort of macroparasitism we call civilization" (p. 111). And second, in Jared Diamond's 1997 book *Guns, Germs, and Steel,* one chapter is entitled "From Egalitarianism to Kleptocracy." Civilization, in these two books, is either "macroparasitology," the few living off the many, or "kleptocracy," the few stealing from the many.

Civilization as Cage

There are two sources for my own understanding of civilization as discussed in this book—a very long and detailed one from 1986 and a very short and general one from 2004. The latter does not cite the former, but they are in substantial and independent agreement.

The very detailed source, once again, is Michael Mann's ongoing, multivolume investigation of the comparative sociology of imperial power. In the first volume, the standard term he uses for civilization is "the cage"; for instance, "the city-walls symbolized and actualized the cage of authoritative power" (p. 100).

Mann defines social power as "mastery exercised over other people" (p. 6), but he distinguishes between power in earlier *precivilization* and in later *civilization*. In precivilized societies or cultures, "authority was freely conferred, but recoverable; power, permanent and coercive, was unattainable" (p. 39). How, then, did civilization's violent injustice become normal? When did the very many begin to be ruled by the very few—in, as the latter claimed, the former's best interests? If "the general capacities of human beings faced with their early environment gave rise to the first societies—to agriculture, the village, the clan, the lineage, and the chiefdom—but not to civilization, stratification, or the state" (p. 40), how did "civilization, stratification, and the state" begin, continue, and eventually prevail?

Civilization was created in at least four (but maybe six or seven) independent locations around the world. The floodplains of great alluvial rivers—such as the Tigris and Euphrates in Mesopotamia, the Nile in Egypt, the Indus in modern Pakistan, and the Yellow River in China—provided especially fertile ground for the invention of irrigated agriculture, a system that involved the establishment of written records, walled cities, and sacred temples by an ascendancy of literate, urban, and religious elites who could project, plan, prepare, and oversee masses of peasants in large-scale irrigation projects. "Civilization was an abnormal phenomenon" because, as Mann concludes,

> it involved the state and social stratification, both of which human beings have spent most of their existence avoiding. The conditions under which, on a very few occasions, civilization did develop, therefore, are those that made avoidance no longer possible. The ultimate significance of alluvial agriculture, present in all "pristine" civilizations, was the territorial constraint it offered in a package with a large economic surplus. When it became irrigation agriculture, as it usually did, it also increased social constraint. The population was caged into particular authority relations. (p. 124)

The "cage" of civilization protects those within, but it both proscribes and tempts those without. From the beginning, then, civilization became imperial as it attempted to expand social power as mastery over other people through ever-widening circles of security. It would only be a question, at any given time or place, of who had lost, who had gained, and who still wanted imperial control over others. The evolution of the "cage" led from the domestication of wild grains through the irrigation of floodplains and the building of cities to the steady thrust for imperial expansion. From Mann once again: "The gigantic *protection racket* of political history began: Accept my power, for I will protect you from worse violence—of which I can give you a sample, if you don't believe me" (p. 100, emphasis mine).

Civilization as Trap

The short and general source for my understanding of "civilization" is Ronald Wright's 2004 book *A Short History of Progress,* first delivered as the Massey Lectures and broadcast on CBC Radio's *Ideas* series. Wright spends much less time than Mann arguing about how many independent inventions of civilization have occurred in human history. Like Mann, however, Wright defines "'civilization' and 'culture' in a technical, anthropological way":

> Civilizations are a specific kind of culture: large, complex societies based on the domestication of plants, animals, and human beings. Civilizations vary in their makeup but typically have towns, cities, governments, social classes, and specialized professions. All civilizations are cultures, or conglomerates of cultures, but not all cultures are civilizations. (pp. 32–33)

Between 3000 and 1000 BCE, the great experiment of "civilization ringed the world" (p. 33). Wright, again like Mann, notes that "people afraid of outsiders are easily manipulated. The warrior caste, supposedly society's protectors, often became *protection racketeers*" (p. 49, emphasis mine). But just as Mann's term for civilization was the cage, Wright's term is "the progress trap—or, more simply, "the trap":

> I want to see what we can deduce from the first progress trap—the perfection of hunting, which ended the Old Stone Age [only about twelve thousand years ago]—and how our escape from that trap by the invention of farming led to our

greatest experiment: worldwide civilization. We then have to
ask ourselves this urgent question: Could civilization itself be
another and greater trap? (pp. 31–32)

That ultimate trap is both biological and social. The biological trap
concerns the dilemma of food, population, and pollution: "Adding
200 million after [the population of the world at the time of]
Rome took thirteen centuries; adding the last 200 million took
only three years" (p. 109). The social trap concerns the violence of
hierarchy, oppression, and war: "All civilizations become hierarchical; the upward concentration of wealth ensures that there will
never be enough to go around" (p. 108). In other words, "violence
is as old as man but civilizations commit it with a deliberation that
lends it special horror" (p. 73).

Think of how much progress civilization has made with violence and how exponentially faster its weapons have developed.
"From the first chipped stone to the first smelted iron took
nearly three million years; from the first iron to the hydrogen
bomb took only 3,000 years" (p. 14). It took us only three thousand years to learn how to destroy the world. "Violence is bred
by injustice, poverty, inequality, and other violence. This lesson
was learnt very painfully in the first half of the twentieth century,
at a cost of some 80 million lives. Of course, a full belly and a
fair hearing won't stop a fanatic; but they can greatly reduce the
number who *become* fanatics" (p. 126). Even more significantly, a
just and fair distribution of the world's resources would help
separate the hundreds of *fanatics* who kill from the thousands of
supporters who help them and the millions of *sympathizers* who
defend them.

During the Paleolithic or Old Stone Age, from around 3,000,000
to 12,000 BCE, we humans learned to control, organize, and domesticate tools, fires, and hunts. Later, during the Neolithic or New
Stone Age, from around 3,000 to 1,000 BCE, we learned to control,
organize, and domesticate plants and grains, animals and herds,

peoples and communities. We are so terribly, terribly clever, but where in all that human evolution is there any sign of wisdom?

Civilization as Protection

I italicized the words "protection racket" and "protection racketeers" in the separate quotations from Mann and Wright because they remind me of one famous and one infamous statement on the same theme.

On May 13, 1798, James Madison wrote an oft-quoted letter to his close friend and fellow Virginian, Thomas Jefferson, in which he warned prophetically that

> the management of foreign relations appears to be the most susceptible of abuse, of all the trusts committed to a Government, because they can be concealed or disclosed, or disclosed in such parts and at such times as will best suit particular views; and because the body of the people are less capable of judging and are more under the influence of prejudices, on that branch of their affairs, than of any other. Perhaps it is a universal truth that the loss of liberty at home is to be charged to provisions against danger, real or pretended, from abroad.

Madison cited the two possibilities of "danger, real or pretended, from abroad." But of course, there is the third and best type of all, namely, a real danger that is extended and expanded, overemphasized, overtrumpeted, and oversensationalized.

On April 18, 1946, Reichsmarchal Herman Göring was interviewed in his jail cell at Nuremberg by Captain Gustave Gilbert, a U.S. Army intelligence psychologist, who later reported these words of Göring's in his 1947 book *Nuremberg Diary*:

> Naturally, the common people don't want war; neither in Russia nor in England nor in America, nor for that matter

in Germany. That is understood. But, after all, it is the *leaders* of the country who determine the policy and it is always a simple matter to drag the people along, whether it is a democracy or a fascist dictatorship or a Parliament or a Communist dictatorship.... The people can always be brought to the bidding of the leaders. That is easy. All you have to do is tell them they are being attacked and denounce the pacifists for lack of patriotism and exposing the country to danger. It works the same way in any country.

And once again, it is best if there is a real attack that can be magnified, a true danger that can be exaggerated out of all proportion.

Finally, then, I follow Mann and Wright in using the term "civilization" as that imperial drive invented during the Neolithic Revolution, and I see empire—be it Roman or American—as no more and no less than the violent normalcy of civilization created again and again at specific times and places with specific conditions and opportunities. My point is, once again, that to resist empire-as-such we must know what we are up against. It is something inherent in civilization itself. Non-imperial civilization is something yet to be seen upon our earth.

That leads immediately into the next and last part of this chapter and to this rather terrible question: *Is the normalcy of human civilization's violence our inevitable destiny?* Is violence and especially escalatory violence (is there another type?) our inherent destiny and therefore our inherent doom? Or can we change the normal brutality of civilization? My own answer is affirmative, and the reason is that certain individuals and institutions have witnessed clearly to us that normalcy is not destiny, that the normalcy of civilization's brutality is not humanity's inevitable fate. The nonviolence of pacifists and martyrs has always been such a witness, but in the next section I look not at an *individual* witness but at an *institutional* one.

NORMALCY AND INEVITABILITY

In the ordinary and everyday world, most people speak regularly to one another and argue aplenty; they eat and drink what they want; and they make love, have babies, and raise families. Why, then, do certain individuals vow before God to commit themselves to permanent silence, lifelong asceticism, and perpetual celibacy? Why do people enter monasteries? Or better, why do monasteries exist?

I do not ask why an individual monk chooses or is chosen for such a life. There may be as many reasons as there are vocations, reasons private and personal, reasons familial and public, reasons based in repentance for a past crime or in entreaties for a future life.

In my own case, I entered an Irish monastery in 1950, straight out of high school at sixteen, because, first, being a missionary monk was the most exciting life I could imagine, and second, it was my considered teenage judgment that God had the greatest game in town. By contrast, I knew another novice, older than myself, who became a monk because his wartime job with Bomber Command in Britain had been going inside the gun turrets of the B–17 "Flying Fortresses" that had limped home from raids over Europe and removing the bullet-riddled bodies and cleaning the blood-spattered seats.

I repeat my question. What are the professional, institutional, and public reasons (not the personal, individual, and private ones) that monasteries exist? In reply, I go back to origins, to the first time the word *monasterion*—from the Greek word *monos,* or "alone"—was used in our Western tradition. I go back to Judaism, where the monastic life was already present before it came into Christianity.

Injustice by Reason of Inequality

In the first century, Alexandria sprawled along a spur of land connected by a mile-long causeway to Pharos Island's lighthouse in the north and bordered in the south by salty Lake Mareotis, which extended much farther than today's Lake Mariot. The city, second-largest of the empire and capital of Egypt's wealth, sent huge grain ships lumbering across the Mediterranean to sustain the daily bread-dole for about 200,000 of Rome's poorest inhabitants. The large and powerful Jewish population lived in the northeast section of the city, and among them were two very famous brothers. According to Josephus's *Jewish Antiquities,* one of them, Alexander, "surpassed all his fellow citizens both in ancestry and birth" (20.100), and the other, Philo, was "a man held in the highest honor" and "no novice in philosophy" (18.259).

In his essay *On the Contemplative Life,* Philo tells us in great detail about a Jewish community of female and male Therapeutics, so-called from the Greek *therapeuein,* "to heal." They practiced a medicine not for bodies but for souls, "which are under the mastery of terrible and almost incurable diseases, which pleasures and appetites, fears and griefs, and covetousness, and follies, and injustice, and all the rest of the innumerable multitude of other passions and vices, have inflicted upon them" (1.1).

There were four important characteristics of the common life of the Therapeutics. First of all, "because of their anxious desire for an immortal and blessed existence, thinking that their mortal life has already come to an end," they gave up all their possessions to their children, relatives, or friends. Why? Because "great anxiety concerning the means of subsistence and the *acquisition of money engendered injustice by reason of the inequality which it produced,* while the contrary disposition and pursuit produced *justice by reason of its equality*" (2.17, emphasis mine). Therapeutics abandoned the communal injustice of human normalcy and found the communal justice of divine radicality.

Second, they left the world they had known to "take up their abode outside of walls, or gardens, or solitary lands, seeking for a desert place beyond the Mareotic lake" to the south (2.20, 3.21). The Therapeutics had their own individual cells, surrounded by walled courtyards and containing shrine-rooms, where they spent six days of each week in prayer, meditation, and the study of sacred scripture as philosophical allegory. They did not eat until sunset each day, and some went for three or even six days without eating (4.34–35).

Third, apart from their individual cells, they had two communal buildings. One was the Assembly Room, where all met together on the seventh day—with women and men separated by a dividing wall—to hear the eldest expound the scriptures. Another was the Banquet Room, where all met "at the end of seven weeks"; again, the women were on one side and the men on the other, and all were seated on "rugs of the coarsest materials, cheap mats of the most ordinary kind of the papyrus of the land" (9.69). The feast began with instruction by the president while all listened, and then individuals rose to sing a hymn, with "both men and women" joining in choral unity (10.80). The feast continued with a banquet of bread, salt, and the herb hyssop (no blood), with cold or hot water (no wine). It concluded with the female and male choirs singing and dancing antiphonally until "they join[ed] together, and the two [became] one chorus," just as, at the Red Sea during the Exodus, the Israelites "sang hymns of thanksgiving to God the Savior, Moses the prophet leading the men, and Miriam the prophetess leading the women" (11.83–87).

Finally, there is this very important aspect of their common life. "They do not use the ministrations of slaves, looking upon the possession of servants or slaves to be a thing absolutely and wholly contrary to nature, for nature has created all men free, but the *injustice and covetousness of some men who prefer inequality*, that cause of all evil, having subdued some, has given to the more powerful authority over those who are weaker" (9.70, emphasis mine). You may remember that, to the contrary, the great Greek philosopher Aristotle considered slavery to be quite natural.

The Therapeutics were *semi-hermits,* and their ascetic lifestyle is called *semi-eremitic*: individuals are primarily isolated in private cells but come together periodically for certain communal activities. That mode of asceticism stands on a spectrum between two other ways of abandoning the unjust violence of civilization's normalcy. The first such separated lifestyle is *eremitic* (from the Greek word *eremos,* or "desert"): individuals practice asceticism in total human isolation. Of course, truly successful hermits are utterly unknown to history. Some abandon their world forever, and if they do not manage total disappearance, semi-hermits often cluster around them. The other separated life is *coenobitic* (from the Latin word *coena* for common "meal"): individuals live in total human community, with everyone praying, working, studying, and worshiping together.

This inaugural usage of the terms "monastery" and "monk" was gender-neutral and included women as well as men. I follow Philo's usage and do not distinguish between "monastery" and "convent" or between "monk" and "nun," especially since those male/female words often refer not just to gender but to hierarchy. My point here is that Philo explains clearly that the function of the monastery was to allow individuals to withdraw from the normalcy of human injustice to live and celebrate the radicality of divine justice. In my terms, therefore, the first monastery was a living witness that civilization's escalatory violence was not humanity's inevitable destiny. People, whether few or many, could and did live quite differently from that normalcy.

In chapter 4, I return to the subject of justice-as-equality and injustice-as-inequality (italicized in the quotations from Philo). Here I conclude by looking at the most extreme example of a monastery I know or can even imagine. I do so because my own experience with this site struck me as a minor paradox mirroring the major paradox of monastery-as-such.

An Incredible, Impossible, Mad Place

When NASA's weather satellites find a clear day over Ireland, three islets appear as faint specks eight miles out in the Atlantic Ocean off Bolus Head on Kerry's Iveragh Peninsula. In line, east to west, come first Lemon Rock, then Skellig Beag or Small Skellig, and finally Great Skellig or Skellig Michael. The last site is a steep-cliffed island, a rocky sea-crag, a UNESCO World Heritage Site, a splinter of my native country, and a searing question mark against the normalcy of civilization's violence. The island rises "from the gray Atlantic like a jagged tooth," says Chet Raymo in his 2004 book *Climbing Brandon,* Ireland's second-highest mountain on the Dingle Peninsula of County Kerry. That rock-island looks, he adds, "as if it were the first thrust of the creation itself, a tentative emergence of order from chaos, God's cautious finger to the wind" (pp. 19, 151). Three times in forty-five years I have attempted to reach that one tiny spot on the vast surface of our earth.

During my first attempt to visit Skellig Michael, in late July 1961, drizzle had become rain, mist had become fog, and everyone agreed that it was a "softdaythankGod." No boat was available, no trip was possible, and neither of the Skelligs was visible, not even from the coast. (The coast was not even visible from itself.) I wanted to climb the island's six hundred or so steps to the monastic ruins because I was then an Irish monk, Skellig Michael was a place to kneel, since, as T. S. Eliot wrote of another sacred ruin, prayer had once been valid there. And if ever, then always. But I never made it.

Twenty years later my second attempt was even more disappointing. A residual storm wind had created perfect visibility, but the sea-swell was far too great for docking at Skellig Michael. I was warned that even if a boat landed me safely that morning, it might not be able to get me off again that evening. It was August 28, 1981, and I was staying at the Parknasilla Great Southern Hotel at Sneem overlooking the Kenmare River on the southern stretch of the Ring of Kerry. George Bernard Shaw, Dublin-born and London-based, had stayed at that same hotel in 1910, but he had managed to dock on Skellig Michael, which he called "the most fantastic and impossible rock in the world." Shaw got there in an "open boat, 33 feet long, propelled by ten men on five oars" rowing at "49 strokes a minute." In a letter dated September 18 from Parknasilla Hotel, the popular playwright and political activist described the Skelligs to his friend Barry Jackson as "pinnacled, crocketed, spired, arched, caverned, minaretted; and these gothic extravagances are not curiosities of the islands: they are the islands: there is nothing else."

By the time Shaw visited Skellig Michael, it had changed from a monastic to a pilgrimage site. Even though his letter spent more space describing—admiringly—the boat's rowers, he also described—less admiringly—the rock's pilgrims. "An incredible, impossible, mad place, which still tempts devotees to make 'stations' of every stair landing, and to creep through 'Needle's eyes' at impossible altitudes, and kiss 'stones of pain' jutting 700 feet above the Atlantic." After more than half a millennium, hermits and monks had ceded place to pilgrims and penitents. What, by the way, does monastic life have to do with penitential life, and what do monks have to do with penitents? Penance, clearly—but why and for what? In any case, remember this comment of Shaw's for later. "I tell you," he wrote to his friend, "the thing does not belong to any world that you and I have lived and worked in: it is part of our dream world." It was, as monasteries always claim to be, out of this world.

On Monday, July 11, 2005, a high-pressure front settled firmly over Ireland. "Costa del Irlanda basked in near-record temperatures," quipped the front page of the next day's *Irish Independent,* with "glorious sunshine" and "scorching temperatures" in the upper eighties inland and the lower eighties on the coast. The Borgs and Crossans were leading a pilgrimage to explore Celtic Christianity, and our group arrived from Clonmacnoise to Killarney that Sunday evening. By then we knew that our trip's climactic but "weather-permitting" visit to Skellig Michael was certain for the next day. By 10:00 AM the next morning, the sun, the sea, and the breeze were Mediterranean as the boats picked us up at Portmagee Harbor across from Valentia Island on the northwest coast of the Iveragh (or Ring-of-Kerry) Peninsula. Our small boat—Michael O'Sullivan's Aquastar Fisherman, the *Ursula Mary,* from Waterville, County Kerry—had a closed cockpit for its two-man crew, an open, seated well for its fourteen passengers, and a 380 Volvo engine that had a top speed of twenty-two knots but was kept at around twelve knots for the forty-five-minute run to the island's narrow docking steps by eleven o'clock that morning.

Skellig Michael is named for the Archangel Michael, and were it not for its monastic history, you might think that only an angel could live on that twin-pinnacled sea-crag off Ireland's roughest coast. The tiny forty-four-acre island is shaped like a Western saddle, with the front rising to a precipitous seven-hundred-foot-high peak and the back rising to a slightly less pointed six-hundred-foot-high peak along the island's southwest-to-northeast axis. Access to the latter peak is gained by a sloping ascent from the landing dock to the bottom of about six hundred steps that are easy and wide enough for anyone not deterred by the absence of guardrails and the presence of sheer drops.

On top of that saddle's lower back-peak, a monastery—a mini-monastery necessarily—was built at the end of the sixth century. Inside its sacred enclosure were six cells, a large oratory with an outside altar, and a smaller oratory, also with an outside altar but built atop a rather awesome artificial terrace reclaimed from the sheer cliff face. The cells and oratories were built by drystone corbeling, a masonry technique in which upper stones inch steadily inward upon lower ones to form eventually an elegant dome. Get a layer's center of gravity wrong, and you have built yourself a heap of fallen stones; get it right all around, and you have a beehive building that is perfectly watertight and free of mustiness even in Ireland's coastal rain.

The smallest cell is eight feet by eight feet, with a height of ten feet, while the largest (the abbot's?) is fifteen feet by twelve feet,

with a height of sixteen feet. The corbeled walls range correspondingly from three and a half feet to six feet thick at their
bases. "The winds of the Atlantic played over their heartstrings like
Aeolian harps," says Chet Raymo's *Climbing Brandon* of those
rock-bound monks. "They were, to be sure, pilgrims of the Absolute, seeking their God in a raw, ecstatic encounter with stone,
wind, sea, and sky" (pp. 151, 159). Island, mountain, and sea were
particularly holy sites for Celtic Christianity. They were thin and
translucent places where another world most nearly merged with
our everyday one. What, then, could be holier than a mountain on
an island above the sea? But even that ascetic isolation was not
enough.

On top of the saddle's higher front-peak, the monks constructed
an even more isolated and vertiginous hermitage during the ninth
century. It may have been for one special monk or for any and all
of the monks in turn, but it was certainly a communal project. The
construction and occupation of the Skellig's hermitage made
building and living in the Skellig's monastery look downright easy
and almost comfortable. In 1990 Walter Horn and Jenny White
Marshall, both University of California professors, collaborated
with Grellan Rourke, an Irish architect in charge of the conservation of the island's monastic heritage, to produce a book, *The Forgotten Hermitage of Skellig Michael,* as a magnificent celebration of
that awesome site:

> [On] an island at the western edge of the European land
> mass—at the time the monastery was founded, the western
> edge of the Christian world—was a hermitage ... seven hun-
> dred feet above the sea, clinging to the narrow ledge of an
> austere pinnacle ... a visual wonder and a marvelous feat of
> construction.... [It was one] of the most daring architectural
> expressions of early Irish monasticism: a hermitage built vir-
> tually in the air on the treacherous ledges of an Atlantic rock
> rising straight up from the ocean.... [L]evel surfaces on which
> to build the structures necessary for a hermitage did not exist.

They had to be created—and were created—by the erection
of walls at the brink of steeply slanting ledges, along the very
boundary between life and death. (pp. 2, 23)

Granted that the Gulf Stream was near the Kerry coast, granted
that the ocean in the first millennium was warmer off western
Ireland than in the second one, and granted that the wind rising
up those cliff faces left a more humane microclimate around the
monastery, that site nevertheless demands an answer to this question: why, across six centuries, did some human beings abandon
mainland for island, and then abandon the semi-isolation of the
monastery for the total isolation of the hermitage? And beyond
that specific example, there is this section's more general question:
why do monasteries exist as a religious institution?

Normalcy Is Not Inevitability

Think now of those two extraordinary monasteries half a millennium apart—one Jewish on the fringes of Egypt's western desert,
the other Christian on the fringes of Ireland's western coast, both
with several individual cells and certain communal buildings.
Think of how monasticism vaulted first from Judaism into Christianity and then from the vast Christian deserts of the East to the
tiny Christian islands of the West, as if the once great but now tot-
tering cities of the Roman center had never existed. Think, finally,
of how those late-third-century Egyptian hermits, Paul and
Anthony, are the most frequently depicted nonbiblical figures on
Ireland's eighth- to tenth-century high crosses.

Ireland had no sun-bleached deserts, so what was to be the Irish
equivalent of Egypt's monastic, out-of-this-world location? For
Celtic Christianity, an island's separation from the mainland was
the equivalent of the desert's separation from the town. Apart from
Irish mainland monasteries like St. Kevin's at Glendalough or St.
Ciaran's at Clonmacnoise, what could approach or even surpass
the ascetic rigors of Egypt better than a monastery or a hermitage

on a sea-crag like Skellig Michael? But still, why do monasteries exist? What is their transcultural function, their transtemporal purpose?

Take this comment from the three intrepid archaeologists who drew and photographed *Forgotten Hermitage* atop Skellig Michael's southern precipice. "Christian monasticism," they say, "had its conceptual roots in the belief that union with God could best be obtained by withdrawal from civilization into harsh and isolate regions" (p. 1). Since God is everywhere and union with God is surely possible anywhere, I focus on one phrase in that explanation, "withdrawal from civilization," and within that phrase, on the word "civilization" itself. Here, then, is my own suggestion for why the monastery exists as an institution.

The monastery presents an alternative lifestyle that implicitly criticizes the greed, injustice, and oppression of our everyday world. It is a mode of semicommunal or fully communal life witnessing that *violence is not the inevitability of human nature but only the normalcy of human civilization.* As mentioned earlier, the word "civilization" is often used to refer to all those magnificent aspects of our human life together—art and architecture, poetry and literature, music and dance, play, thought, and learning. But civilization also has darker aspects. Its magnificent cultural gifts are often built upon violence against the earth and injustice against the world.

Greek Orthodox coenobitic monasteries—from St. Catherine's at the foot of Mount Sinai to Vatopédhi at the top of Mount Athos, from Eski Gümüs, carved inside volcanic tufa at Nigde in central Turkey, to Metamorfosis, perched atop a rock-pinnacle at Meteora in central Greece—are certainly "out-of-this-world" sites. But I have never known and cannot even imagine anything quite like Skellig Michael's monastery and hermitage. I take it, therefore, as my supreme example of monastic life and use it to focus and emphasize my answer to this section's question: why do monasteries exist? Monasteries (and especially Skellig Michael) are witnesses that *the escalatory violence of civilization is not the inevitable destiny of humankind,* even though the brutal normalcy of civilization will seek to co-opt and corrupt that monastic witness.

There is another reason for taking Skellig Michael as my paradigmatic example, and it explains why I have detailed my own attempts to get there. Any monastery is a *paradox* in the original Greek meaning of being beyond or even against the standard view of things or the normal opinion about them. Here is another paradox: You cannot get to Skellig Michael on a bad day. You can only get there with a clear sky and a calm sea. The days you *cannot* reach it let you experience what it would have been like to live there—if you had reached it. And the days you *can* reach it do not let you experience what it was like to live there—because you reached it. When I finally got there under a blue Mediterranean sky, it felt more like Anacapri than Skellig Michael. That paradox of island access mirrors in miniature the paradox of monastic existence.

The normalcy of civilization's violence is not the inevitability of humanity's destiny. So, yes, we can change. But as Ronald Wright's *A Short History of Progress* argues, "The future of everything we have accomplished since our intelligence evolved will depend on the wisdom of our actions over the next few years" (p. 3), since "these years may be the last when civilization still has the wealth and political cohesion to steer itself towards caution, conservation and social justice" (p. 125). In other words, "the 10,000-year experiment of the settled life will stand or fall by what we do, and don't do, now" (p. 131).

It would be nice to turn now from the "Bad Empire" in chapter 1 to the "Good Book" in chapter 2, as if the Christian Bible were all about dreams or hopes or plans for a just and peaceful earth and nothing else. But that Bible is far more powerful and far more dangerous than any such simple fantasy. Read it, read it all, read it in both its Old Testament and New Testament, read it especially in its final terrible book, the Apocalypse, or the Revelation to John. If you do, you will never again be able to make the lie-libel claim that the Old Testament has a violent God of war while the New

Testament has a nonviolent God of peace. The Bible is about God and the ambiguity of divine power.

The rest of this book is about the Christian Bible, especially its depiction of divine power as violent or nonviolent. Before I discuss Jesus of Nazareth, Paul of Tarsus, and John of Patmos in chapters 3 through 5, chapter 2 looks at the prior biblical tradition they would have known. As you will see, Christian Jews were certainly not the first to practice nonviolent resistance to Rome: both violent resistance to imperial injustice and nonviolent resistance were already operative among first-century non-Christian Jews.

GOD AND THE AMBIGUITY OF POWER

For no thought is contented. The better sort,
As thoughts of things divine, are intermix'd
With scruples, and do set the word itself
Against the word:
As thus, "Come, little ones"; and then again,
"It is as hard to come as for a camel
To thread the postern of a needle's eye."
—WILLIAM SHAKESPEARE (1595)

In these lines from *The Tragedy of King Richard the Second* (act 5, scene 5), King Richard, a prisoner in Pomfret Castle, has been forced by the ambiguity of royal imprisonment to consider the ambiguity of biblical imprisonment. How do you decide a king against a king in the Realm or a word against a word in the Bible?

In another play, *As You Like It* (act 4, scene 1), Shakespeare writes that "the poor world is almost six thousand years old." That date is very general compared to the precise dates propounded within the next half-century by two theologians. First, around 1642–44, John Lightfoot, Vice-Chancellor of England's Cambridge University, dated the creation of the universe to Sunday, September 12, 3928 BCE, at 9:00 AM. Then, in 1650, James Ussher, Archbishop of Armagh, Primate of All Ireland, and Vice-Chancellor of Dublin's Trinity College, dated it to Sunday, October 23, 4004 BCE (but gave no time of day). Ussher also estimated that Eve and Adam were ejected from Eden on November 10, 4004 BCE, and that the flood receded from the earth on May 5, 2348 BCE.

Those precise dates make ridicule almost too temptingly easy, but they also raise another question. Granted that *some* Christians date our universe in the low thousands of years and that *all* scientists date it in the low billions of years, here is my question for this chapter's first section. Why does the Bible itself date creation to around 4000 BCE? Why date creation around four thousand years before Christ and not any other nice round number, such as 10,000 or 100,000 BCE? What is special about a date around six thousand years ago?

When the biblical tradition raised inaugural and fundamental questions of meaning in Genesis 1–11, it selectively adopted and serenely adapted very ancient stories passed down from the Sumerians, those intensely competitive and magnificently creative people who lived in southern Mesopotamia from about 4500 to 2500 BCE. What they were attempting to think through in those narratives was the Neolithic Revolution of their own contemporary world. In, for example, their parables about the disputes between summer and winter, between cattle and grain, between plow and pickax, or (as discussed later) between shepherd and farmer, the divine judgment is always given to what we might call the evolutionary future among those options.

Genesis 1–11 was using, in other words, stories that dated back to the Neolithic Revolution and were originally formulated in Sumer to think through its implications. In more ways than we might want to imagine or face, therefore, our world was "created" about six thousand years ago.

HOW THE BIBLE STARTS ITS STORY

In what follows, I look at four major parables: on the primacy of distributive justice in Genesis 1; on the responsibility of human morality in Genesis 2–3; on the tragedy of inaugural fratricide in

Genesis 4; and on the divine punishment of the flood-destruction and the divine promise of "never again" in Genesis 6–9. These four parables recounted as the Bible begins its story must be read as stages in an ongoing narrative where the failure of divine violence by the end of Genesis 1–11 demands a new and nonviolent start in Genesis 12. The ambiguity of these divergent models of God-power is already established as the Bible starts its story and continues through to its ending in the apocalyptic Book of Revelation.

Justice: Creation and Sabbath

The creation story in Genesis 1:1–2:4a is not from ancient Sumerian traditions but emphatically and uniquely from Israel's priestly concerns. Those authors had no intention of writing about the *origin* of the world—about which they knew they knew nothing—but about the *meaning* of the world, about which they thought they knew a lot. And they did.

First of all, those priestly authors imagined God as an architect who first builds a house and then furnishes it. There would therefore be an equal balance between days for separating and preparing the house-universe and days for decorating and filling the house-universe. Next, they looked around their world and organized it into eight great chunks of materials that God had created. So there should have been four days of building and a corresponding four days of furnishing as God created the world. In conceiving seven days rather than nine for creation, they revealed their purpose as clearly as possible.

Look at the figure on the next page and notice that the repeated inaugural sequence of "God said, let ..." (that is, *let* something be created) appears eight times but must be doubled for the third and sixth days if eight chunks of divine creation are to fit into six days of divine work. Why? So that God could rest on the seventh day, not the ninth day. In other words, in creating the universe, not even God could skip the Sabbath. Put yet another way: in creating the universe, God crowned it with the Sabbath.

Day 1:
(1) *Then God said,*
"*Let* [LIGHT be]."
And there was
And God saw that it was good.
And there was evening and
there was morning,
the first day.

Day 2:
(2) *And God said,*
"*Let* [FIRMAMENT be]."
And it was so.
And there was evening and
there was morning,
the second day.

Day 3:
(3) *And God said,*
"*Let* [SEA/LAND be]."
And it was so.
And God saw that it was good.
(4) *Then God said,*
"*Let* [PLANTS/TREES be]."
And it was so.
And God saw that it
was good.
And there was evening and
there was morning,
the third day.

Day 4:
(5) *And God said,*
"*Let* [SUN/MOON be]."
And it was so.
And God saw that it was good.
And there was evening and
there was morning,
the fourth day.

Day 5:
(6) *And God said,*
"*Let* [BIRDS/FISHES be]."
And God saw that it was good.
And there was evening and
there was morning,
the fifth day.

Day 6:
(7) *And God said,*
"*Let* [ANIMALS be]."
And it was so.
And God saw that it was good.
(8) *Then God said,*
"*Let* [HUMANS be]."
And it was so.
God saw everything
was very good.
And there was evening and
there was morning,
the sixth day.

There absolutely cannot be more than six days of divine creation because it must all be finished before this conclusion:

> [God] rested on the seventh day from all the work that he had done. So God blessed the seventh day and hallowed it, because on it God rested from all the work that he had done in creation. (2:2b–3)

You probably noticed in that quotation that "rested from all the work that he had done" is repeated both before and after "blessed the seventh day and hallowed it." It is not humanity on the sixth day but the Sabbath on the seventh day that is the climax of creation. And therefore our "dominion" over the world is not ownership but stewardship under the God of the Sabbath.

We may think of the Sabbath—Saturday for Jews and Sunday for Christians—as time off from work to leave space for worship. Keeping the Sabbath is one of the Ten Commandments: "The seventh day is a sabbath to the Lord your God; you shall not do any work—you, or your son or your daughter, or your male or female slave, or your ox or your donkey, or any of your livestock, or the alien resident in your towns" (Deuteronomy 5:14). But here is the reason given for that commandment:

> Six days you shall do your work, but on the seventh day you shall rest, *so that* your ox and your donkey may have relief, and your homeborn slave and the resident alien may be refreshed. (Exodus 23:12, emphasis mine)

> The seventh day is a sabbath to the Lord your God; you shall not do any work—you, or your son or your daughter, or your male or female slave, or your ox or your donkey, or any of your livestock, or the resident alien in your towns, *so that* your male and female slave may rest as well as you. (Deuteronomy 5:14, emphasis mine)

The Sabbath Day was not rest *for* worship but rest *as* worship. It was a day of equal rest for all—animals, slaves, children, and adults—a pause that reduced all to equality both symbolically and regularly. The Sabbath Day was about the just distribution of basic rest-from-labor as symbol and reality of God's own distributive justice. Later in this chapter, we will find that same association of Sabbath and divine distributive justice extended from the Sabbath Day to the Sabbath Year and then to the Sabbath Jubilee. In summary, the Sabbath was about the justice of equality as the crown and climax of creation itself.

In the middle of the second century BCE, the Jewish writer Aristobulus claimed in his *Fragment 5* that Sabbath observance was not just ethnic and legal but also cosmic and natural. "God, who established the whole cosmos, also gave us the seventh day as a rest, because life is laborious for all. According to the laws of nature, the seventh day might be called first also, as the genesis of light in which all things are contemplated." The just distribution of a world not our own is indeed the light in which everything must be considered, organized, and established.

There is also, by the way, one very special feature in that account of creation. In this serene vision of an all-peaceful creation, *both beasts and humans are vegetarians.* In Genesis 1:29–30, God informs humans that

I have given you every plant yielding seed that is upon the face of all the earth, and every tree with seed in its fruit; you shall have them for food. And to every beast of the earth, and to every bird of the air, and to everything that creeps on the earth, everything that has the breath of life, I have given every green plant for food.

Inaugurally, there would have been nonviolence in both the animal and the human world.

Morality: Adam and Eve

The preceding parable is about God's establishment of distributive justice as the crowning climax of creation—or in the language of a different vision, about equitable distribution as the imperative demand of human evolution.

The parable of Adam and Eve in Genesis 2:3b–3:24 is about the human choice of moral knowledge over eternal life. It is usually called "the Story of the Fall" without adequate thought given to the question of fall *from* what or *to* what. It is, however, a much more sophisticated story than one of single divine command and simple human disobedience. It is not a story of God drawing a line on the ground and commanding the First Humans not to cross it, their doing so, and then being punished for it. It is about our human fall (or rise?) from nature into culture.

The Epic of Gilgamesh

Unlike the story of the Sabbath's creation in Genesis 1, the biblical narrative of Eden has Mesopotamian antecedents that date back to the Neolithic Revolution and its invention of civilization by the third millennium BCE. In Tablet 1 of *The Epic of Gilgamesh,* for example, that divine-human ruler of the Sumerian city of Uruk "carved on a stone stele all of his toils, and built the walls of Uruk-Haven, the wall of the sacred Eanna Temple, the holy sanctuary." Remember from chapter 1 that written record, walled city, and sacred temple are three constitutive elements of civilization. That trilogy reappears a few lines later with mention of "the Ishtar Temple, three leagues and the open area of Uruk the wall encloses.... Take and read out from the lapis lazuli tablet how Gilgamesh went through every hardship." Literacy, City, and Temple are the elements and tokens of civilization's invention.

Unlike Genesis 2–3, the Gilgamesh tale is not about the *arrival* but about the *acceptance* of humanity's mortal destiny. "All living creatures born of the flesh shall sit at last in the boat of the West, and when it sinks, when the boat of Magilum sinks, they are gone," because, "when the gods created man, they allotted to him death, but life they retained in their own keeping."

The plot begins to unfold, not through a male-and-female marriage, as in Genesis 2–3, but through a male-and-male companionship. Gilgamesh is two-thirds divine and one-third human, created from heaven and divinity downwards. He rules Uruk with injustice, violence, and rape—"like a wild bull he makes himself mighty, head raised over others."

To remedy this situation the creator-god Aruru decides to make Enkidu "equal to Gilgamesh's stormy heart, let them be a match for each other so that Uruk may find peace." But Enkidu, as Gilgamesh's counterpart, was created not from heaven and divinity downwards, but from earth and animality upwards. "Aruru washed her hands, she pinched off some clay and threw it into the wilderness ... she created valiant Enkidu ... he ate grasses with the gazelles, and jostled at the watering hole with the animals."

Next, just as Eve persuades Adam, so a female protagonist, Shamsat, seduces Enkidu from nature into culture: when she tells him, "Enkidu, you have become like a god," he realizes that "his understanding had broadened." Proclaiming that "he whose strength is mightiest is the one born in the wilderness ... he splashed his shaggy body with water, and rubbed himself with oil, and turned into a human. He put on some clothing and became like a warrior." With that, I leave Gilgamesh and Enkidu for now but will return to them later.

The Trees of Eden

There were two special trees, says Genesis 2:9, in the center of the magnificent paradise-garden of Eden: "Out of the ground the Lord

God made to grow every tree that is pleasant to the sight and good for food, the tree of life also in the midst of the garden, and the tree of the knowledge of good and evil." Two trees—the Tree of Eternal Life and the Tree of Moral Knowledge—stood side by side, as it were, in the center of Eden. Divinity had the attributes of both trees, but humanity could only have one or the other. Humans could have eternal life *or* moral knowledge, but not eternal life *and* moral knowledge. That was for God alone. God therefore told the First Humans in 2:16–17: "You may freely eat of every tree of the garden; but of the tree of the knowledge of good and evil you shall not eat, for in the day that you eat of it you shall die." And then came temptation:

> Now the serpent was more crafty than any other wild animal that the Lord God had made. He said to the woman, "Did God say, 'You shall not eat from any tree in the garden'?" The woman said to the serpent, "We may eat of the fruit of the trees in the garden; but God said, 'You shall not eat of the fruit of the tree that is in the middle of the garden, nor shall you touch it, or you shall die.'" But the serpent said to the woman, "You will not die; for God knows that when you eat of it your eyes will be opened, and you will be like God, knowing good and evil." (3:1–5)

Actually, in the story so far, both God and the Serpent have told the truth, but not the whole truth. On the one hand, God has said of the Tree of Moral Knowledge, in 2:17, that "in the day that you eat of it you shall die." Yes, they will die eventually, but not immediately on the day of eating. Still, on that day they will know what none of the other animals know: that they will someday die. Then they will move from eternal life to moral knowledge and shift forever out of nature into culture. On the other hand, the Serpent is correct in saying that moral knowledge will make them like God and that they will not immediately die.

Notice that Shamsat persuades Enkidu to choose culture over nature, civilization over wilderness, knowledge over ignorance, and human-mortality over animal-immortality. Eve, however, persuades Adam to choose not just understanding, knowledge, and wisdom, but "the knowledge of good and evil"—that is, to choose morality.

In the Bible, God alone is Lord of both nature and culture (or as we might say, of evolution). Humanity cannot be lord of both, and so this great parable must end with this statement from God:

> Then the Lord God said, "See, the man has become like one of us, knowing good and evil; and now, he might reach out his hand and take also from the tree of life, and eat, and live forever"—therefore the Lord God sent him forth from the garden of Eden, to till the ground from which he was taken. He drove out the man; and at the east of the garden of Eden he placed the cherubim, and a sword flaming and turning to guard the way to the tree of life. (3:22–24)

The banishment from the garden is not so much divine punishment as human consequence. We could have had *eternal life,* says the parable, at least in the sense that, like all the other animals, we would not have known that we would surely and eventually die. But we chose *moral knowledge* instead, became self-conscious about ourselves (naked!), and learned that we would surely and inevitably die.

Carnivores do not generally kill and eat their own kind; if they did, they would soon be extinct. The lioness does not normally have her cubs for appetizers and her mate for the main course. All animals are protected from that kind of extinction by instinct—except humans. We have no instinct against killing members of our own species, although we do seem to have one against eating them afterwards. Instead of instinct, we have only morality, and that is the great lesson of Genesis 2–3. Morality, not instinct, stands between us and extinction.

So what happened as soon as we humans, armed with our new-found knowledge of good and evil, left Eden forever?

Fratricide: Cain and Abel

Recall from the previous chapter that the Neolithic Revolution's invention of civilization involved the control and manipulation of cereals, animals, and humans. Recall also that it happened, not exclusively but inaugurally and paradigmatically, along the irrigated floodplains of the Euphrates and Tigris Rivers within the constricted and protected space of a city-state. As I said there, you can find that history by reading the much longer discussion in the first volume of Michael Mann's *Sources of Social Power* or the much shorter booklet by Ronald Wright, *A Short History of Progress.* You can also get it in even more succinct summary from the fourth chapter of Genesis.

Genesis 4 adopted and adapted the story of Cain and Abel from much earlier Mesopotamian antecedents; those more ancient traditions—first oral and then written—represented meditations on the Neolithic Revolution itself. They convey sober and somber thoughts about the creation of civilization by some of its earliest inventors.

The Sumerian Tradition

The Mesopotamian tradition of Dumuzi and Enkimdu—respectively, the Shepherd-god and the Farmer-god—as the divine embodiment of herding and farming goes back, like *The Epic of Gilgamesh,* to Sumerian origins in the third millennium BCE. The sun-god Utu advises his sister, Inanna, to marry the Shepherd, since "his fat is good, his milk is good." Inanna, however, rejects the Shepherd and prefers the Farmer, who "makes grain grow abundantly." The Shepherd criticizes the Farmer as "the man of dike, ditch, and plow," and after a detailed comparison of Shepherd-Farmer products, the Shepherd asks rhetorically, "The farmer—what has he more than I?"

Next, the Shepherd takes his sheep to the banks of the river, whose water links the worlds of herding and farming together. There he tries to start a quarrel with the Farmer. But the Farmer refuses to fight and instead offers peace. "I against you, why shall I strive? Let your sheep eat the grass of the riverbank. In my meadowland let your sheep walk about. In the bright fields of Erech let them eat grain. Let your kids and lambs drink the water of my canal."

Then, in return, the Shepherd accepts the Farmer as his friend and invites him to his marriage with a now-willing Inanna. "As for me, who am a shepherd, at my marriage, o farmer, may you be counted as my friend. O farmer Enkimdu, as my friend. O farmer, as my friend, may you be counted as my friend."

In this Mesopotamian tradition, therefore, the goddess first prefers the Farmer, then accepts the Shepherd, but far from killing the Shepherd, the Farmer refuses even to quarrel with him, and they become friends. So far, so good. But then Inanna decides to travel into the underworld and is trapped there forever unless she returns to earth and gets somebody to replace her. As you might guess, she sends her Shepherd-husband down to the underworld as her proxy. So, in the end, the Shepherd is a doomed species—killed, if not by the Farmer, then by his own wife, the divine Inanna.

The Biblical Tradition

In the biblical tradition (Genesis 4), the first event after humans are expelled from Eden is the birth to Adam and Eve of two sons, named Cain and Abel. As everyone knows, civilization began immediately with fratricide: the murder of one brother by another. But the story is more detailed than that. "Abel was a keeper of sheep, and Cain a tiller of the ground" (4:2), and "when they were in the field, Cain rose up against his brother Abel, and killed him" (4:8). That inaugural fratricide was the murder of a shepherd by a farmer on his own farm. That is the first act in the invention of human civilization—the farmer displacing the shepherd—and God does not punish the farmer but only marks him forever as the future of a lost past. There is no counterviolence from God—not even the appropriate divine vengeance when, as God says, "your brother's blood is crying out to me from the ground!" (4:10).

Next comes the second act in the rise of civilization's normalcy. After the birth of his first son from an unnamed wife, Cain "built a city, and named it Enoch after his son Enoch" (4:17). The farmer displaces the shepherd and builds a city—with a few biblical sentences covering several evolutionary millennia. As Robert S. McElvaine of Millsaps College in Jackson, Mississippi, wrote in his 2001 book *Eve's Seed: Biology, the Sexes, and the Course of History,* "Cain, the introducer of violence, is, moreover, identified as the father—or grandfather—of sedentary culture or 'civilization.'... This story corresponds neatly with the understanding that agricultural surplus eventually led to an increase in individualism, aggression, warfare, and greed" (p. 100).

Whether one reads the nonviolent Sumerian prototype about the interaction between the Shepherd and the Farmer or its more violent—and accurate—biblical adaptation, it is clear that in both cases the Shepherd represents the decreasing past and the Farmer represents the increasing future of human evolution's cutting edge (pun intended). The Bible, working from Sumerian models, says that civilization began in fratricide. With the Neolithic Revolution, the *cage* is closed for Mann, the *trap* is set for Wright, and *escalatory violence* has begun for Genesis. Watch that escalation as you read through Genesis 4. It begins in 4:8 with a single murder of Abel by Cain. Next, in 4:15, God refuses to avenge it with divine capital punishment but warns that, if Cain is killed by anyone, his family (presumably) would execute a "sevenfold" revenge. Finally, Lamech proclaims, in 4:23–24:

I have killed a man for wounding me,
A young man for striking me.
If Cain is avenged sevenfold,
Truly Lamech seventy-sevenfold.

The Bible summarizes both Mann and Wright in 24 verses: the farmer kills the herder, he builds a city, and human violence escalates exponentially.

It is fascinating that the tradition of Rome's urban origins also begins in fratricide, and as the next stage, or act three, to those preceding ones. Romulus and Remus were the twin sons of the war-god Mars and a human mother. As Livy records the story in his *History of Rome* (1.3), when Romulus starts to build walls around the new city of Rome, Remus mocks his activity by jumping over the first low layers. He jeers that Romulus's enemies will jump over his walls just as he has done, and Romulus, killing his brother, says that he will then slay them, just as he is slaying Remus. Cain, Abel, and inaugural fratricide. Romulus, Remus, and inaugural fratricide. Are we destined to violence by human civilization or by human nature? Is the normalcy of human civilization simply the inevitability of human nature? Put bluntly: are we as doomed as the dinosaurs—but by earthly violence, not heavenly meteor?

Ambiguity: Noah and Abraham

To pick up *The Epic of Gilgamesh* from where we left it, Enkidu and Gilgamesh start by fighting one another, then become friends, and finally set out as warrior-companions on a series of heroic exploits. When Enkidu dies, the distraught Gilgamesh goes to seek Utanapishtim, who survived the great flood and was granted the gift of immortality. Utanapishtim tells him where to find a prickly, roselike plant called "the old man becomes a young man," which will give him and the inhabitants of Uruk eternal life. "I will eat it," says Gilgamesh in Tablet XI, "and return to the condition of my youth." But on his way home, "a snake smelled the fragrance of the plant, silently came up, and carried off the plant." You will recognize the snake who steals eternity from humanity in its later incarnation in the Bible's Garden of Eden; here I focus first, however, on the Mesopotamian Utanapishtim and the Israelite Noah, then on the biblical ambiguity of Noah and Abraham.

The stories of Utanapishtim and Noah are extremely similar. In the Mesopotamian version, after the assembly of the gods decides to destroy everyone, the god Ea warns Utanapishtim to "tear down the house and build a boat. Abandon wealth and seek living things. Spurn possessions and keep alive living beings. Make all living beings go up into the boat."

Next comes the construction of the boat, with specific details about its dimensions, provisions, and logistics. "The boat was finished by sunset," but "the launching was very difficult." Then the waters envelop the land and destroy its inhabitants, and even "the gods humbly sat weeping, sobbing with grief."

Then, "on Mount Nimush, the boat lodged firm." Utanapishtim sends out successively a dove, a swallow, and a raven to determine whether the earth is dry once again. "Then I sent out everything in all directions and sacrificed a sheep," and "the gods smelled the sweet savor, and collected like flies over the sacrifice."

Finally, the supreme god, Enlil, repents of what he has done to the world and declares that "previously Utanapishtim was a human being. But now let Utanapishtim and his wife become like us, the gods."

The contacts and parallels between that story and the biblical version in Genesis 6–9 are quite obvious—down to the mountain in 8:4 where the boat is grounded; the three exploratory birds (raven, dove, dove) in 8:6–11; the exit sacrifice ("when the Lord smelled the pleasing odor") in 8:21; and the divine repentance ("never again") in 9:11–15. I am concerned here, however, not so much with the variations on the "Great Flood" story from Sumer to Israel, but with the ambiguity of what I call the Noachic solution versus the Abrahamic solution.

The Noachic solution was God's answer to the problem of increasing evil upon the earth. Here is the reason for God's destruction of everyone except Noah and his family:

The Lord saw that the wickedness of humankind was great in the earth, and that every inclination of the thoughts of their hearts was only evil continually. And the Lord was sorry that he had made humankind on the earth, and it grieved him to his heart. So the Lord said, "I will blot out from the earth the human beings I have created—people together with animals and creeping things and birds of the air, for I am sorry that I have made them." But Noah found favor in the sight of the Lord.... Noah was a righteous man, blameless in his generation; Noah walked with God.... Now the earth was corrupt in God's sight, and the earth was filled with violence. And God saw that the earth was corrupt; for all flesh had corrupted its ways upon the earth. (Genesis 6:5–11)

Given the earth's increasing evil, violence, and corruption, God's solution is to kill everyone except the one just and righteous family of Noah. That is certainly one divine solution to the problem of evil.

Clearly, however, the Noachic solution does not work because, in Genesis 10–11, the declining years of life expectancy announce that humanity is once again getting not better but worse. So, then, in Genesis 12:1–3, a new divine solution appears:

The Lord said to Abram, "Go from your country and your kindred and your father's house to the land that I will show you. I will make of you a great nation, and I will bless you, and make your name great, so that you will be a blessing. I will bless those who bless you, and the one who curses you I will curse; and in you all the families of the earth shall be blessed."

The method of the nonviolent Abrahamic solution reverses that of the violent Noachic solution. Instead of the Just One being preserved while all others are slaughtered, the Just One is chosen to bring blessings to all the "families of the earth." Throughout this chapter and especially in the book's final chapter, we encounter these twin divine solutions to humanity's corruption by violence—

the Noachic solution, which *exterminates* the many for the few, and the Abrahamic solution, which *converts* the many by the few.

Two themes emerge from this opening discussion. One is that there is continuity from the Neolithic Revolution's climactic invention of civilization through the Mesopotamian meditations on its meaning and on into the biblical mutations of those traditions in Genesis 1–11. The other is the ambiguity of a God whose Noachic solution has failed by the end of Genesis 1–11 and who starts all over with the Abrahamic solution in Genesis 12. It is that ambiguity between a violent and a nonviolent God that is the subject of the rest of this chapter—and this book.

THE LAW: DISTRIBUTIVE OR RETRIBUTIVE JUSTICE?

In ordinary speech, the term "justice" has primarily, if not exclusively, come to mean retributive justice, or punishment—that sanction by which the innocent are freed and the guilty condemned. Think for a moment about this example. In a tragic accident, a young child is killed by a driver, who flees the scene. On the local evening news, the anguished parents cry out for "justice." That is both an absolutely understandable and absolutely valid use of the term "justice" to mean retributive justice—the requirement that the perpetrator be found, held accountable, and punished. But what if the identified driver turns out to be someone so important and influential that it looks like he may avoid any punishment for his crime? Would we not immediately go from retributive to distributive justice and insist that punishments must be distributed fairly, equitably, justly? In other words, we know that the primary and even the exclusive use of justice should be to designate distributive justice. Retributive justice is, at best, a subdivision—maybe even a minor subdivision—of distributive justice.

Therefore, when the Bible insists repeatedly that God is a God of "justice and righteousness," that redundant expression names God as a God of distributive justice who does what is right by doing what is just, and does what is just by doing what is right. But how exactly does that work—specifically within the Torah, or the Divine Law of Israel?

A God of Cosmic Distribution

What does the Torah say about buying and selling land, that original material basis of life itself? In the Book of Leviticus, God decrees that "the land shall not be sold in perpetuity, for the land is mine; with me you are but aliens and tenants" (25:23). All peasants know that their land is their life. In the Torah of Israel, therefore, it is taken off the market—it is not an ordinary economic commodity to be bought and sold like sheep or goats. Behind and beneath that commandment is a theology of creation in which the land belongs to a just God who distributed it fairly and equitably to the tribes and families of Israel and who demands that it be administered fairly and equitably by those who do not own it but simply administer it as resident aliens or tenant farmers for its Owner. And of course, land-as-life is a microcosm for earth-as-life because, according to the Psalms, "the earth is the Lord's and all that is in it, the world, and those who live in it" (24:1). And that same distributive justice, however it has been established and guaranteed, both *then and now,* applies to all the earth.

Still within the Torah, we find that command repeated in the Book of Deuteronomy: "You must not move your neighbor's boundary marker, set up by former generations, on the property that will be allotted to you in the land that the Lord your God is giving you to possess" (19:14). Boundary stones mark out a cartography of justice, a geography of equity, and a divine fairness of distribution. That at least was the theory, and it demanded the people's acceptance in this antiphonal exchange: "'Cursed be anyone who moves a neighbor's boundary marker.' All the people shall say, 'Amen!'" (27:17).

We can see that theology at work in the story about the vineyard of Naboth the Jezreelite in 1 Kings 21:1–15. King Ahab offers Naboth a good price or a fair exchange for his vineyard because it is near the king's palace. Naboth replies: "The Lord forbid that I should give you my ancestral inheritance." Ahab's consort, the Canaanite Queen Jezebel, takes that refusal as a calculated insult, so she has Naboth murdered and gives the vineyard to her husband. There is no need, by the way, to demonize Jezebel. She simply came, let us say, from a different economic theology, one we could call MAFTA—the Mediterranean Area Free Trade Association for the buying and selling of everything, including land.

How, then, do ordinary people deal with a God of cosmic distributive justice both local and global? If I cannot buy and sell land, how do I keep mine and get yours? If the Torah decrees that land-as-life cannot be bought and sold, how does the unjust normalcy of civilization defeat the radicality of God? The prophet Isaiah warns against those "who join house to house, who add field to field, until there is room for no one but you, and you are left to live alone in the midst of the land!" (5:8). How do we attain that triumphant individualism if we cannot buy and sell land? Well, what about borrowing and lending with land as collateral? If you default on your mortgage loan, I can foreclose and take your land. That plan B is precisely why the Torah spends so much time legislating against it and so much time on laws about borrowing and lending, about interest and collateral. Watch, then, five steps in the Torah's relentless attempt to stay the growth of inequality and bring its bright shining manifesto down to specific social program. Always read the small print in contract, covenant, or constitution.

Forbidding Interest

In one code after another, interest is forbidden among those who lend under the Torah. Of course, if foreigners lend with interest, reciprocal interest is acceptable. Exodus commands: "If you lend money to my people, to the poor among you, you shall not deal with them as a creditor; you shall not exact interest from them" (22:25). So does Deuteronomy: "You shall not charge interest on loans to another Israelite, interest on money, interest on provisions, interest on anything that is lent" (23:19). The priestly code of holiness in Leviticus is even more emphatic:

> If any of your kin fall into difficulty and become dependent on you, you shall support them; they shall live with you as though resident aliens. Do not take interest in advance or otherwise make a profit from them, but fear your God; let them live with you. You shall not lend them your money at interest taken in advance, or provide them food at a profit. (25:35–37)

Controlling Collateral

Two laws constrain what and how collateral can be taken. From Exodus: "If you take your neighbor's cloak in pawn, you shall restore it before the sun goes down; for it may be your neighbor's only clothing to use as cover; in what else shall that person sleep?" (22:26–27). And from Deuteronomy: "No one shall take a mill or an upper millstone in pledge, for that would be taking a life in pledge" (24:6). Or again from Deuteronomy: "When you make your neighbor a loan of any kind, you shall not go into the house to take the pledge. You shall wait outside, while the person to whom you are making the loan brings the pledge out to you" (24:10–11). By divine command, both human life and human dignity are to be respected in borrower-lender relations.

Remitting Debts

We now move steadily into ever more radical attempts to prevent the relentless growth of inequality. Deuteronomy declares that "every seventh year you shall grant a remission of debts.... Every creditor shall remit the claim that is held against a neighbor, not exacting it of a neighbor who is a member of the community, because the Lord's remission has been proclaimed" (15:1–2). This applies, once again, to all—and only those—who live under the Torah. The Law adds this obvious warning: "Be careful that you do not entertain a mean thought, thinking, 'The seventh year, the year of remission, is near,' and therefore view your needy neighbor with hostility and give nothing; your neighbor might cry to the Lord against you, and you would incur guilt" (Deuteronomy 15:9).

Freeing Slaves

When it comes to the management of slaves, once again, we have laws in both Exodus and Deuteronomy. The seventh-year liberation applies to both male and female slaves, but with special and different provisions. To give some social protection to a female slave after the loss of her virginity during enslavement, Exodus specifies:

> When a man sells his daughter as a slave, she shall not go out as the male slaves do. If she does not please her master, who designated her for himself, then he shall let her be redeemed; he shall have no right to sell her to a foreign people, since he has dealt unfairly with her. If he designates her for his son, he shall deal with her as with a daughter. If he takes another wife to himself, he shall not diminish the food, clothing, or marital rights of the first wife. And if he does not do these three things for her, she shall go out without debt, without payment of money. (21:7–11)

To remunerate a male slave for the loss of his labor during enslavement, Deuteronomy specifies:

When you send a male slave out from you a free person, you shall not send him out empty-handed. Provide liberally out of your flock, your threshing floor, and your wine press, thus giving to him some of the bounty with which the Lord your God has blessed you.... Do not consider it a hardship when you send them out from you free persons, because for six years they have given you services worth the wages of hired laborers; and the Lord your God will bless you in all that you do. (15:13–14, 18)

Reversing Dispossession

In what is surely the crowning glory of the Bible's divine covenant of distributive justice, the seventh-year (or Sabbath Year) liberations from debt obligation and debt enslavement culminate in the reversal of rural dispossession in the year after seven seven-year celebrations—that is, in the fiftieth year, or the Sabbath Jubilee. Not surprisingly, this ultra-radical decree is found only in Leviticus. "You shall hallow the fiftieth year and you shall proclaim liberty throughout the land to all its inhabitants. It shall be a jubilee for you: you shall return, every one of you, to your property and every one of you to your family" (25:10). Every fiftieth year, in other words, the land is to revert to its original just distribution.

It is often asserted, probably quite correctly, that the Jubilee Year was not really observed half-century after half-century in the Jewish homeland. On the one hand, it is clearly important because it derives from the priestly heart of Torah and concerns the very purity of the land itself. On the other hand, if it can be quietly skipped without even debate, why should other purity rules be observed? If the Torah is only a menu, maybe the Ten Commandments are simply suggestions and perhaps acceptance of any five or six would suffice?

Throughout these sequential laws, from Sabbath Day through Sabbath Year to Sabbath Jubilee, we can see clearly the demand of

God for a just distribution of land-as-life based on the creation theology in Genesis 1:1–2:4a.

A God of Cosmic Retribution

That emphasis on God's *distributive* justice is clearly and definitely present all over the Torah. But so is an equal—if not greater—emphasis on God's *retributive* justice. Consider, for example, Deuteronomy 28, which may stand here for the entire Deuteronomic theology: its sequence of sin, punishment, repentance, and deliverance runs through huge swaths of the biblical books that follow it and is still regularly invoked today whenever disaster is seen as divine punishment (*What did I/we do to deserve this?*).

The most obscenely egregious invocation of God as Divine Punisher occurred recently in a conversation on the Christian Broadcasting Network's show *The 700 Club* between Jerry Falwell and Pat Robertson immediately after 9/11. John F. Harris, reporting in the *Washington Post* for September 14, 2001, quoted the Reverend Falwell's claim that the 9/11 tragedy was simply God's punishment of America for its sins.

> The abortionists have got to bear some burden for this because God will not be mocked. And when we destroy 40 million little innocent babies, we make God mad. I really believe that the pagans, and the abortionists, and the feminists, and the gays and the lesbians who are actively trying to make that an alternative life-style, the ACLU, People for the American Way—all of them who have tried to secularize America—I point the finger in their face and say, "You helped this happen."

It is a strange God, by the way, who punishes Christian secularism with Islamic terrorism. But back to Deuteronomy 28.

The Book of Deuteronomy insists elsewhere that God's *distributive* justice be established in God's land on God's earth. The Lord "your God is God of gods and Lord of Lords, the great God, mighty and awesome, who is not partial and takes no bribe, who executes justice for the orphan and the widow, and who loves the strangers, providing them food and clothing" (10:17–18). It is therefore mandatory that "you shall not deprive a resident alien or an orphan of justice; you shall not take a widow's garment in pledge" (24:17). God's distributive justice demanded that special concern be shown for those who were structurally vulnerable in that time and place: the widow who lacked a husband and the orphan who lacked a father in a patriarchal society, or the resident alien who lacked clan protection in a tribal society. But for here and now, I focus on the claims of God's *retributive* justice in Deuteronomy 28.

The book imagines Moses repeating the Sinai covenant between God and Israel just before entering the Promised Land—hence the Greek title *Deuteros Nomos,* or "Second (giving of the) Law." Deuteronomy 28 is very unevenly divided between promised blessings ("if you will only obey the Lord your God, by diligently observing all his commandments that I am commanding you today, the Lord your God will set you high above all the nations of the earth" [1–14]) and threatened curses ("if you will not obey the Lord your God by diligently observing all his commandments and decrees, which I am commanding you today, then all these curses shall come upon you and overtake you" [15–68]). Besides the fertility of humans, animals, and fields, the much shorter list of blessings includes this special promise: "The Lord will cause your enemies who rise against you to be defeated before you; they shall come out against you one way, and flee before you seven ways" (7). The much longer list of curses includes the infertility of humans, animals, and fields—and this special threat: "The Lord will cause you to be defeated before your enemies; you shall go out against them one way and flee before them seven ways" (25). For the moment, however, I leave aside the parallel but very uneven promise in Deuteronomy of rewards (fourteen verses) and punishments (fifty-four verses) for obedience or disobedience to

God. And I also leave aside any discussion of the literal or meta-phorical nature of the anthropomorphic personification of God as angry punisher. I ask only about the integrity and validity of the Deuteronomic theology.

The land of Israel was a tiny piece of real estate positioned at the hinge of the European, Asian, and African continents. When empires clashed along a north-south axis between the Nile Delta and whoever controlled the Anatolian Plateau or the Mesopota-mian Plain, tiny Israel was there in the middle. When the axis of empire changed to an east-west direction and the clash was be-tween Persians and Greeks or Parthians and Romans, little Israel was still right there in the middle. So here is the geopolitical truth. If the people of Israel had all been saints and had spent their lives on their knees praying, the only difference would have been death kneeling down rather than standing up.

I consider it bad or even obscene theology to tell such people that invasion (or drought or any other disaster) is a divine punish-ment for sin. Nothing they could ever have done or not done would have changed a destiny of oppression—by imperialism marching north and south or east and west. Their Promised Land was simply the cockpit of empire. And when a theology of divine punishment was accepted and internalized, the Bible was filled with pleas for mercy, cries for clemency, and prayers for forgive-ness. If imperial oppression were God's punishment for sin, a plea for forgiveness from corporate sin was an appeal for divine deliv-erance from imperial oppression. "Forgive us our sins [the alleged cause]" meant "Send those imperialists [the alleged effect] back from whence they came."

Divine justice as distributive *and/or* retributive is the first biblical ambiguity to be considered. On the one hand, both of these attri-butes or emphases stretch from one end of the Christian Bible to the other. It is not as if retributive justice were only in the Old Tes-tament and distributive justice were only in the New Testament. Both strands are there from Genesis through Revelation. On the other hand, is there any evidence—apart from biblical assertions and human fears—that God ever punishes anyone? There is terribly clear evidence of human consequences, but unless one equates human consequences with divine punishments—which I, for one, do not—is there any similar evidence for divine punishments?

In his 2004 book *Dresden: Tuesday, February 13, 1945*, Frederick Taylor describes the deliberate burning to the ground of Germany's largest synagogue, in Dresden on Kristallnacht, November 9, 1938, while SA and SS forces restrained the city's firefighters from doing anything to save it. "A grizzled Dresden street character named Franz Hackel ... muttered: 'This fire will return! It will make a long curve and then come back to us!'" (p. 75). During the night between Shrove Tuesday and Ash Wednesday, February 13–14, 1945, the city of Dresden was deliberately struck twice by a combination of high-explosive and incendiary bombs from British and American planes to create a perfect firestorm with the greatest destruction of any single night-raid of the war. I do not believe that was divine punishment, but it was a terrible human consequence. I therefore rephrase my question about the biblical ambiguity of divine justice as a deeper question about divine violence: is God violent or nonviolent? That most basic question of all continues into the next subject.

PROPHECY: REVOLUTION OR INDICTMENT?

Biblical prophecy (from the Greek *pro-phe⁻mi*) was not just about "speaking before," about "fore-telling" the future, but about "speaking for" God, especially as an indictment against those who failed to observe the covenant of distributive justice at the heart of Israel's Torah. When we hear of the biblical prophets, we might think only of Amos and Micah, Isaiah and Jeremiah, Ezekiel and Zechariah. But I begin here with two earlier prophets, Elijah and his disciple Elisha in the late 800s and the early 700s BCE. Recall that the Jewish homeland was divided into the northern Kingdom of Israel and the southern Kingdom of Judah in those centuries. I begin with Elijah and Elisha in the Kingdom of Israel because these earliest of the prophets were engaged in *violent* revolution and, compared with the *nonviolent* later prophets, they continue that biblical ambiguity between a violent or a nonviolent God. Surely the character of a prophet's God determines the content of that prophet's program.

God's instructions to Elijah are quite clear: "You shall anoint Hazael as king over Aram. Also you shall anoint Jehu son of Nimshi as king over Israel; and you shall anoint Elisha son of Shaphat of Abel-meholah as prophet in your place. Whoever escapes from the sword of Hazael, Jehu shall kill; and whoever escapes from the sword of Jehu, Elisha shall kill" (1 Kings 19:15–17). Regime change, both foreign and domestic, by violent rebellion is the divine program to be started by Elijah and completed by Elisha, who becomes his disciple in 1 Kings 19:19–21 and obtains a double share of his spirit in 2 Kings 2:9–11. Here is how Elisha delivers God's mandate to Jehu:

Then the prophet Elisha called a member of the company of prophets and said to him, "Gird up your loins; take this flask of oil in your hand, and go to Ramoth-gilead. When you arrive, look there for Jehu son of Jehoshaphat, son of Nimshi; go in and get him to leave his companions, and take him into an inner chamber. Then take the flask of oil, pour it on his head, and say, 'Thus says the Lord: I anoint you king over Israel.' Then open the door and flee; do not linger."

So the young man, the young prophet, went to Ramoth-gilead. He arrived while the commanders of the army were in council, and he announced, "I have a message for you, commander." "For which one of us?" asked Jehu. "For you, commander." So Jehu got up and went inside; the young man poured the oil on his head, saying to him, "Thus says the Lord the God of Israel: I anoint you king over the people of the Lord, over Israel. You shall strike down the house of your master Ahab, so that I may avenge on Jezebel the blood of my servants the prophets, and the blood of all the servants of the

Lord. For the whole house of Ahab shall perish; I will cut
off from Ahab every male, bond or free, in Israel." (2 Kings
9:1–8)

First of all, remember that we met King Ahab earlier trying to ac-
quire Naboth's ancestral vineyard. Second, when Elisha sends the
young prophet on that mission of high treason, he advises him to
"flee [and] do not linger." That is certainly very prudent but not
exactly very brave of Elisha. Third, Ahab belonged to the dynasty
of Omri, which ruled the northern Kingdom of Israel from
around 880 to 841 BCE, so this divinely certified and prophetically
delivered mandate is for the new dynasty of Jehu to replace violently the previous one of Omri. Here is how that transition
occurs as Joram, the last king of Omri's line, falls to the treachery
of Jehu.

Both King Ahaziah of the southern Kingdom of Judah and
King Joram of the northern Kingdom of Israel "set out, each in
his chariot, and went to meet Jehu; they met him at the property
of Naboth the Jezreelite" (2 Kings 9:21). Of course, you are probably thinking, where else! The plot concludes in 2 Kings 9:22–24:

When Joram saw Jehu, he said, "Is it peace, Jehu?" He answered, "What peace can there be, so long as the many
whoredoms and sorceries of your mother Jezebel continue?"
Then Joram reined about and fled, saying to Ahaziah, "Treason, Ahaziah!" Jehu drew his bow with all his strength, and
shot Joram between the shoulders, so that the arrow pierced
his heart; and he sank in his chariot.

So began the dynasty of Jehu, which ruled the northern Kingdom
of Israel from around 841 to 753 BCE. With God, prophecy, treachery, and violence on its side, how did it do? Did the actions of
Elijah and Elisha improve the lot of Israel's suffering peasants and
oppressed poor?

What happened is this. Omri's dynasty had produced Ahab, who ruled for about twenty years (873–853 BCE). Omri's dynasty was replaced by Jehu's dynasty, which produced Jeroboam II, who ruled for about thirty years (782–753 BCE). In promoting this regime change, Elijah and Elisha simply took Israel out of the frying pan into the fire. Eventually the nonviolent prophet who spoke vehemently against Jeroboam II was Amos, who risked his own life by confronting Jeroboam's injustice directly and nonviolently:

> Then Amaziah, the priest of Bethel, sent to King Jeroboam of Israel, saying, "Amos has conspired against you in the very center of the house of Israel; the land is not able to bear all his words. For thus Amos has said, 'Jeroboam shall die by the sword, and Israel must go into exile away from his land.'" And Amaziah said to Amos, "O seer, go, flee away to the land of Judah, earn your bread there, and prophesy there; but never again prophesy at Bethel, for it is the king's sanctuary, and it is a temple of the kingdom." (Amos 7:10–13)

From Amos onwards, the biblical prophets worked always on that same dangerous interface between politics and religion and spoke always in the name of God and Torah, justice and equity, but never again did a biblical prophet promote a violent internal revolution as the will and plan of God.

HOW THE BIBLE ENDS ITS STORY

There is probably no idea more subject to mystification and misunderstanding than *eschatology,* or *apocalypticism,* except maybe their combination as *apocalyptic eschatology.* Yet not only are these terms conceptually simple, but they represent almost inevitable conclusions from certain basic beliefs. "Eschatology" comes from the Greek *eschata* + *logos* and concerns last things or endings—but the end of what? "Apocalyptic" comes from the Greek *apokalypsis* and concerns a special revelation (from the Latin *revelatio*)—but a special revelation about what?

The Great Divine Cleanup of the World

Suppose, on the one hand, that your communal *faith* is based on a just God who controls the earth. Suppose, on the other, that your communal *experience* is based on internal royal injustice and external imperial control. What then? How do you hold on to both fundamental faith and continual experience confronted with such cognitive dissonance? One answer is that the Creator-God would transform—would *have to* transform—an evil and unjust earth into a world of justice and peace. Faith, and not just hope, demanded that God would overcome, someday. There would, someday, be a Great Divine Cleanup of the world. Before proceeding, however, I need to remove two serious misunderstandings about God's ultimate cleanup of the earth.

First, we misunderstand ancient Jewish and/or Christian eschatology if we think it was about the end of the world—if we think it was about the divine destruction of this physical earth. In the King James Version of the Bible, the phrase "end of the world" is repeated in Matthew 13 (verses 39 and 49) and in chapter 24 (verses 3 and 20). But the Greek term translated there as "world" is actually *aiōn*, from which we get our word *eon*, meaning a period, a time, an era. What is to end is this present "era" of evil and injustice, suffering and oppression.

Our problem is that we can easily imagine the earth's destruction because we ourselves can now do it atomically, biologically, chemically, demographically, and environmentally—and that brings us only up to the letter *e* in the alphabet. For ancient Jews and Christians, by contrast, only God *could* destroy the earth, but God *would* never do that. Why? Because six times during creation God declared the product "good," and when all was finished, "God saw everything that he had made, and indeed, it was very good"

(Genesis 1:31). On the one hand, therefore, God would never destroy God's own creation. On the other, what God could do was not to destroy but to transform the earth. And God would do just that—someday.

Second, we misunderstand ancient Jewish and/or Christian eschatology if we think it was about evacuating a destroyed earth for a new heavenly location. Instead, that transformation would take place here below on an earth transfigured from violence to peace. It was not, as it were, a movement from earth to heaven, but rather one from heaven to earth. Recall, for example, that for Jesus in the Lord's Prayer the Kingdom of God is about the will of God "on earth as in heaven." The original mock-up for God's earthly kingdom has been retained in heaven—like the model in an architect's office—but the final construction site will be on the earth itself.

In imagining that transformed earth, eschatology spoke of a physical world, an animal world, and a social world transmuted from violence to nonviolence. I choose as an example of that triple alteration a text from the Jewish *Sibylline Oracles* that dates from around 150 years before the time of Jesus. It is one of the best and clearest summaries of how that three-part world will be transformed by God's redemptive action.

First, the transfigured *physical* world is a place of unlabored fertility with abundant food or drink:

For the all-bearing earth will give the most excellent unlimited fruit to mortals, of grain, wine, and oil and a delightful drink of sweet honey from heaven, trees, fruit of the top branches, and rich flocks and herds and lambs of sheep and kids of goats. (3.744–48)

The Mediterranean triad of grains, grapes, and olives appears, of course, in first place.

Next, the transfigured *animal* world will turn carnivores into herbivores and wild animals into domesticated playmates for children. There will no longer be any violence in all the world:

Wolves and lambs will eat grass together in the mountains. Leopards will feed together with kids. Roving bears will spend the night with calves. The flesh-eating lion will eat husks at the manger like an ox, and mere infant children will lead them with ropes. For he will make the beasts on earth harmless. Serpents and asps will sleep with babies and will not harm them, for the hand of God will be upon them. (3.788–95)

As you may have recognized, that ecstatic hyperbole recapitulates the famous rhapsody of Isaiah 11:6–9 from almost six hundred years earlier. He too envisioned a future earth where, even in the animal world,

the wolf shall live with the lamb, the leopard shall lie down with the kid, the calf and the lion and the fatling together, and a little child shall lead them. The cow and the bear shall graze, their young shall lie down together; and the lion shall eat straw like the ox. The nursing child shall play over the hole of the asp, and the weaned child shall put its hand on the adder's den. They will not hurt or destroy on all my holy mountain; for the earth will be full of the knowledge of the Lord as the waters cover the sea.

That ancient vision concedes that even the natural violence of the feral carnivore will be abolished in God's new creation. No longer will there be conflict between animal and animal or between animals and humans. We are back, in other words, to that nonviolent, vegetarian world seen at the creation in Genesis 1:29–30.

Finally, the transfigured *social* world in the *Sibylline Oracles* will see the cessation of violence, the end of warfare, and, especially, the establishment of "just wealth among men":

There will be no sword on earth or din of battle, and the earth will no longer be shaken, groaning deeply. There will no longer be war or drought on earth, no famine or hail, damaging to fruits, but there will be great peace throughout the whole earth. King will be friend to king to the end of the age. The Immortal in the starry heaven will put in effect a common law for men throughout the whole earth.... And then, indeed, he will raise up a kingdom for all ages among men, he who once gave the holy Law to the pious, to all of whom he promised to open the earth and the world and the gates of the blessed and all joys and immortal intellect and eternal cheer. From every land they will bring incense and gifts to the house of the great God.... Prophets of the great God will take away the sword for they themselves are judges of men and righteous kings. There will also be just wealth among men for this is the judgment and dominion of the great God. (3.751–58, 767–73, 781–84)

That is a standard scenario for a full-service eschatology, and as is quite clear, it is not about humanity's evacuation from a destroyed earth to a heavenly alternative, but about physical, feral, and social life in a transfigured world on a transformed earth.

It is so terribly easy to mock this magnificent scenario, to laugh at images of lettuce for leopards and pesto for panthers. But do not think that the incredibility of these perfected physical and animal worlds makes the vision of a just and nonviolent social world equally incredible. Since we first invented *culture* (or it us), violence has been our drug of choice, but since we first invented *civilization* (or it us), violence has escalated along with all of civilization's other increases and improvements. Our present problem is that escalatory violence has now reached a level where withdrawal will be only slightly less painful than continued addiction. How much time to detoxify do we have left before it is too late for the social and/or the animal and/or the physical world? Recall: three million years from stone to iron weapons, but three thousand years from iron to atomic weapons. Not bad progress that, for a smart ape from Africa.

One final point. Eschatology is a vision of God's own cleanup of God's own world now grown toxic from evil and impurity, injustice and oppression, war and violence. An *apocalypse* adds to that expectation claims of a special *revelation* about it. Strictly speaking, an apocalyptic seer could be proclaiming anything about any aspect of that eschatological faith, but primarily and predominantly, an *apocalyptic eschatology* claims a special revelation about the imminence of God's transformative action. It is to happen soon, the apocalyptic seer asserts, any day now, certainly in our lifetime. Those who are foolhardy give a precise date. Those who are wise do not.

Final War or Final Banquet?

Along with that faith in the imminent arrival of God's cosmic fumigation of violence and injustice, there arises one very obvious question: what will God do about non-Jews, about those whom Jews called the "Gentiles" (from Latin *gentes,* "nations" or "peoples")? Here we encounter another misunderstanding. That question is not simply one of xenophobia, chauvinism, or discrimination against all others except themselves. Israel was not worried about the Irish or the Japanese. "The Gentiles" meant the great *empires.* For about five hundred years before the time of Jesus, his ancestors had known the Gentiles/nations only as conquering empires—as the Assyrians, the Babylonians, the Persians, the Macedonians, the Greco-Egyptians, the Greco-Syrians, and finally the Romans. The question was simply this: when the Great Divine Cleanup begins, what will God do with the contemporary Great Empire? More proximately and immediately: what in the first century CE will God do about the Romans? More generally and widely: what is God's final solution to the problem of evil?

By now you will probably not be surprised to find, in answer to that question, another example of the biblical ambiguity I have been exploring in this chapter. And it arises, once again and always, from whether one envisages a God of distributive or retributive justice—that is, even more basically, a God of nonviolence or a God of violence—in the Law or the Prophets. As we have seen already, both visions are there—and here as well. As prologue, I repeat one point to avoid another long-held misunderstanding. It is positively, absolutely *not* that one solution is found exclusively in the Old Testament and/or the Jewish tradition while another is found exclusively in the New Testament and/or the Christian tradition. It is not ecumenical courtesy, political correctness, or post-Holocaust sensitivity, but simply biblical and historical accuracy to insist that *both* solutions run side by side, and often in the same books, from one end of the biblical tradition to the other. They are asserted relentlessly as the twin train tracks of the Divine Express, and they are utterly persuasive for those who have never imagined a Divine Monorail.

Extermination

One answer to the question of what God will do about empires (and recall that empire has always been the normalcy of civilization's brutality) is quite simply extermination. We saw it earlier as the Noachic solution: God will destroy the contemporary Gentile empire that violently and unjustly rules Israel and the world. In this vision, God's solution to the problem of human violence is the Great Final Battle in which good triumphs over evil—and triumphs, let us be clear, by divine violence. The symbolic place of that cosmic cleanup as cosmic slaughter is at Har Megiddo in Hebrew (hence our English "Armageddon"), the mountain pass where the spine of Israel's central hill country cuts westward toward the coast and skirts a great plain suitable for battle.

I will cite only two examples of this vision of ethnic or ethic cleansing of the earth by divine violence, but as noted earlier, you can find it from one end of the biblical tradition to the other. Here is God according to the prophet Micah:

In anger and wrath I will execute vengeance on the nations that did not obey.... Then my enemy will see, and shame will cover her who said to me, "Where is the Lord your God?" My eyes will see her downfall; now she will be trodden down like the mire of the streets.... The nations shall see and be ashamed of all their might; they shall lay their hands on their mouths; their ears shall be deaf; they shall lick dust like a snake, like the crawling things of the earth; they shall come trembling out of their fortresses; they shall turn in dread to the Lord our God, and they shall stand in fear of you. (5:15; 7:10, 16–17)

Sometimes physical extermination is muted into abject social servitude, but in either scenario, divine violence destroys the nations/empires one way or another. Again, I emphasize that this solution is found in both the Old and New Testaments and that in fact it consummates our Christian Bible in its final book, the Apocalypse, or Revelation:

And the wine press was trodden outside the city, and blood flowed from the wine press, as high as a horse's bridle, for a distance of about two hundred miles.... Then I saw an angel standing in the sun, and with a loud voice he called to all the birds that fly in midheaven, "Come, gather for the great supper of God, to eat the flesh of kings, the flesh of captains, the flesh of the mighty, the flesh of horses and their riders—flesh of all, both free and slave, both small and great." Then I saw the beast and the kings of the earth with their armies gathered to make war against the rider on the horse and against his army. And the beast was captured, and with it the false prophet who had performed in its presence the signs by which he deceived those who had received the mark of the beast and those who worshiped its image. These two were thrown alive into the lake of fire that burns with sulfur. And the rest were killed by the sword of the rider on the horse, the sword that came from his mouth; and all the birds were gorged with their flesh. (14:20, 19:17–21)

I leave that vision of terminal divine violence aside for now but will return to it in much greater detail as the subject for this book's final chapter.

Conversion

There is another scenario for God's final solution to the problem of evil; we saw it earlier as the Abrahamic solution. It is not the Great Final War but the Great Final Banquet, and its symbolic place is not Mount Megiddo for fighting but Mount Zion for feasting.

The primary text here is famous not only for its content but because it is repeated, more or less verbatim, in two different but contemporary biblical prophets from the southern Kingdom of Judea in the late eighth century. It is given in Isaiah 2:2–4 and also in Micah 4:1–3, but with an additional verse in Micah 4:4. Here is the longer Micah version:

In days to come the mountain of the Lord's house shall be established as the highest of the mountains, and shall be raised up above the hills. Peoples shall stream to it, and many nations shall come and say: "Come, let us go up to the mountain of the Lord, to the house of the God of Jacob; that he may teach us his ways and that we may walk in his paths." For out of Zion shall go forth instruction, and the word of the Lord from Jerusalem. He shall judge between many peoples, and shall arbitrate between strong nations far away; they shall beat their swords into plowshares, and their spears into pruning hooks; nation shall not lift up sword against nation, neither shall they learn war any more; but they shall

all sit under their *own* vines and under their *own* fig trees, and
no one shall make them afraid; for the mouth of the Lord of
hosts has spoken. (Micah 4:1–4, emphasis mine)

That opening phrase, "in days to come," expresses the unspecified
time of the future eschatological moment. At that time, all peoples
and nations will convert to the God of nonviolence in a world
without weapons and to the God of justice in a world without
empires.

Another text, Isaiah 25:6–8, describes the eschatological con-
vention of all peoples on Mount Zion as not only a divine seminar on nonviolence but a divine feast of the best food and drink:

On this mountain the Lord of hosts will make for all peoples
a feast of rich food, a feast of well-aged wines, of rich food
filled with marrow, of well-aged wines strained clear. And he
will destroy on this mountain the shroud that is cast over all
peoples, the sheet that is spread over all nations; he will swallow up death forever. Then the Lord God will wipe away the
tears from all faces, and the disgrace of his people he will take
away from all the earth, for the Lord has spoken.

Cosmic peace is celebrated at and by a cosmic banquet on Mount
Zion, and it is not a battle-feast for the vultures of the air but a
peace-feast for the nations of the earth.

A final example from a prophet of the late sixth century appears
in Zechariah 8:20–23, and it raises a very important question
about this envisioned *conversion:*

Thus says the Lord of hosts: Peoples shall yet come, the inhabitants of many cities; the inhabitants of one city shall go
to another, saying, "Come, let us go to entreat the favor of
the Lord, and to seek the Lord of hosts; I myself am going."
Many peoples and strong nations shall come to seek the Lord
of hosts in Jerusalem, and to entreat the favor of the Lord.

Thus says the Lord of hosts: In those days ten men from nations of every language shall take hold of a Jew, grasping his garment and saying, "Let us go with you, for we have heard that God is with you."

Here is the final question and the final possible misunderstanding of Jewish and then Jewish Christian eschatology. Is that conversion to Judaism or to God?

First, there is no vision of everyone having their own God and their own religion within that moment of cosmic peace, feast, and unity. The biblical prophets who wrote those texts had seen the Gods of the nations and experienced the Gods of the great empires, and they thought of them as part of the problem, not part of the solution. No, they said, all peoples and all nations will have to convert to the one true God of nonviolence, justice, and peace. Second, then, there is nothing in those texts about a Great Cosmic Circumcision for all Gentile males, nor does the question arise as to whether the final banquet will be kosher or not. No doubt, most eschatological seers would find these questions quite meaningless, and it is hard to find an eschatological vision that raises such issues for God's transfigured earth.

Equality

I conclude with one extra-biblical Jewish text that dates from the time of the emperor Augustus immediately before and after the birth of Jesus. In *Sibylline Oracles,* an apocalyptic seer gives us another vision of the eschatological world here below upon this transformed earth:

The earth will belong equally to all, undivided by walls or fences. It will then bear more abundant fruits spontaneously. Lives will be in common and wealth will have no division. For there will be no poor man there, no rich, and no tyrant, no slave. Further, no one will be either great or small anymore. No kings, no leaders. All will be on a par together. (2.319–24)

I cite this passage lest you think that the dream of human equality is something recently invented by us and that I am simply retro-jecting it back into a first century that would never have under-stood it.

In summary, then, the two final divine solutions for the prob-lem of the Gentile empires, the Noachic solution of extermina-tion by force and violence and the Abrahamic solution of conversion to justice and peace, are never reconciled anywhere in the biblical tradition. They are there together from one end of it to the other. Indeed, they often coexist in the same book or even in the same chapter. So once again, are we to take them both and worship a God of both violence and nonviolence, or must we choose between them and recognize, as I am arguing, that the Bible proposes the radicality of a nonviolent God strug-gling with the normalcy of a violent civilization? Is that its dignity, its integrity, its authority—for any Christian—and its value for any human being?

RESISTANCE: VIOLENCE OR NONVIOLENCE?

In this final section, I go outside biblical traditions and first-century documents to look at resistance itself. Apart completely from a Jesus or a Paul, how did other first-century Jews respond as their homeland became a tiny colonial part of the great Roman Empire?

The first choice was between *collaboration* and *resistance,* and of course, each could be theologically motivated. The priest-historian Josephus, an aristocratic Jew for whom nonresistance to the Roman Empire was the will of Israel's God, was a classic example of religio-political collaboration. Here, from his *Jewish War,* are three faith-based points.

First, it was the divine will that Rome rule the world: "God who went the round of the nations, bringing to each in turn the rod of empire, now rested over Italy" (5.367). Next, it was the divine will that the new Flavian dynasty rule Rome: "[Titus] was still at Alexandria, assisting his father [Vespasian] to establish the empire which God had recently committed to their hands" (5.2). Finally, therefore, in revolting against imperial control, "you are warring not against the Romans only, but also against God....The Deity has fled from the holy places and taken His stand on the side of those with whom you are now at war" (5.378, 412).

The alternative to collaboration was resistance, but that immediately raised the options of violent or nonviolent resistance. I insist emphatically that both of these options were programmatically present in the first-century Jewish homeland. I also insist that Jewish nonviolent resistance to Rome is not an invalid retrojection of our own knowledge of nonviolent resistance to oppression—from Ireland with Daniel O'Connell, through North and South America with Martin Luther King Jr. and Oscar Romero, to South Africa with Nelson Mandela and Desmond Tutu. Nonviolent resistance to injustice was not invented quite that recently. Like violent resistance, it was already there in the first-century Jewish homeland. As therapy against the presumption that modernity invented both the violent resistance of terrorism and the nonviolent resistance of pacifism, I offer an example of each from first-century Jewish responses to Roman imperialism.

Violent Resistance: The Daggers of the Sicarii

It was anti-Roman Jewish rebels who invented urban terrorism, although, to be accurate, they never used it against their ordinary fellow citizens but only against the Jewish high priests who collaborated with Rome. The time was in the late 50s to early 60s CE; this is Josephus's account in his *Jewish War:*

In Jerusalem, the so-called *sicarii* ... committed murders in broad daylight in the heart of the city. *The festivals were their special seasons,* when they would mingle with the crowd, carrying short daggers [*sicae* in Latin] concealed under their clothing, with which they stabbed their enemies. Then, when they fell, the murderers joined in the cries of indignation and, through this plausible behavior, were never discovered. The first to be assassinated by them was Jonathan the [ex-]high priest [from 36 to 37 CE]; after his death there were numerous daily murders. *The panic created was more alarming than the calamity itself;* every one, as on a battlefield, hourly expected death. Men kept watch at a distance on their enemies and would not trust even their friends when they approached. Yet, even while their suspicions were aroused and they were on their guard, they fell; so swift were the conspirators and so crafty in eluding detection. (2.254–57, emphasis mine)

Notice two important sentences (italicized) in that account. First, "the festivals were their special seasons." With large crowds in a small space within the temple, the assassinations had both maximum anonymity and maximum publicity. Second, "the panic created was more alarming than the calamity itself." That description is what justifies my term "urban terrorists" for the *sicarii,* or dagger-men. Their intent was not just to murder but to terrorize high-profile Jewish collaborators with the Roman occupation. I would emphasize, however, that they did not kill at random and they did not kill ordinary civilians.

Josephus adds one further detail to their story, and this, once again, is something we might think was invented only in the last few decades of our own contemporary world. Here is what happened when some of the *sicarii* were captured:

[The *sicarii*] kidnapped the secretary of the captain [of the Temple] Eleazar—he was the son of Ananias the high priest—and led him off in bonds. They then sent to Ananias saying that they would release the secretary to him if he would induce Albinus [the Roman prefect from 62 to 64 CE] to release ten of their number who had been taken prisoner. Ananias under this constraint persuaded Albinus and obtained this request. This was the beginning of greater troubles; for the brigands contrived by one means or another to kidnap some of Ananias' staff and would hold them in continuous confinement and refuse to release them until they had received in exchange some of the *sicarii*. When they had once more become not inconsiderable in number, they grew bold again and proceeded to harass every part of the land. (*Jewish War*, 2.254–57)

The *sicarii* counter-captured from within the high priestly family and exchanged at the rate of one for ten, and of course, once that tactic was so successful, they adopted kidnapping as a permanent counterstrategy. That led, concludes Josephus, to even "greater troubles."

Nonviolent Resistance: God, Not Caesar, Is the Only Lord

After the death of Herod the Great in 4 BCE, Rome divided Herod's realm between his sons. Archelaus got the center and south but lasted only ten years before being exiled for incompetence. Rome then took over direct control of his territories, sent in Coponius as the first governor, and ordered the standard census to prepare for tax assessments. Here is what happened next, according to Josephus's *Jewish War:*

Under his administration, a Galilean, named Judas, incited his countrymen to revolt, upbraiding them as cowards for consenting to pay tribute to the Romans and tolerating mortal masters, after having God for their Lord. (2.117)

Josephus groups all types of Roman resistance under the rubric of a "fourth philosophy," thereby ignoring any distinction between nonviolent and violent action but also quarantining resistance safely separate from the three philosophies or ideologies of the Essenes, the Pharisees, and the Sadducees. Those Jewish philosophical options, he hints, are just like the Roman philosophical options of, respectively, Pythagoreans, Stoics, and Epicureans. But he also hints that this "fourth philosophy" is almost radically un-Jewish. Or, as he continues:

> [Judas] was a teacher who founded a sect of his own, having nothing in common with the others. Jewish philosophy, in fact, takes three forms. The followers of the first school are called Pharisees, of the second Sadducees, of the third Essenes. (2:118)

Despite all that apologetic damage control, the theological motivation of Judas is quite clear. Only God, not Caesar, is Lord, and to submit to a census for taxation is to accept Rome as God's replacement. That description, however, does not make it clear whether Judas was advocating violent or nonviolent revolt. I conclude, however, that he sought a nonviolent response, for two major reasons.

First, about twenty years later, when Josephus wrote *Jewish Antiquities,* he went into much more detail about Judas and his movement. Watch the rather tortuous rhetoric, which indicates that he is not describing something simple, like a straightforward armed rebellion. Here is one example:

> A certain Judas, a Gaulanite from the city of Gamala [east of the Sea of Galilee], who had enlisted the aid of Saddok, a Pharisee, threw himself into the cause of rebellion. They said that the assessment carried with it a status amounting to downright slavery, no less, and appealed to the nation to make a bid for independence. They urged that in case of success the Jews would have laid the foundation of prosperity, while if they failed to obtain any boon, they would win

honor and renown for their lofty aim; and that Heaven would be their zealous helper to no lesser end than the furthering of their enterprise until it succeeded—all the more if with high devotion in their hearts they stood firm and did *not shrink from the bloodshed that might be necessary.* (18:4–9, emphasis mine)

Now that a Pharisee is working alongside Judas, Josephus's clear separation of the "fourth philosophy" from all other Jewish options is not as absolute as he made it sound earlier. Notice also the phrase I italicized, "necessary bloodshed." In an ordinary violent revolt, bloodshed could be taken for granted on both sides. But Judas is announcing nonviolent resistance and inviting his followers to be ready for their own bloodshed—as martyrs.

That admitted closeness between Pharisees and the "fourth philosophy" reappears a few paragraphs later:

As for the fourth of the philosophies, Judas the Galilean set himself up as leader of it. This school agrees in all other respects with the opinions of the Pharisees, except that they have a passion for liberty that is almost unconquerable, since they are convinced that God alone is their leader and master. They think little of submitting to death in unusual forms and permitting vengeance to fall on kinsmen and friends if only they may avoid calling any man master. Inasmuch as most people have seen the steadfastness of their resolution amid such circumstances, I may forgo any further account. For I have no fear that anything reported of them will be considered incredible. The danger is, rather, that report may minimize the indifference with which they accept the grinding misery of pain. (18:23–25)

My conclusion is that Judas the Galilean invented a mode and program of nonviolent resistance backed, of course, by readiness for martyrdom.

Second, whenever armed revolts broke out in the Jewish homeland, some or all of the four Roman legions stationed near Antioch on the Orontes to guard the Euphrates frontier marched
southward for brutal and punitive suppression. But they did not
move from their Syrian base camps against Judas and his followers.
That confirms for me that their resistance was nonviolent and
could therefore be handled by the prefect's own police forces and
auxiliary troops. Thus, Judas, not Jesus, was the first Galilean to
proclaim nonviolent resistance to violent injustice in the first
quarter of the first century CE.

JESUS CHRIST, THE LAND OF THE LIVING

The ambiguity of divine power suffuses the Christian Bible in *both*
its Testaments and therefore presses this question for us Christians:
how do we reconcile the ambiguity of our Bible's violent and/or
nonviolent God? My proposal is that *the Christian Bible presents the
radicality of a just and nonviolent God repeatedly and relentlessly confronting the normalcy of an unjust and violent civilization.* Again and
again throughout the biblical tradition, God's radical vision for
nonviolent justice is offered, and again and again we manage to
mute it back into the normalcy of violent injustice.

The Christian Bible records the ongoing struggle between the
normalcy of civilization's program of religion, war, victory, peace (or
more succinctly, peace through victory), seen in chapter 1, and the
radicality of God's alternative program of religion, nonviolence, justice, peace (or more succinctly, peace through justice), seen here in
chapter 2. But that struggle is depicted *inside the Bible* itself. That is
its integrity and its authority. If the Bible were only about peace
through victory, we would not need it. If it were only about
peace through justice, we would not believe it.

The Christian Bible forces us to witness the struggle of these
two transcendental visions *within its own pages* and to ask ourselves
as Christians how *we* decide between them. My answer is that *we*

are bound to whichever of these visions was incarnated by and in the historical Jesus. It is not the violent but the nonviolent God who is revealed to Christian faith in Jesus of Nazareth and announced to Christian faith by Paul of Tarsus.

I conclude with an image to hold in imagination as we move from this chapter to the next one. Istanbul's Church of St. Savior was originally called "in chora" because it was situated "in the country" or "in the land" outside the walls of Constantine's new city of Constantinople. Later, when it was included inside Theodosian's walls, that title was changed in a superb pun to mean Jesus Christ as himself "the land of the living." Having gone from church to mosque to museum, it is today the Kariye Müzesi.

As you pass from outer to inner narthex, the doorway is crowned with a magnificent mosaic of Christ *Pantokrator.* That title, by the way, meant "All-Powerful" at a time when the Christian Byzantine emperors still held the title *Autokrator,* or "Self-Powerful," once held by the pagan Roman emperors. As in all such Eastern icons, frescoes, or mosaics of Christ, his right hand is raised in an authoritative teaching gesture, with his fingers separated into a twosome and a threesome to command Christian faith in the two natures of Christ and the three persons of the Trinity. As usual, he holds a book in his left hand. But he is not reading the book— it is not even open, but securely closed and tightly clasped.

Christ does not read the Bible, the New Testament, or the Gospel. He is the norm of the Bible, the criterion of the New Testament, the incarnation of the Gospel. That is how we Christians decide between a violent and nonviolent God in the Bible, New Testament, or Gospel. The person, not the book, and the life, not the text, are decisive and constitutive for us.

3

JESUS AND THE KINGDOM OF GOD

A double constraint has always been at the heart of Mediterranean history: poverty and the uncertainty of the morrow.
—FERNAND BRAUDEL,
*The Mediterranean and the
Mediterranean World in
the Age of Philip II* (1972)

In the straitened Mediterranean, the kingdom of Heaven had to have something to do with food and drink.
—PETER BROWN,
*Protocol of the Forty-second
Colloquy of the Center for
Hermeneutical Studies in Hellenistic
and Modern Culture* (1982)

Three questions guide this chapter's discussion of Jesus's life. The first two are general ones. In the prologue of our co-authored 2001 book *Excavating Jesus: Beneath the Stones, Behind the Texts*, Jonathan Reed and I ask these two questions: "Why did Jesus happen when he happened? Why then? Why there? Sharpen the question a little. Why did two popular movements, the Baptism movement of John and the Kingdom movement of Jesus, happen in territories ruled by Herod Antipas in the 20s of that first common-era century? Why not at another time? Why not in another place?" (p. xvii).

At the start of this chapter, I add another and more specific question: why is Jesus so often found around the Sea of Galilee, the Lake of Tiberias, the harp-shaped Lake Kinneret? In the concluding paragraph of his magnificent 1906 book on *The Quest of the Historical Jesus,* Albert Schweitzer said of Jesus that "he comes to us as one unknown, without a name, as of old, by the lakeside, he came to those men who did not know who he was" (p. 487). It is almost discourteous to interrupt that soaring peroration and ask: What was Jesus doing "of old, by the lakeside"? Why precisely there? Why precisely then?

Since Nazareth was Jesus's native village and he was always called "Jesus of Nazareth," why does this relocation occur in Matthew 4:13: "He left Nazareth and made his home in Capernaum by the sea," that is, by the inland Sea or Lake of Galilee? He moved not just from a very tiny village to a somewhat larger one, but from a hillside village to a lakeside one.

Or again: Jesus's two most famous disciples were closely connected with lakeside fishing villages. First, Mary. She is "of Magdala," the most important town on the lake before Herod Antipas built Tiberias around 19 CE. That town's Hebrew name comes from *migdal,* a tower, presumably a lighthouse. Its Greek name, Tarichaeae, means salted fish. Next, Peter. He came from a fishing village, Bethsaida, and so did Philip and Andrew, according to John 1:14. Peter seems to have moved to his wife's house in Capernaum, that is, from one fishing village to another, because it is his mother-in-law who ministers to Jesus at that house in Mark 1:31.

Furthermore, the first and most important members of the Twelve, the brothers Peter and Andrew as well as the brothers James and John, the sons of Zebedee, were all called by Jesus to join him as he "passed along the Sea of Galilee" (Mark 1:16). All four are called from their boats and their nets by Jesus's command to "follow me and I will make you fish for people" (1:17). In

Mark's gospel, Jesus in Galilee is seldom far from lake, boat, net, and fish. Why?

With these three questions, and especially the final one, constantly in mind, I begin with an overview of the geographical and historical matrix in which Jesus lived his life. I use the term "matrix" deliberately to avoid the term "background." If you are having a studio portrait taken and the photographer asks you to choose a computer-generated snow, forest, meadow, beach, or jungle scene—that is background. The scene is there, but it has no interaction with you—you will not be cold in the snow or warm on the beach. A matrix, on the other hand, is interactive and reciprocal—it changes you and you change it. Southern racism was matrix, for example, not just background, for the Reverend Martin Luther King Jr. Here, then, is the geographical and historical matrix for Jesus—first in the generation of Herod the Great during the thirty or so years before Jesus's birth, and then in the generation of Herod Antipas during the thirty or so years of Jesus's life.

KING OF THE JEWS AND FRIEND OF THE ROMANS

Herod the Great's rule over the Jewish homeland by imperial appointment in the generation before Jesus made Henry VIII look both merciful and monogamous. Apart from multiple dynastic marriages and royal executions, he simultaneously undertook two of the largest contemporary construction projects in the world. Leaving aside Rome itself as one giant construction site, Herod's creation of the port of Caesarea on the Mediterranean and his extension of the plaza of the Temple in Jerusalem were state-of-the-art construction in his time.

Caesarea on the coast was dubbed Maritima to distinguish it from Caesarea Philippi to the north. The site lacked a natural harbor and water supply, so Herod started from scratch on a brand-new city with a brand-new port. It had inner, middle, and outer harbors with an anchorage of around forty acres; for double emphasis, that port was also named for Caesar as Sebastos in Greek, or Augustus in Latin. The foundations of the giant breakwaters—still clearly visible by helicopter if the sea is calm—were constructed with huge wooden frames filled with the just-invented hydraulic cement, which could harden underwater. That required volcanic sand called *pozzolana* from the Bay of Naples, and with it probably came Italian architects and engineers as well. The breakwaters themselves reached out eight hundred feet into the Mediterranean, and with widths between one hundred and two hundred feet, they easily supported extremely large warehouses.

Jerusalem meant the Temple, and Herod expanded its plaza to the size of five football fields from north to south and three from east to west. That giant esplanade would have been impressive on flat ground, but Herod was building atop a hill with ravines on either side. To the north his workers dug deep into the hill and used those stones to build up the plaza to the south. The mortarless support walls were built with blocks weighing two to five tons, but some were fifty tons, and one monster was around four hundred tons. Herod's purpose was this above all: he was creating a giant "Court of the Gentiles"—and by the way, we have absolutely no evidence that anyone opposed that inclusivity. Hard, is it not, to think of Herod the Great as an earlier Apostle of the Gentiles?

I think, however, that we have to put Caesarea and Jerusalem together to see Herod's plans for those two immense construction projects. The creation of Caesarea's harbor established Herod's commitment to Rome's first order of imperial business—an all-weather infrastructure of ports, roads, and bridges. The extension of Jerusalem's Temple established Herod's commitment to Rome's second order of imperial business—Romanization by urbanization for commercialization. And of course, the establishment of cities increased the productivity of the countryside by converting local aristocrats into good Romans.

Taken in tandem, Caesarea and Jerusalem were a deepening immersion of the Jewish homeland within the program of Rome's imperial system. Into his great port on the coast would come not just Jews for their major feasts but pious pagan pilgrims and even tourists to visit what was now the greatest temple of the Mediterranean world. Herod's harbor-lighthouse in Caesarea might not displace the Pharos of Alexandria as one of the seven wonders of the ancient world—but maybe his great temple in Jerusalem could displace Diana's in Ephesus as another of those seven wonders?

Furthermore, Herod built three temples to Rome and Augustus, that divine couple at the heart of the New World Order (recall them from chapter 1?): in Caesarea Maritima, in his other new city of Sebaste in Samaria, and far to the north in what would eventually be Caesarea Philippi. But by now you may have begun to see a pattern. In all that construction, what about Galilee? Is Herod deliberately skipping Galilee? Maybe he was afraid of the Galileans because of their fierce opposition when the empire first declared him "Friend of the Romans," gave him his title "King of the Jews," and sent him home to work it out if he could. Or maybe he was just annoyed because of that initial resistance and wished to punish Galilee. Under Herod the Great, therefore, and for whatever reason, the imperial program of Romanization did not strike Galilee as it did Judea. What does that mean?

THE RISE AND FALL OF HEROD ANTIPAS

It means that Romanization by urbanization for commercialization struck Galilee forcibly not under Herod the Great in the generation *before* John and Jesus, but under his son Herod Antipas in the generation *of* John and Jesus. I turn now to look at the life of Herod Antipas in general before focusing on the late 20s, when the Baptism movement of John and the Kingdom movement of Jesus started in Perea and Galilee under Antipas's rule. Think of Antipas's life as a drama of acute disappointment over six sequential acts.

The first act took place as Herod the Great was close to death. His will designated Antipas the heir to his throne as King of the Jews. But then he changed his mind and designated Antipas's older brother, Archelaus, as the heir to both title and kingdom. When Herod finally died in 4 BCE, both Antipas and Archelaus appeared before Caesar Augustus in Rome to plead their opposing cases. The Herodian family members preferred direct rule by a Roman governor, but failing that, they supported Antipas over Archelaus. Augustus, however, compromised on all sides. He gave half the Jewish homeland—Idumeaea, Judea, and Samaria—to Herod Archelaus, but entitled him *ethnarch* ("people-ruler"), not *monarch*. He divided the rest between two *tetrarchs* ("quarter-rulers"), with Herod Antipas getting Galilee and Perea on either side of the Jordan and Herod Philip getting the far northern reaches of the country. Antipas began his rule sorely disappointed.

The second act began immediately as, in the words of Josephus's *Jewish War,* "Herod fortified Sepphoris to be the ornament of all Galilee, and called it Autocratoris" (18.27). *Autocrator* is the standard Greek translation for the Latin *Imperator*—the first title of the Imperator Caesar Augustus—and is best translated into English not just as "Emperor" but as "World-Conqueror." Sepphoris, of course, was nowhere near the world-class level of Herod the Great's construction projects, but still, Antipas began his program of Romanization by urbanization for commercialization when he dedicated his rebuilt capital city to Augustus. Thereafter, he stayed very quiet as long as Augustus was alive, and maybe especially after Archelaus was ordered into exile in 6 CE and a Roman governor took over direct control of his territory in the southern half of the country. Well did Luke 13:32 have Jesus call Antipas "that fox."

The third act began in 14 CE when Augustus died and Tiberius became emperor. At that point, Antipas made his second move to become King of the Jews. To replace his older capital city, Sepphoris, he started to create a new one about twenty miles to the east on the western shore of the Sea of Galilee. He named it Tiberias, in honor of the new emperor Tiberius. But why a new capital, and why a new one there and not somewhere else? Antipas could have given Sepphoris the new name Tiberias and built, say, a major new basilica there to celebrate Tiberius's ascension to the throne. Once again, then, why build a new capital city, and why build it there on the lake?

Think about it. If you were Antipas and wanted to become King of the Jews, you would have to increase your tax base in Galilee so that Rome might grant you that royal promotion. If Antipas did this as *tetrarch* of Galilee and Perea, Rome might think, what would he not accomplish as *monarch* of the entire Jewish homeland? Antipas could not squeeze more taxation from his peasant-farmers without risking resistance or even revolt. But having learned, as it were, how to multiply loaves in the valleys around Sepphoris, he would now learn how to multiply fishes in the waters around Tiberias.

The fourth act was the necessary tandem step to the preceding one; this internal, or home-directed, maneuver was Antipas's second step toward kingship. He needed Roman approval, but he also needed Jewish acceptance, and for that he needed to forge a Herodian-Hasmonean connection. The Hasmoneans were a native dynasty that had ruled the Jewish homeland for one hundred years before the Romans arrived in the middle of the first century BCE and appointed the Herodians in their place. Herod the Great, for example, had first chosen a Hasmonean princess, Mariamme, as his queen, but later executed her—rightly or wrongly?—for conspiracy against him. Antipas obtained his Hasmonean consort by divorcing his Nabatean wife and marrying Herodias, wife of his own half-brother Philip and granddaughter of the murdered Mariamme.

The fifth act was supposed to establish Antipas as a major player on the world stage of high imperial politics. When the Roman governor of Syria met the Parthian ruler Artabanus to discuss peaceful relationships, Antipas gave a great feast for them on the river Euphrates and immediately—but unwisely—got his report of that meeting back to Rome before the governor's own report had arrived.

The sixth act ran Antipas out of time. Herodias's brother, Herod Agrippa, grew up in Rome as the friend of Caligula, and when Caligula became emperor, he made Agrippa the King of the Jews, ruling over the entire Jewish homeland. Antipas and Herodias hastened to Rome in 41 CE to plead their case—this time against Agrippa as earlier against Archelaus—but instead of becoming King and Queen of the Jews, they both ended up in exile. After thirty-seven years of patient and careful planning, it was all over for Antipas.

The saga of Antipas the would-be king concluded over a decade after the time of John and Jesus, but I have given it in full in order to help you understand that third act, when he was founding Tiberias to commercialize the lake and its fishes in the name of Rome's empire and both John and Jesus clashed with him in the name of Israel's God.

THE BIRTH OF A SON OF GOD

Each of the four New Testament gospels begins, not with a first *chapter,* but with a parabolic *overture.* On the one hand, therefore, they are all quite different: each must summarize, synthesize, and symbolize the full story that is to follow. On the other hand, and after that opening, each moves immediately to Jesus's public life so that there are no missing chapters or missing years. None of that is particularly unusual in contemporary biographical texts.

Here is an example very deliberately and precisely chosen. Upon his death in 14 CE, as we saw in chapter 1, Augustus Caesar left behind a political autobiography about 2,500 words long to be inscribed in bronze at the entrance of his new dynastic mausoleum in Rome's Campus Martius. We have Greek chunks and Latin fragments of the text from Pisidian Antioch in the museum at Yalvach and can still see most of those two versions carved on the walls of the Temple of Rome and Augustus in Old Ankara.

What is most striking, however, is the autobiography's opening: "At the age of nineteen...." In some cases there might be no knowledge about the birth of somebody who became famous only later in life, but that is not the case here. Had Augustus wanted, he could have detailed his infancy and youth—at least in summary—up to that fateful nineteenth year when the will of his assassinated grand-uncle, Julius Caesar, declared him both adopted son and designated heir. He simply ignored his earlier life as irrelevant and started with his first act of political and moral courage in opposing and attacking the murderers of Caesar.

It is, Augustus judged, the public life that counts, but of course, the conception, birth, and infancy of Octavian as Augustus-to-be might well become symbolic overture or dramatic prophecy for others. Almost immediately after his victory over Antony and Cleopatra off Cape Actium, the tale of Octavian's conception was recorded in his *Theologoumena* by Asclepias of Mendes in Egypt. And Suetonius, the early-second-century Roman imperial historian and tabloid journalist, repeated Mendes' tale about Octavian's conception—but only at the very end of Augustus's life, when readers might be ready to accept a claim that the conception of so great an individual had required human-divine collaboration. This is his account in "The Deified Augustus" section of *The Lives of the Caesars* (94.4):

When Attia had come in the middle of the night to the solemn service of Apollo, she had her litter set down in the temple and fell asleep, while the rest of the matrons also slept. On a sudden a serpent glided up to her and shortly went away. When she awoke, she purified herself, as if after the embraces of her husband, and at once there appeared on her body a mark in colors like a serpent, and she could never get rid of it; so that presently she ceased ever to go to the public baths. In the tenth month after that Augustus was born and was therefore regarded as the son of Apollo. Attia too, before she gave him birth, dreamed that her womb was borne up to the stars and spread over the whole extent of land and sea, while Octavius dreamed that the sun rose from Attia's womb.

Toward the end of that same century, another historian, Dio Cassius, repeated the story in his *Roman History,* but added that, in adopting Octavian, Julius Caesar "was influenced largely by Attia's emphatic declaration that the youth had been engendered by Apollo" (45.1).

Only Matthew 1–2 and Luke 1–2 work within that same tradition of a divinely conceived and prophetically predestined child in creating an *overture* to Jesus's public life. Nobody else in the New Testament or the earliest Christian literature knows those stories, which differ quite clearly in the details of their content but also agree on certain more fundamental aspects. Those important agreements concern events that did not happen and are symbolical rather than actual, fictional rather than factual. Put bluntly: what did not happen historically is what counts parabolically. To say, for example, as they both do, that Jesus was *born in Bethlehem,* the city of King David, is to proclaim him as the awaited Davidic Messiah—just as a politician *born in a log cabin* could mean a new Lincoln for modern Americans.

From that basis, therefore, the twin stories in Matthew 1–2 and Luke 1–2 not only exalt Jesus within his own Jewish tradition but place his birth and destiny in deliberate contradiction to Roman imperial theology's story of Augustus's birth and destiny.

First of all, Jesus's genealogical descent goes back to Abraham for Matthew (1:17) and to Adam for Luke (3:23–38). That rather outdoes Augustus's claims for descent from the goddess Aphrodite-Venus and the Trojan hero Anchises through Aeneas and Ascanius-Julus at the time of the Trojan War only one thousand years earlier. Also recall from chapter 1 that Augustus's Trojan ancestors had been led from Troy to Italy by Venus's western star.

Turn now to the continuing story in Matthew 1–2. Herod was officially appointed King of the Jews by Roman authority. But then, as Matthew says in 2:1–2, "in the time of King Herod, after Jesus was born in Bethlehem of Judea, wise men from the East came to Jerusalem, asking, 'Where is the child who has been born king of the Jews? For we observed his star at its rising, and have come to pay him homage.'" A new and therefore a replacement King of the Jews has been appointed by God and not by Rome. Moreover, a new and therefore replacement star has appeared in the sky; instead of guiding three individuals westward from Troy to Rome, as the old star did, it guides three individuals westward from Persia to Jerusalem. (No wonder, then, that the post-Matthean tradition came up with *three* wise men!) Whether you take star and counter-star as both factual or both fictional, or one factual and the other fictional, recognize that Matthew's first-century counter-story is high treason, not just a cute Christmas carol whose historicity we can discuss once a year in our media. Herod, of course, did not debate historicity—he got the message and decreed murder.

The story in Luke 1–2 is both totally different in detail and incident and totally similar in meaning and purpose. Luke mentions Caesar Augustus in the opening verse of 2:1. With that name on his readers' or hearers' minds, he records this event at the birth of Jesus:

> In that region there were shepherds living in the fields, keeping watch over their flock by night. Then an angel of the Lord stood before them, and the glory of the Lord shone around them, and they were terrified. But the angel said to them, "Do not be afraid; for see—I am bringing you good news of great joy for all the people: to you is born this day in the city of David a Savior, who is the Messiah, the Lord. This will be a sign for you: you will find a child wrapped in bands of cloth and lying in a manger." And suddenly there was with the angel a multitude of the heavenly host, praising God and saying, "Glory to God in the highest heaven, and on earth peace among those whom he favors!" (2:8–14)

Maybe we are too jaded with that story's annual appearance along with the tinsel, mistletoe, and Christmas decorations. But "Savior" and "Lord" were titles of Caesar Augustus because he had brought "peace" to this earth.

Out of thousands of examples, one carved inscription for "Savior" and one literary text for "Lord" will suffice. The inscription is from Halicarnassus, modern Bodrum in southwestern Turkey:

> The eternal and immortal nature of everything has bestowed upon mankind the greatest good with extraordinary benefactions by bringing Caesar Augustus in our blessed time the father of his own country, divine Rome, and ancestral Zeus, *Savior* of the common race of men, whose providence has not only fulfilled but actually exceeded the prayers of all. For land and sea are at *Peace* and the cities flourish with good order, concord and prosperity.

The literary text is from the *Tristia,* or *Sorrow,* of a belatedly repentant Ovid, exiled by Augustus to the western Black Sea coast. He addresses the emperor as "Jupiter" and then calls him "*Lord* of Empire ... not less mighty than the world you govern" (5:2).

A cynic might say, of course, that Augustus had saved the Roman world from Roman civil war. Still, the phrase "peace on land and sea" became almost an Augustan mantra at the heart of Roman imperial theology. The only question, of course, was whether peace on earth was to be established as Augustus's peace through victory or Jesus's peace through justice.

THE DAY THE ROMANS CAME

All that the gospels tell us about the youth of Jesus is Luke's story of the incident in the Temple at Jerusalem when Jesus was twelve years of age. He separated from his parents at the Feast of Passover, and "after three days they found him in the temple, sitting among the teachers, listening to them and asking them questions. And all who heard him were amazed at his understanding and his answers"

(2:46–47). This is surely a deliberate parable, a typical symbol-story, a portrait of the prophet as a young prodigy. Compare it, for example, with this account of his own youth in Josephus's *Life:* "While still a mere boy, about fourteen years old, I won universal applause for my love of letters; inasmuch that the chief priests and the leading men of the city used constantly to come to me for precise information on some particular in our ordinance" (9).

There is, however, one aspect of Jesus's youth about which I am willing to speculate—but to speculate close to history rather than to parable. At the time of Herod the Great's death in 4 BCE, revolts broke out all over the Jewish homeland. It eventually took three of the four legions of the Syrian governor Varus to put down all the rebellions. The primary military function of those legions was to guard Rome's Euphrates frontier against the Parthian Empire; by deploying them and client-rulers' auxiliary troops in the Jewish homeland, Rome was dangerously weakening that protective screen. In other words, when the Syrian legions moved southward, they marched not just offensively but punitively. We will teach you a lesson, they said, so that we will not need to return for another few generations. And check the dates—they came in 4 BCE, in 66 CE, and, finally, in 132 CE. After that, they never had to come again.

Jesus was born, as best we can reconstruct the date, around 4 BCE with all of that strife as natal background. "At Sepphoris," according to Josephus's *Jewish War,* a rebel named Judas "broke open the royal arsenals, and, having armed his companions, attacked the other aspirants to power" (2.56). And the result? "Varus at once sent a detachment of his army into the region of Galilee adjoining Ptolemais, under the command of his friend Gaius; the latter routed all who opposed him, captured and burnt the city of Sepphoris and reduced its inhabitants to slavery" (2.68). (You may recall Varus's eventual fate from chapter 1.)

Jesus grew up in Nazareth, a tiny village about four miles—a walk of one and a half hours—over the ridge and across the valley floor from Sepphoris. What do you think happened to Nazareth when Varus's legionary troops struck nearby Sepphoris in 4 BCE? Josephus does not give any detailed description of those events, but we can apply to Sepphoris and its villages in 4 BCE what his *Jewish War* describes as having happened during Vespasian's attack when next the Syrian legions marched southward, in 67–68 CE. At Gerasa, or Jerash, on the other side of the Jordan from Sepphoris, Lucius Annius "put to the sword a thousand of the youth, who had not already escaped, made prisoners of women and children, gave his soldiers license to plunder the property, and then set fire to the houses and advanced against the surrounding villages. The able-bodied fled, the feeble perished, and everything left was consigned to the flames" (4.488–89).

In Nazareth around the time Jesus was born, men, women, and children who did not hide successfully would have been, respectively, killed, raped, and enslaved. Those who survived would have lost everything. I speculate, therefore, that the major stories Jesus would have heard while growing up in Nazareth would have been about "the year the Romans came." I push the speculation a little further: At some chosen moment in Jesus's youth, did Mary bring him up to the top of the Nazareth ridge, point out Sepphoris, and talk about "the Year of the Romans"? From all such talk, what did the young Jesus decide about God, Rome, resistance, and violence?

GOD'S KINGDOM: IMMINENT OR PRESENT?

As discussed earlier, my proposal is that Antipas built a new capital in 19 CE, called it Tiberias, and located it on the lakeshore because he was beginning his second attempt to become King of the Jews by commercializing the lake and thereby vastly increasing his tax base. Maybe then, he thought, the new emperor Tiberius would be impressed enough to grant what the old emperor Augustus had denied him. It was precisely then that two alternative visions of God's Kingdom rather than Rome's were proclaimed against him, one by John and the other by Jesus.

Consider these two texts, one from John and the other from Jesus, and imagine how these two accusations could have derailed Antipas's hope for a popularly applauded Herodian-Hasmonean marriage alliance. First, in Mark 6:18, John the Baptist tells Herod, "It is not lawful for you to have your brother's wife." Second, in Mark 10:11–12, Jesus announces that "whoever divorces his wife and marries another commits adultery against her; and if she divorces her husband and marries another, she commits adultery." Criticism of his marriage by two popular prophets was not exactly part of Antipas's plan.

I now take chapters 1 and 2 of this book and fine-focus them here in chapter 3 to see how the radicality of God's nonviolent justice confronts the normalcy of human civilization's violent injustice *at a very specific time and a very specific place*. The time is the 20s of the first common-era century, and the place is the twin territories ruled by Herod Antipas—Perea to the east and Galilee to the west of the river Jordan.

I compare that divine radicality as understood first within John's Baptism movement in Perea and then within Jesus's Kingdom movement in Galilee. To understand the Jewish matrix from which they both operated and to understand how they diverged from one another in it, recall my description of apocalyptic eschatology as the Great Divine Cleanup of the present world here below upon the earth (see chapter 2). That is absolutely presumed in what follows.

John and God's Imminent Kingdom

John was an eschatologist who proclaimed the imminent arrival of the avenging God. Any day now, but certainly very soon, God would come to purify and justify an earth grown old in impurity and injustice. John's theory was close to the Deuteronomic theology (see chapter 2): oppression by Roman power was a punishment for Israel's sins, and that sinfulness impeded the promised advent of God. What was needed, therefore, was a great sacrament of repentance, a popular repetition of ancient Israel's coming out of the desert, crossing the Jordan, and entering the Promised Land. In that process, the Israelites would repent of their sins as they were "baptized" or immersed in the Jordan, their moral cleansing symbolized by the physical washing.

A critical mass of repentant people who had "retaken" their Promised Land would prepare for, or possibly even hasten, the start of God's Great Divine Cleanup. In the meantime, of course, and no matter how nonviolent his proclamation was in theory, John was planting ticking time bombs of eschatological expectation all over the Jewish homeland. So Antipas executed him. Notice one very important aspect of that action. If Antipas had considered John a violent threat, he would have also rounded up as many of John's followers as he could catch. The fact that he did not, and that he executed only John, tells us that Antipas was responding to somebody who opposed the Roman system nonviolently.

We know about John from both the New Testament and Josephus's *Jewish Antiquities* (18:116–19), but each source has one major difficulty. Josephus never wants to admit that Jewish apocalyptic eschatology was a powerful first-century force, and so he explains John's execution very vaguely. "Eloquence that had so great an effect on mankind might lead to some form of sedition," he informs us, "for it looked as if they would be guided by John in everything that they did." The content of that eloquence is never mentioned.

The canonical gospels insist that John's message was about the imminent advent of Jesus, not the imminent advent of the apocalyptic God. Mark, for example, has John announce: "The one who is more powerful than I is coming after me; I am not worthy to stoop down and untie the thong of his sandals. I have baptized you with water; but he will baptize you with the Holy Spirit" (1:7–8). For John, the more powerful one was God, but for Mark it was, of course, Jesus. That is made even clearer in the rather fiercely apocalyptic language of Luke 3:7–9, 16:

John said to the crowds that came out to be baptized by him, "You brood of vipers! Who warned you to flee from the wrath to come? Bear fruits worthy of repentance. Do not begin to say to yourselves, 'We have Abraham as our ancestor'; for I tell you, God is able from these stones to raise up children to Abraham. Even now the ax is lying at the root of the trees; every tree therefore that does not bear good fruit is cut down and thrown into the fire....

"I baptize you with water; but one who is more powerful than I is coming; I am not worthy to untie the thong of his sandals. He will baptize you with the Holy Spirit and fire."

This would be totally inaccurate as a prophecy of Jesus's character, but it fits very well with John's fiery image of a coming God who will destroy evil in a world overcome by it. The language here comes from John himself, but it is humanely softened by Luke's own insertion in 3:10–14:

And the crowds asked him, "What then should we do?" In reply he said to them, "Whoever has two coats must share with anyone who has none; and whoever has food must do likewise." Even tax collectors came to be baptized, and they asked him, "Teacher, what should we do?" He said to them, "Collect no more than the amount prescribed for you." Soldiers also asked him, "And we, what should we do?" He said to them, "Do not extort money from anyone by threats or false accusation, and be satisfied with your wages."

In one sense, John was right that the Kingdom of God was imminent, but it would not come as he or anyone else expected.

Jesus and God's Present Kingdom

One of the surest things we know about Jesus is that he was baptized by John. What makes this fact so certain is the growing nervousness it evokes as you move from Mark, through Matthew and Luke, into John.

Mark's gospel is quite matter of fact: "In those days Jesus came from Nazareth of Galilee and was baptized by John in the Jordan" (1:9). But that baptism is immediately overshadowed by this vision for Jesus in 1:10–11: "And just as he was coming up out of the water, he saw the heavens torn apart and the Spirit descending like a dove on him. And a voice came from heaven, 'You are my Son, the Beloved; with you I am well pleased.'"

Matthew's gospel is much more defensive. Jesus arrives for baptism in 3:13, but this interaction ensues in the next two verses: "John would have prevented him, saying, 'I need to be baptized by you, and do you come to me?' But Jesus answered him, 'Let it be so now; for it is proper for us in this way to fulfill all righteousness.' Then he consented." Thereafter, as in Mark, the heavenly vision and revelation overshadow the baptism.

Luke's gospel is almost evasive, and unless you are reading carefully you might miss any mention of Jesus's baptism: "Now when all the people were baptized, and when Jesus also had been baptized and was praying, the heaven was opened" (3:21). In this case, however, the revelation from God is not accompanied by any vision for Jesus.

John's gospel has the final solution in 1:26–33. He omits any mention of John's baptism of Jesus and insists instead on the Baptist's testimony to Jesus as "Son of God" and "Lamb of God." John the Baptist explicitly identifies Jesus (and not God) with the one greater than himself whom he had foretold as coming soon. The heavenly vision now assists the Baptist to identify Jesus, not Jesus to recognize his own identity: "John testified, 'I saw the Spirit descending from heaven like a dove, and it remained on him. I myself did not know him, but the one who sent me to baptize with water said to me, 'He on whom you see the Spirit descend and remain is the one who baptizes with the Holy Spirit'" (1:32–33).

But all of this only emphasizes that John baptized Jesus and therefore that Jesus had *at least originally* accepted John's message of the imminent advent of an apocalyptic and avenging God. That would explain, for example, Jesus's defense of John, the desert-hardened prophet, in contrast with Antipas, the wind-shaken reed, in Luke 7:24–27, quoting from Malachi 3:1:

> Jesus began to speak to the crowds about John: "What did you go out into the wilderness to look at? A reed shaken by the wind? What then did you go out to see? Someone dressed in soft robes? Look, those who put on fine clothing and live in luxury are in royal palaces. What then did you go out to see? A prophet? Yes, I tell you, and more than a prophet. This is the one about whom it is written, 'See, I am sending my messenger ahead of you, who will prepare your way before you.'"

But the very next verse (7:28) both reiterates that accolade in its first half and then drastically downgrades it in the second half: "I tell you, among those born of women no one is greater than John; yet the least in the kingdom of God is greater than he."

Since I consider that both these statements came from the historical Jesus, I think that Jesus started by accepting John's theology of God's *imminence* but, precisely because of what happened to John, changed from that to a theology of God's *presence*. John expected God's advent, but Antipas's cavalry came instead. John was executed, and God still did not come as an avenging presence. Maybe, thought Jesus, that was not how God acted because that is not how God is. Jesus's own proclamation therefore insisted that the Kingdom of God was not imminent but present; it was already here below upon this earth, and however it was to be consummated in the future, *it was a present-already and not just an imminent-future reality.*

Jesus could hardly have made such a spectacular claim without immediately appending another one to it. You can speak forever about the *future-imminence* of the Kingdom, but unless you are foolish enough to give a precise date, you can hardly be proved

right or wrong. We are but waiting for God to act; apart from preparatory faith, hope, and prayer, there is no more we can do. When
God acts, it will be, presumably, like a flash of divine lightning
beyond all categories of time and place. But to claim an *already-
present* Kingdom demands some evidence, and the only such that
Jesus could have offered is this: it is not that we are waiting for
God, but that God is waiting for us. The present Kingdom is a *collaborative eschaton* between the human and divine worlds. The
Great Divine Cleanup is an interactive process with a present beginning in time and a future (short or long?) consummation.
Would it happen without God? No. Would it happen without believers? No. To see the presence of the Kingdom of God, said Jesus,
come, see how we live, and then live likewise.

GOD'S KINGDOM: MONOPOLY OR FRANCHISE?

It is rather unfortunate that the expression "Kingdom of Heaven"
ever entered the Christian vocabulary. In the New Testament it is
used over thirty times, but only by Matthew, while "Kingdom of
God" is used twice as often, and by different authors (Mark, Luke,
John, Acts, and Paul). Matthew himself uses "Kingdom of God"
about five times. "Kingdom of Heaven"—in Greek it is actually
"Kingdom of the Heavens"—is all too often misinterpreted as the
Kingdom of the future, of the next world, of the afterlife. For
Matthew, "Heaven" was simply a euphemism for "God," the
Dwelling used interchangeably with the Dweller, as when we say,
"The White House announces ..." when we mean, "The president
announces...." In other words, "Kingdom of Heaven" meant ex-
actly the same as "Kingdom of God." But what was that?

"The Kingdom of God" was a standard expression for what I
have been calling the Great Divine Cleanup of this world. It was
what this world would look like if and when God sat on Caesar's
throne, or if and when God lived in Antipas's palace. That is very
clear in these parallel phrases of the Lord's Prayer in Matthew 6:10:
"Your kingdom come. Your will be done, *on earth* as it is in

heaven." The Kingdom of God is about the Will of God for this earth here below. That earthly presence agrees, of course, with everything we have seen so far about apocalyptic eschatological expectation. It is about the transformation of this world into holiness, not the evacuation of this world into heaven.

It is clear, I hope, that the Kingdom of God is inextricably and simultaneously 100 percent political and 100 percent religious. "Kingdom" is a political term, "God" is a religious term, and Jesus would be executed for that "of" in a world where, for Rome, God already sat on Caesar's throne because Caesar was God. I was once told by a colleague that the difference between us was that I considered earliest Christianity a political movement with religious overtones while he considered it a religious one with political overtones. I replied that, to the contrary, my position was that earliest Christianity was absolutely both at the same time because nobody in the first century made such a distinction. Remember that Caesar's coins said he was DIVI F, that is, DIVI FILIUS, or SON OF GOD; how could one distinguish politics from religion in that title? For Jesus, "the Kingdom of God" raised a politico-religious or religio-political question: to whom did the world belong, and how, depending on the answer, should it be run?

There was one other major difference between John and Jesus besides the one over the imminence or presence of God's Kingdom on earth, and it was almost a necessary concomitant to this first distinction. I put it this way: *John had a monopoly, but Jesus had a franchise.* John was "the Baptist" or "the Baptizer"—that was his nickname in both Josephus and the New Testament. It was not that lots of baptizing stations lined the Jordan and you simply went to the one nearest your own home. You went to John and only to John. To stop his movement, therefore, Antipas had only to execute John. His movement might linger on in memory, nostalgia, and sorrow for one or two generations, but since it depended on John's life, it ended with John's death. Once again, I think, Jesus watched and learned. Here is how his strategy differed from John's.

First of all, recall that Jesus announced the presence of the Kingdom of God by inviting all to come and see how he *and his companions* had already accepted it, had already entered it, and were already living in it. To experience the Kingdom, he asserted, come, see how *we* live, and then live like us. This invitation presumes that Jesus was promulgating not just a vision or a theory but a praxis and a *communal* program, and that this program was not just for himself but for others as well. What was it?

Basically it was this: *heal the sick, eat with those you heal, and announce the Kingdom's presence in that mutuality.* You can see that communal program at work in such texts as Mark 6:7–13, Luke 9:1–6, Matthew 10:5–14, and Luke 10:1–11. Notice some unusual features of these texts. First, Jesus does not settle down at Nazareth or Capernaum and instruct his companions to bring people to him as monopolist of the Kingdom. Second, he tells others to do exactly what he himself is doing—healing the sick, eating with the healed, and proclaiming the Kingdom's presence. Third, he does not tell them to heal in his name or even to pray to God before they heal—nor does he himself pray before he heals. This approach is actually quite extraordinary and can only be explained by the Kingdom's presence and our participation in it—if we are in the already-present Kingdom, we are already in union with God and can act accordingly.

The logic of Jesus's Kingdom program is a mutuality of healing (the basic spiritual power) and eating (the basic physical power) shared freely and openly. That program built a *share*-community from the bottom up as a positive alternative to Antipas's Roman *greed*-community established from the top down. That food is the material basis of life and that the control of eating controls all else is clear enough. Even if we are normally well fed, we realize our absolute dependence on food before all else—after food is furnished, much else is needed as well, but first and foremost, with no food, there is no life. So eating as a basic physical power is relatively clear, but healing as a spiritual power is much more difficult to understand.

It is certainly quite clear that, however we explain it, Jesus was a great healer. This passage from Arthur Kleinman's famous 1980 book *Patients and Healers in the Context of Culture* helps us to understand the effectiveness of Jesus's healing:

> A key axiom in medical anthropology is the dichotomy between two aspects of sickness: disease and illness. *Disease* refers to a malfunctioning of biological and/or psychological processes, while the term *illness* refers to the psychosocial experience and meaning of perceived disease. Illness includes secondary personal and social responses to the primary malfunctioning (disease) in the individual's physiological or psychological status (or both).... Viewed from this perspective, illness is the shaping of disease into behavior and experience. It is created by personal, social, and cultural reactions to disease. (p. 72)

Thus, diseases are *cured,* while illnesses are *healed.* Sometimes a disease can be cured, but very often the best that can be done is to heal the illness that surrounds it. That was especially true for ancient medicine, and it is still very often true today, especially for those suffering from chronic or terminal pain.

When I tried to explain the distinction between curing disease and healing illness to my undergraduate students at DePaul University, they usually understood the disease-illness complex in psychosomatic terms and interpreted healing as a mind-over-matter phenomenon. They were seldom able to comprehend it as what I called a sociosomatic complex until they saw the 1993 movie *Philadelphia.* Tom Hanks plays Andrew Beckett, a gay lawyer fired by his law firm because his AIDS infection came from homosexual encounters. My students all understood that Beckett's *disease* cannot be *cured,* but they could also see eventually that his *illness* is being *healed* by the support of his partner, his family, and his lawyer's successful suit against his law firm's illegal discrimination. Curing is not available, but healing is still possible.

Here is an example from another book by Arthur Kleinman, his 1988 study *The Illness Narratives.* He is quoting "Lenore Light ... an intense twenty-nine-year-old internist who comes from an upper middle class black family and works in an inner-city ghetto clinic." This experience, she says, has "radicalized me: it is a revolutionary encounter with the social sources of mortality and morbidity and depression. The more I see, the more appalled I am at how ignorant I have been, insensitive to the social, economic, and political causes of disease." She provides an example:

> Today I saw an obese hypertensive mother of six. No husband. No family support. No job. Nothing. A world of brutalizing violence and poverty and drugs and teenage pregnancies and—and just plain mind-numbing crises, one after another after another. What can I do? What good is it to recommend a low-salt diet, to admonish her about control of her pressure: She is under such real outer pressure, what does the inner pressure matter? What is killing her is her world, not her body. In fact, her body is the product of her world. She is a hugely overweight, misshapen hulk who is a survivor of circumstances and lack of resources and cruel messages to consume and get ahead impossible for her to hear and not feel rage at the limits of her world. Hey, what she needs is not medicine but a social revolution.

Lenore is right that "what we need is prevention, not the Band-Aids I spend my day putting on deep inner wounds" (pp. 216–17). Healing is what happens within a community of concern, support, and assistance, and that is a sociosomatic and not just a psychosomatic reality.

The healing of illness by Jesus and his companions must be understood in the framework of a preventive social revolution, in Light's terms, and in the framework of the Kingdom of God's Great Divine Cleanup of the world, in the even more radical terms of Jesus and his followers. We should not be surprised, of course, if a great and famous healer, like the Jewish Jesus or the Greek Asklepios, is reputed to raise the dead, that is, to bring life emphatically and triumphantly out of death. And we should not be surprised to see such claims in the advertisements of the healer's followers. What would be very surprising, however, is to hear that claim in the testimonials of his patients. Claims that great healers "raise the dead" come from their publicity, not from their medical departments.

THE EXCAVATION FROM HELL

I conclude with an archaeological discovery that I use not as historical proof but as dramatic symbol of Jesus's focus on the Sea of Galilee under Herod Antipas in the later 20s CE. It is a sad emblem of what the life of peasant-fishers was like once Antipas had created Romanization by urbanization for commercialization on the Lake of Tiberias. This discovery is also a symbolic answer to the three opening questions of this chapter, especially the one about why Jesus was so often by the lake.

In the summer of 1985, a severe drought had lowered the water level in the Sea of Galilee and exposed beach all along its shoreline. In late January 1986, two brothers, Moshe and Yuval Lufan of Kibbutz Ginnosar, discovered on the lake's northwest corner a large boat sunk in the mud opposite Migdal, or Magdala, just south of their home. In his 1995 book *The Sea of Galilee Boat: An Extraordinary 2,000-Year-Old Discovery,* Shelley Wachsmann records in fascinating detail the painstaking restoration work on "the Galilee Boat" conducted by Orna Cohen from the Conservation Laboratory of the Hebrew University's Institute of Archaeology. The boat's timbers were the consistency of wet cardboard or soft cheese, and it is no wonder that Wachsmann calls the work "the excavation from hell" (p. 59). It took a decade of restoration work before the boat could be put on public display at Kibbutz Ginnosar in the Yigal Allon Museum (named to honor the Israeli soldier-statesman who had once lived at the kibbutz).

The original boat was about twenty-seven feet long by about seven and a half feet wide and had mast and sail, two large oars on either side, and a large double-oared rudder in the stern. It was certainly the type of workhorse-boat imagined in those stories about Jesus and the Twelve on the lake. Wachsmann dates the life of the boat "from about 100 BC to AD 67. At present I do not believe that it is possible to be more accurate than that" (p. 349). The boat was constructed by cannibalizing older boats. Half of its keel was quite adequate—but reused—cedar wood, and the other half was rather inadequate jujube wood. Furthermore, its planking had been replaced not with new boards but with bits and pieces patched together. "The craft contained a total of at least seven different types of timber," notes Wachsmann. "Whoever built this boat had indeed scraped the bottom of the barrel for timber" (p. 252). Finally, one day, it was no longer seaworthy. Its mast, sail, oars, stempost, and sternpost were removed for further use in other boats, and every single iron nail was removed from the wood for future use. It was then pushed out from the Magdala boatyard into the sea, where it sank in a graveyard for boats no longer suitable even for cannibalization.

The boat represents what Antipas's Romanization by urbanization for commercialization did to the ordinary peasant-fishers who used the lake before Tiberias was built. They could no longer cast their nets freely from the shore. They could no longer own a boat or beach a catch without taxation. They probably had to sell what they caught to Antipas's factories, which dried or salted fish and made that execrable fish sauce called *garum*. The boat vividly symbolizes the harder times in the 20s when excellent artisans had to work with very inadequate resources and nurse their boats for as long as possible. As Wachsmann concludes: "The Galilee at this time was economically depressed; the timbers used in the boat's construction are perhaps a physical expression of this overall economic situation" (p. 358). This was the violent normalcy of civilization, in Roman time and Galilean place.

Jesus spent his time on and beside the lake because it was precisely and specifically by the shores of the Sea of Galilee that *the radicality of Israel's God confronted the normalcy of Rome's civilization under Herod Antipas in the 20s of the first century* CE.

INTERLUDE: THE KINGDOM OF GOD AND
THE SON OF MAN

Before continuing from Jesus's life in Galilee to his death in Judea, I want to consider one very special phrase: "the Son of Man." It is a term as important as "the Kingdom of God" for understanding Jesus and, especially, for confirming that he claimed not just the imminence but the presence of God's Kingdom here below within our world. But "Son of Man" is a term that requires a lot of explanation before we moderns can see its implications. Very often today, for example, "Son of God" is used in media interviews to denote that Jesus was divine and "Son of Man" to indicate that he was human. But this usage is most inadequate, and indeed, if anything, "Son of Man" is an even more exalted title than "Son of God." So be patient as I locate this title within its matrix in Jewish eschatology.

The ancient world had a tradition of expecting the rise of four worldwide empires, to be followed by a climactic fifth one. At the start of the second century BCE, for example, Aemilius Sura gave us this version: "The Assyrians were the first of all races to hold world power, then the Medes, and after them the Persians, and then the Macedonians. Then ... the world power passed to the Romans." As you might expect, Sura was a Roman, and his scenario was recorded by Velleius Paterculus, a Roman of the first century CE, in his *History of Rome* (1.6.6).

In the 160s BCE, slightly later than that Roman scenario, the biblical tradition offered a rather different application of the classic sequence of five kingdoms in the Book of Daniel. There the fifth and final kingdom would not be that of Rome but of God. This interpretation requires very close reading indeed.

The Vision

The first part of the vision in Daniel 7:1–8 has "four great beasts" arising from the stormy sea—with the sea in the Old Testament always symbolizing pre-creation or anti-creation chaos. The first three beasts are described as "like a lion ... like a bear ... [and] like a leopard"; the "fourth beast" was "terrifying and dreadful and exceedingly strong. It had great iron teeth and was devouring, breaking in pieces, and stamping what was left with its feet. It was different from all the beasts that preceded it, and it had ten horns." Scholars agree that the four beasts represent the Babylonian, Medean, Persian, and Macedonian Empires, with Alexander's west-to-east dominion, of course, being the most fearsome of them all. This first part concludes as Alexander's empire was divided up among his generals after his death, and the emphasis shifts to one of those successors, the fourth beast's "little horn," representing Antiochus IV Epiphanes and his Greco-Syrian Empire.

The second part of the vision in 7:9–12 describes God as the Ancient One calling a heavenly tribunal where, surrounded by angelic throngs, "the court sat in judgment and the books were opened." The judgment was that rule would be taken from "the beasts" and the final "little horn" would be destroyed.

The third part of the vision, in 7:13–14, shows the conclusion of that heavenly condemnation of all imperial power. We move from sea to sky and from the bestial to the human. Instead of multiple ones "like a beast," there appears a single "one," who is "like a son of man," and he comes before God on the clouds of heaven. But that strange term requires some special explanation.

In English male chauvinism, the terms "man" and "mankind" are often used for "a human being" and "humanity." In Hebrew or Aramaic male chauvinism, "man" and "son of man" are used in similar fashion. Thus, for example, the King James Version translates Psalm 8:8 and 144:3 literally, with a parallelism of "man" and "son of man," while the New Revised Standard Version does so with a parallelism of "human beings" and "mortals." Similarly here in Daniel 7:13. The older translation of "one like a son of man" is now "one like a human being," but the meaning is exactly the same in either case. "Man" and "son of man" are simply poetic (and chauvinistic) parallelism for the same reality: "humans" and "humanity."

It is, then, to this "one like a son of man"—or "one like a human being"—that God grants "dominion and glory and kingship, that all peoples, nations, and languages should serve him. His dominion is an everlasting dominion that shall not pass away, and his kingship is one that shall never be destroyed" (Daniel 7:14). This is, once again, a version of the fifth and final kingdom of universal rule here below upon the earth. In Daniel 7:13–14, a New World Order replaces the Old World Order of 7:1–8. Notice that the older order is always bestial, while only the newer one is truly human.

The Interpretation

The basic interpretation is already quite clear as summarized in Daniel 7:17–18: "As for these four great beasts, four kings shall arise out of the earth. But the holy ones of the Most High shall receive the kingdom and possess the kingdom forever—forever and ever." None of this is imagined as a simple political or military or even religious conflict. It is a transcendental struggle between heaven and earth over control of the world here below. It is a struggle between the holy angels of God and the imperial powers of earth. This anti-imperial vision so affronts the violent normalcy of civilization's brutality that it requires a heavenly engendered alternative. Notice especially that God's Kingdom comes from heaven down to earth and not—or ever—from earth up to heaven. It is always about the holiness of this earth as God's creation.

That Kingdom is given into the care of "one like a human being" ("one like a son of man"); originally, in the 160s BCE, that probably denoted Michael the Archangel, leader of the angelic hosts (7:13) and guardian of heaven. Next it is passed from his protection to that of those angelic hosts, "the holy ones of the Most High" (7:18, 21, 22, 25). Finally, they deliver God's Kingdom to the earth, to "the people of the holy ones of the Most High" (7:27). God's Kingdom will ultimately be granted to God's people, and it will be exactly the Kingdom prepared for them and protected in heaven by Michael and the angels. (By the way, as you will recall from chapter 2, that is the thinking behind "on earth as in heaven" in the Lord's Prayer.)

The description of God's Kingdom as given to Michael in 7:14 is repeated when given to the people of God in 7:27: "The kingship and dominion and the greatness of the kingdoms under the whole heaven shall be given to the people of the holy ones of the Most High; their kingdom shall be an everlasting kingdom, and all dominions shall serve and obey them." Need I repeat once more that God's Kingdom is prepared in heaven above to be established on earth here below? That, of course, is a mythological scenario and a parabolical vision, but unless it is also historically accurate for our future, we are destined for the normalcy of civilization's eternal imperialism. Granted the equal normalcy of escalatory violence, our species has a very uncertain future.

The Application

Along with his Baptism by John, Jesus's proclamation of the Kingdom of God is as sure as something historical can ever be. But there has always been controversy about whether Jesus proclaimed the Kingdom as *future-only*—even if imminent—or as *already-present*—even if still to be consummated. My argument so far is that Jesus differed precisely from John in emphasizing not the *future-presence* but the *already-presence* of God's Kingdom as the Great Divine Cleanup of the world.

One very strong proof of that is how the Son of Man is used to interpret the Kingdom of God. Here again, scholarly debate has obscured the most important point. The main discussion has been about whether Jesus spoke of himself as the Son of Man or whether it was placed on his lips by the later tradition. What I emphasize here is how the title "Son of Man" for Jesus—be it from him or from the evangelists (and I think it was from the evangelists)—reinforces and rephrases the claim that the Kingdom of God is now *already* in collaborative process.

I take Mark as my example because he is the earliest of the four gospels and the others all used his data. The terms "Kingdom of God" and "Son of Man" are equally distributed throughout his gospel—each is used about fourteen times. But what is most striking about the latter term as Mark's very special title for Jesus is that he gives it three aspects in present-to-future continuity:

First aspect: Jesus as Son of Man with earthly authority
   (2:10, 28)
Second aspect: Jesus as Son of Man in death and resurrection
   (8:31; 9:9, 12, 31; 10:33, 45; 14:21, 41)
Third aspect: Jesus as Son of Man returning with heavenly
   power and glory (8:38; 13:26, 34; 14:62)

First, Mark identifies Jesus as the Son of Man, or "the Human One," from Daniel 7:13. Next, he has Jesus, as that Son of Man, offer God's Kingdom to any who would receive it and thereby become the people of the saints of the Most High. Finally, even though the Kingdom will be consummated in the future, it is already present on earth. That Kingdom has yet to be revealed in power and glory, but it is already here in humility and service. Its presence is now known only to *faith* (1:15), but one day it will be revealed to *sight* (9:1). Mark thought that day would be "within this generation," but of course, he was wrong on that by at least two thousand years. Apart from that, his claim is clear: God has given the Kingdom to Jesus, and all are invited to enter it—but that involves following Jesus through death into resurrection and a life here below absolutely opposite to the way of the world's imperial normalcy.

THE CROWD AND THE DEATH OF JESUS

The residents of the Bavarian village of Oberammergau have staged a Passion Play every decade on the decade and also on special anniversaries in gratitude for protection from a 1634 plague. When I saw the second production after World War II, in 1960, it was the same one that Hitler had seen in 1930 and 1934, before and after he became Chancellor of Germany. Later, in July 1942, about the time the German armies were beginning their fateful push toward Stalingrad, Hitler commented on what he had seen a decade earlier:

> It is vital that the Passion Play be continued at Oberammergau; for never has the menace of Jewry been so convincingly portrayed as in this presentation of what happened in the times of the Romans. There one sees in Pontius Pilate a Roman racially and intellectually so superior, that he stands out like a firm, clean rock in the middle of the whole muck and mire of Jewry.

Judging from that approval, Hitler would have fully applauded Mel Gibson's 2004 film *The Passion of the Christ*. There the "rock" is portrayed as even rockier and the "muck" as even muckier than anything ever dreamed of at Oberammergau. That reminds us that any dramatization of Jesus's death demands a very particular level of ethical responsibility. You must get it right in the present, because getting it wrong has fed theological anti-Judaism and racial anti-Semitism in the past.

Earlier, in my 1995 book *Who Killed Jesus?* I have discussed the historical reconstruction of what actually happened to Jesus as distinct from the different gospel interpretations of that event. But especially after seeing the reactions to the Mel Gibson film, I realize that most people simply do not know the gospel story. That must come first. However you reconstruct the balance of history and parable in that narrative, your first obligation is to know the story, and to get it right. It was that obligation that compelled my friend and colleague Marcus Borg and myself to collaborate on our 2006 book, *The Last Week: A Day-by-Day Account of Jesus's Final Week in Jerusalem*. As in that book, so also here: I focus on Mark as the earliest of the gospel versions and the major source for Matthew and Luke certainly and for John possibly. But I begin with two authors from outside Christianity.

At the end of the first century, the Jewish historian Josephus, in his *Jewish Antiquities* (18.63–64), and at the start of the second century the Roman historian Tacitus, in his *Annals* (4.282–83), agreed on four details concerning Jesus.

First, there had been a *movement* over there in Judea. Second, its founder, Jesus or Christ, was *executed* under Pontius Pilate. Third, despite the execution of Jesus, the movement *continued*. Fourth, it had now *spread* widely because, as Josephus puts it neutrally, "those who had in the first place come to love him did not give up their affection for him," and as Tacitus puts it nastily, "the pernicious superstition was checked for the moment, only to break out once more, not merely in Judaea, the home of the disease, but in the capital itself, where all things horrible or shameful in the world collect and find a vogue."

Josephus mentions two further details. Jesus "won over many Jews and many of the Greeks," and Pilate crucified him "upon hearing him accused by men of the highest standing amongst us." Those twin aspects of Jesus's fate are also basic to Mark's story. Jesus has the crowd on his side but is opposed by a collaboration of Jewish and Roman authority. Those two points are constitutive for the following discussion.

When I first saw the Oberammergau Passion Play in 1960, one point struck me while watching it as *drama* that I had never appreciated while reading it as *text*. The play takes up the whole day, with a long break for lunch. It starts early in the morning of what we Christians call Palm Sunday, and the stage is filled with a huge crowd of men, women, and children, all applauding and supporting Jesus's entrance into Jerusalem. But later that same afternoon, on what we call Good Friday, the same huge crowd (and in the play it is the same) is screaming to have Jesus crucified.

What struck me forcibly for the first time in 1960 was that the story made no dramatic sense—there was no explanation for that change in the crowd's response to Jesus. What happened between Palm Sunday and Good Friday? That experience was my first close introduction to the problem of the historical Jesus, and the subject of my first scholarly article in a 1965 issue of the journal *Theological Studies.* I focused on that problem of the changeling crowd and concluded that "the [gospel] evidence explicitly and definitely points against any representative Jerusalem crowd shouting for Jesus' death; it is quite possible that the crowd before Pilate was interested primarily in Barabbas as a rebel hero, and in Jesus only in so far as He became a threat to Barabbas' release" (26.204). Now, forty years later, I return once more to that constitutive problem of the crowd during Jesus's last week in Jerusalem and its depiction in Mark's gospel.

The same problem, by the way, should have struck anyone seeing *The Passion of the Christ,* but in a slightly different way. The Gibson film does not open on what we Christians call Palm Sunday, as does the Oberammergau play. It opens instead on the evening of what we call Holy Thursday, when Jesus is arrested in the darkness with the help of Judas. That may seem to avoid the problem of Palm Sunday enthusiasm versus Good Friday rejection, but in fact it simply raises the issue in another manner. If on Friday the crowd is as totally and absolutely against Jesus as the film portrays, why do the authorities need darkness and betrayal in order to arrest Jesus? If everyone (except his own followers) is against him, why not arrest him in the daytime and out in the open?

Indeed, Jesus himself raises that issue against Mel Gibson's portrayal: "Have you come out with swords and clubs to arrest me as though I were a bandit? Day after day I was with you in the temple teaching, and you did not arrest me" (Mark 14:48–49). The problem of the crowd is central, therefore, for understanding the death of

Jesus as gospel story and for recognizing its misinterpretation in passion play and passion film.

A Double Demonstration in Jerusalem

After what happened to John, Jesus would have known that he also was in mortal danger. Indeed, Antipas, as a shrewd ruler who lasted forty-three years, may have hesitated to move against Jesus too soon after his unpopular execution of the Baptist. In Galilee, therefore, Jesus was protected especially by John's death. But what about Pilate in Judea?

We cannot tell if Jesus went to the pilgrim feasts in Jerusalem regularly or only once. In either case, the question is the same: If *often*, what happened this one time? If *once*, why this one time? We can be sure, however, that he went that one (or last) time to make a very public double demonstration. He did not go to get himself killed or to get himself martyred. Mark insists that Jesus knew in very specific detail what was going to happen to him—read Mark 10:33–34, for example—but that is simply Mark's way of insisting that all was accepted by both God and Jesus. Accepted, be it noted, but not willed, wanted, needed, or demanded.

Jesus went to Jerusalem that one (or last) time because it was a *capital* city where *religion* and *violence*—conservative religion and imperial oppression—had become serenely complicit. We can probably compare, for instance, the theology of Caiaphas in the generation of Jesus with that of Josephus in the next one. "God, who went the round of the nations, bringing to each in turn the rod of empire, now rested over Italy," says Josephus in his *Jewish War* (5.367). It was the will of God, therefore, that Rome should rule the world and that the Jews should always cooperate and never resist that divine mandate (recall that Josephan position from chapter 2).

Jesus went to Jerusalem because that was where his deliberate double demonstration against both imperial injustice and religious

collaboration had to be made. It is crucially important, especially
in the light of ancient and enduring Christian anti-Judaism, to be
quite clear that this double demonstration was not against Judaism
as such, not against Jerusalem as such, not against the Temple as
such, and not against the high priesthood as such. *It was a protest
from the legal and prophetic heart of Judaism against Jewish religious cooperation with Roman imperial control.* It was, at least for Christian
followers of Jesus, then or now, a permanently valid protest demonstration against any capital city's collusion between conservative
religion and imperial violence at any time and in any place.

The first demonstration was what we mistakenly call "the Triumphal Entry into Jerusalem." It was actually an anti-triumphal
entry, a calculated alternative to imperial normalcy with a prophetic pedigree going back to an oracle added to the book of
Zechariah in the fourth century BCE. That oracle created a very
deliberate contrast with how Alexander of Macedon had entered
cities like Tyre and Gaza after devastating sieges or, especially,
with how he had entered Jerusalem when it finally decided not
to resist but to submit and throw open its gates to the con-
queror.

Like any city of the ancient world, Jerusalem knew that a con-
queror entered it at best through opened gates and at worst
through shattered walls. In either case, he came on battle chariot
or war horse. But in Zechariah 9:9–10, the prophet imagines this
anti-triumphal future entrance of the Messiah on a donkey:

Rejoice greatly, O daughter Zion! Shout aloud, O daughter
Jerusalem! Lo, your king comes to you; triumphant and victorious is he, humble and riding on a donkey, on a colt, the
foal of a donkey. He will cut off the chariot from Ephraim
and the war horse from Jerusalem; and the battle bow shall be
cut off, and he shall command peace to the nations; his dominion shall be from sea to sea, and from the River to the
ends of the earth.

This is the entrance that Jesus enacted implicitly in Mark and explicitly in Matthew 21:4–5. Notice especially the deliberate and preplanned nature of this prophetic demonstration in Mark 11:1–6. It is all set up ahead of time, and the disciples are told to go and get the donkey from its owner because now "the Lord needs it." The owner awaited his donkey's planned use by Jesus.

The second demonstration was what we mistakenly call "the Cleansing of the Temple." It was actually a symbolic destruction of the Temple, and it too had an ancient prophetic pedigree going back to Jeremiah at the end of the seventh century BCE. In Jeremiah 7 and 26, the prophet is ordered by God to warn worshipers in the Temple not to think that the practice of worship excuses them from the practice of justice. Only, says God, "*if* you truly amend your ways and your doings, *if* you truly act justly one with another, *if* you do not oppress the alien, the orphan, and the widow, or shed innocent blood in this place" (7:5–6), will God continue to dwell with them in the Temple. Otherwise, warns God, "I will do to the house that is called by my name, in which you trust, and to the place that I gave to you and to your ancestors, just what I did to Shiloh" (7:14). In other words, the great Temple in Judea will be destroyed just as was the older shrine in Samaria. Their use of divine worship to avoid divine justice had turned the Temple into a safehouse, a refuge, a hideaway, a "den of robbers" (7:11). Notice, by the way, that a "den" is not where robbers do their robbing but where they flee for safety with the spoils they have robbed elsewhere.

What Jesus did, then, was to fulfill this prophecy of Jeremiah's, just as he had fulfilled Zechariah's prophecy on the preceding day. He shut down, symbolically and prophetically, the perfectly valid fiscal, ritual, and administrative operations of the Temple:

> He entered the temple and began to drive out those who were selling and those who were buying in the temple, and he overturned the tables of the money changers and the seats of

those who sold doves; and he would not allow anyone to carry anything through the temple. He was teaching and saying, "Is it not written, 'My house shall be called a house of prayer for all the nations'? [Isaiah 56:7] But you have made it a den of robbers [Jeremiah 7:11]." (Mark 11:15–17)

Jeremiah's message almost cost him his life, and Jesus's double demonstration would cost him his. Notice, once again, that this second demonstration was also deliberately programmed. Jesus had already entered the Temple (11:11), but waited until the next morning (11:15–17) for the demonstration.

In Mark's story, attention is focused on the demonstrations as twin aspects of the same nonviolent protest. Each gets its own day on what we call Sunday and Monday of that last week. Each is an action accompanied, implicitly or explicitly, by a prophetic message and enacted as its fulfillment. Each is quite deliberate. Each takes place at an entrance—into the City and into the Temple. Together, and in the name of God, these demonstrations are a protest against any collaboration between religious authority and imperial violence. But was Jesus doing all this to get himself executed? To die as a martyr and fulfill, say, Isaiah 52–53? We return once more to the problem of the crowd—a problem that is also a solution.

Protected by What Crowd?

We have already seen that the Jerusalem crowd was on the side of Jesus in the anti-imperial demonstration in Mark 11:8–10 on what Christians call Palm Sunday:

Many people spread their cloaks on the road, and others spread leafy branches that they had cut in the fields. Then those who went ahead and those who followed were shouting, "Hosanna! Blessed is the one who comes in the name of the Lord! Blessed is the coming kingdom of our ancestor David! Hosanna in the highest heaven!"

But watch the importance of that continuing support and protection as Mark's story unfolds day by day from Sunday through Wednesday.

On Monday, after the demonstration in the Temple, Mark 11:18 comments that, "when the chief priests and the scribes heard it, they kept looking for a way to kill him; for they were afraid of him, because the whole crowd was spellbound by his teaching." That sets up a clear distinction between the Jewish authorities and the Jewish crowd concerning Jesus. And it is similar to the divergent reactions to Jesus in Josephus cited at the start of this section.

On Tuesday, there is a series of debates between Jesus and those authorities, in several of which they attempt to drive a wedge between him and his popular support. That, for example, is the logic of the trick question: should we pay taxes to Caesar or not? (12:13–17). If he answers yes, the crowd will desert him; if no, the Romans will arrest him. But three times on that Tuesday, Mark insists, the crowd is on the side of Jesus.

First, with regard to John the Baptist, Jesus shows that the authorities were against John as they are now against him, and thus also against their own people. "The chief priests, the scribes, and the elders ... were afraid of the crowd, for all regarded John as truly a prophet" (11:27, 32). Second, after Jesus tells the parable of the wicked husbandmen who kill the vineyard owner's son, those same authorities "realized that he had told this parable against them [and] they wanted to arrest him, but they feared the crowd. So they left him and went away" (12:12). Finally, after Jesus shows from Psalm 110:1 that the Messiah is not just the Son but the Lord of David, "the large crowd was listening to him with delight" (12:37). Mark mentions Jesus's support and protection from the crowd those three times on Tuesday to lead up to his story's climax the next day.

On Wednesday morning, a final decision is made by the religious authorities: "It was two days before the Passover and the festival of Unleavened Bread. The chief priests and the scribes were looking for a way to arrest Jesus by stealth and kill him; for they said, 'Not during the festival, or there may be a riot among the people'" (14:1–2). In effect, therefore, they have given up hope of moving against Jesus during the festival days, and of course after the festival he might well go home. However big the supporting crowd was, it was big enough to stop the authorities by threatening a riot. At this point within the logic of Mark's story, Jesus is safe: as he expected, he has gotten away with his double demonstration, and the Jewish authorities have been stopped by the Jewish crowd, who support the Jewish Jesus.

It is precisely this impasse that is solved for the authorities by Judas in 14:10–11: "Then Judas Iscariot, who was one of the twelve, went to the chief priests in order to betray him to them. When they heard it, they were greatly pleased, and promised to give him money. So he began to look for an opportunity to betray him." Judas offers to tell them where Jesus is at night, away from the crowd, and no doubt their idea is to have it all over and done before the crowd knows anything about it. Betrayal, secrecy, and speed are now essential—within the logic of Mark's narrative. And so it happens.

Rejected by What Crowd?

Mark's story is clear enough from Sunday morning through Thursday night, but what about that "crowd" demanding Jesus's execution on Friday afternoon? I go back once again to a close reading of Mark 15:6–9 and watch the sequence of these four verses very carefully—once again within the logic of narrativity and abstracting for here and now from the question of historicity:

> Now at the festival he used to release a prisoner for them, anyone for whom they asked. (15:6)
> Now a man called Barabbas was in prison with the rebels who had committed murder during the insurrection. (15:7)
> So the crowd came and began to ask Pilate to do for them according to his custom. (15:8)

Then he answered them, "Do you want me to release for
you the King of the Jews?" (15:9)

The narrative logic of Mark's four-verse sequence is quite clear.
There is a Paschal amnesty open to whomever the crowd chooses.
They come up to get Barabbas out. Pilate, recognizing correctly that
the nonviolent Jesus is far less of a threat than the violent Barabbas,
attempts to free Jesus instead. The crowd demands Barabbas and
rejects Jesus. In the story, there is no evidence that they know or
care about Jesus except as a present threat to the freedom of
Barabbas. There is, by the way, every reason to presume that this
"crowd" is no more than a small delegation of, say, nine or ten
people. Granted the tinderbox atmosphere of Passover, the volatile
character of Pilate, and the dangerous nature of their request, gath-
ering in a crowd of more than that number would be suicidal.

Notice, however, that as you move from Mark through Matthew
and Luke and into John, the number and purpose of that crowd
changes drastically before your eyes. Matthew begins with a
"crowd" in 27:15, then expands to "crowds" in 27:20, and ends
with "the people as a whole" in 27:25. Then Luke reverses Mark's
order so that the crowd comes up against Jesus rather than for
Barabbas. Watch the sequence in 23:18–19: "Then they all shouted
out together, 'Away with this fellow! Release Barabbas for us!'
(This was a man who had been put in prison for an insurrection
that had taken place in the city, and for murder)." Finally, in John,
it is not the crowd, be it big or small, but "the Jews" who reject
Jesus and demand Barabbas. Once again, watch the sequence:
"After [Jesus] had said this, [Pilate] went out to the Jews again and
told them, 'I find no case against him. But you have a custom that
I release someone for you at the Passover. Do you want me to release for you the King of the Jews?' They shouted in reply, 'Not
this man, but Barabbas!' Now Barabbas was a bandit" (18:38–40).

The steady increase in the size of the Friday crowd, along with
the steady change in their primary purpose from pro-Barabbas to
anti-Jesus, as well as the exculpation of Pilate, all bespeak the fact

that, in the first-century Jewish homeland, Christian Jews had more to fear from Jewish than Roman authority and more and more of their fellow Jews were refusing the Christian Jewish option.

But all those expansions on a Markan theme only serve to emphasize his original version in which a (prudently small?) crowd approaches Pilate to obtain freedom under the open Paschal amnesty for their hero Barabbas. He, by the way, was not the loutish buffoon portrayed in *The Passion of the Christ* but simply the Jewish version of the Scottish anti-imperialist *Braveheart* or the American anti-imperialist *The Patriot*. Anyone who wants to dramatize the death of Jesus in play or film should first read the text and get the story right.

THE MEANING OF SACRIFICE

Apart from *narrativity,* let alone *historicity,* there is the deeper question of the *theology* within which Jesus's execution is understood then and now by Christian believers. For *The Passion of the Christ* and millions of Christians, it was a theology of substitutionary atonement or vicarious satisfaction. Here is its content.

God was offended by human sin, and because that sin was a human affront to divinity, no adequate satisfaction was possible. Therefore, in his mercy, God sent his only begotten Son to suffer and die in our place. That is why Mel Gibson's film is two hours of unspeakable suffering as Jesus bears punishment for all the sins against God since the dawn of creation. In that theology, God is imagined as a Divine Judge who can no more forgive everyone than a human judge could walk into the courtroom and forgive all those under indictment. (You will recognize the continuing shadow of Deuteronomic theology and God's retributive justice from chapter 2.) Notice, however, that the traditional metaphor for God is Father rather than Judge, and that in human courts we expect a father to recuse himself from judging his own child. We do not think one can be Judge and Parent at the same time.

My purpose here, however, is not to highlight the transcendental conflict between Divine Parent and Divine Judge, but rather to point out the confusion in that theology between *sacrifice, substitution,* and *suffering,* as well as the mistaken presumption that whenever the New Testament mentions the sacrifice of Jesus, those other two aspects must and do accompany it.

Human beings have always known two basic ways of creating, maintaining, or restoring good relations with one another—the *gift* and the *meal.* Both the proffered gift and the shared meal represent the external manifestation of an internal disposition, and both events have their delicate protocols of what and whom they involve and when and why they take place.

These elements of the gift and the meal came together in animal sacrifice. How was one to create, maintain, or restore good relations between a human person and a divine being? What visible acts could do that with an Invisible Being? If by *gift,* the animal was totally destroyed, at least as far as the offerer was concerned. No doubt the smoke and the smell rising upward symbolized the transition of the gift from earth to heaven and from human being to God. If by *meal,* the animal was transferred to God by having its blood poured over the altar and was then returned to the offerer as divine food for a feast with God. In other words, it was not so much that the offerer invited God to a meal, but that God invited the offerer to a meal.

That understanding of sacrifice clarifies the etymology of the term. It derives from the Latin *sacrum facere,* that is, to make (*facere*) sacred (*sacrum*). In a sacrifice, the animal is made sacred and given to God as a sacred gift or returned to the offerer as a sacred meal.

Sacrificial offerers never thought that the point of sacrifice was to make the animal suffer or that the greatest sacrifice was one in which the animal suffered lengthily and terribly. Whether for a human meal or a divine meal, an animal had to be slain, but that was done swiftly and efficiently—ancient priests were also excellent butchers. Likewise, sacrificial offerers never thought that the animal was dying in their place, that they deserved to be killed in punishment for their sins but that God would accept the slain animal as substitutionary atonement or vicarious satisfaction. Blood *sacrifice* should never be confused with or collapsed into either *suffering* or *substitution,* let alone substitutionary suffering. We may or may not like ancient blood sacrifice, but we should neither caricature it nor libel it.

Think about how we ordinarily use the term "sacrifice" today. A building is on fire, a child is trapped upstairs, and the firefighter who rushes in to save him manages to drop the child safely to the net below. Then the roof collapses and kills the firefighter. The next day the local paper bears the headline "Firefighter Sacrifices Her Life." We are not ancients but moderns, and yet that is still an absolutely acceptable statement. On the one hand, all human life and all human death are sacred. On the other, that firefighter has *made* her own death peculiarly, especially, emphatically *sacred* by giving her life up to save the life of another. So far so good. Now imagine if somebody confused sacrifice with suffering and denied that the firefighter had made a sacrifice because she died instantly and without intolerable suffering. Or imagine if somebody confused sacrifice with substitution and said that God wanted somebody dead that day and accepted the firefighter in lieu of the child. And worst of all, imagine that somebody brought together sacrifice, suffering, and substitution by claiming that the firefighter had to die in agony as atonement for the sins of the child's parents. That theology would be a crime against divinity.

It is certainly correct, therefore, to call Jesus's death—or in fact the death of any martyr—a sacrifice, but substitution and suffering are not the point of sacrifice. Substitutionary atonement is bad as theoretical Christian theology just as suicidal terrorism is bad as practical Islamic theology. Jesus died *because* of our sins, or *from* our sins, but that should never be misread as *for* our sins. In Jesus, the radicality of God became incarnate, and the normalcy of civilization's brutal violence (our sins, or better, Our Sin) executed him. Jesus's execution asks us to face the truth that, across human evolution, injustice has been created and maintained by violence while justice has been opposed and avoided by violence. That warning, if heeded, can be salvation. Was it heeded by Jesus's own first followers? Yes (as we will see in chapter 4) and no (as we will see in chapter 5).

Chapter 3 is the central one of this book. The two preceding chapters set up the struggle between the injustice of civilization's normalcy (chapter 1) and the justice of God's radicality (chapter 2), especially inside the Bible itself. I proposed at the end of chapter 2 that Christians choose between the violent God of human normalcy and the nonviolent God of divine radicality, between peace through violence and peace though justice, according to which one they find incarnate in the historical Jesus—in other words, the Jesus of this chapter. In the succeeding two chapters, I look at two divergent responses to the radical God incarnate in that Jesus—both within the Christian New Testament itself.

In chapter 4, I consider Paul as the apostle who took Jesus's message out from the Jewish homeland into the great big Roman world. I emphatically do not agree with those who think Paul betrayed Jesus or invented Christianity. He accurately and effectively rephrased Jesus's message of the already-present Kingdom of God in his own language for that wider world. And he did so not in some newly invented and peculiarly Christian language but *in* and thereby *against* the public discourse of Roman imperial theology. For, before Jesus had ever spoken and even if he had never spoken, before Paul had ever written and even if he had never written, before Christianity had ever arrived and even if it had never arrived, these were, as noted in chapter 1, already the titles of Caesar: "Divine," "Son of God," "God," "God from God," "Redeemer," "Liberator," "Lord," and "Savior of the World." Used as titles not of Caesar the Augustus but of Jesus the Christ, they were either low lampoon or high treason. Since the Romans did not roll over laughing, I trust their judgment about what it was. Over against "peace through victory" came again the alternative "peace through justice." In chapter 4, we will also see examples of the normalcy of Roman civilization used by post-Pauline Christians to sanitize and

deradicalize Paul on such subjects as slavery, patronage, and patriarchy.

In chapter 5, I turn in point-counterpoint from Paul of Tarsus
to John of Patmos. The last book of the Christian Bible, the Apocalypse, or the Book of Revelation, is the most absolutely and viru-
lently anti-Roman work in all of either Judaism or Christianity.
My question will be this: Is it the final attempt to make Jesus violent, to have Jesus return as the incarnation of divine violence? Is
that book the ultimate attempt—and a Christian attempt—to
assert the violent injustice of civilization's normalcy over the nonviolent justice of God's radicality? At the end, even God must use
our standard solution to evil—kill the evildoers. Paul of Tarsus and
John of Patmos represent, respectively, acceptance and rejection of
the radical nonviolence that Jesus proclaimed to and against Pilate
before he was condemned to death.

4

PAUL AND THE
JUSTICE OF EQUALITY

Equality is the mother of justice. Justice is the offspring of equality.

—Philo of Alexandria
(c. 30 bce)

Paul was an apostle—certainly, emphatically, and repetitively "an apostle of Christ Jesus"—but was he then and is he now an *appealing* or *appalling* apostle?

It seems clear that *Newsweek*'s cover story for May 6, 2002, would choose "appalling." The subject was general problems of biblical sexuality within Christianity and the particular problems of criminal sexuality within Roman Catholicism. The cover mentioned Jesus ("What Would Jesus Do?"), but the inside text cited Paul as pro-slavery, anti-Semitic, misogynistic, and homophobic:

The Biblical defense of slavery is: "Slaves, obey your earthly masters with fear and trembling, in singleness of heart, as you obey Christ," writes Saint Paul [in Ephesians 6:5]. Anti-Semitism was long justified by passages like this one from 1 Thessalonians [2:14–15]: the Jews "killed both the Lord Jesus and the prophets." And the subjugation of women had a foundation in 1 Timothy [actually 1 Corinthians 14:33–35]: "As in all the churches of the saints, women should be silent in the churches.... If there is anything they desire to know, let them ask their husbands at home. For it is shameful for a woman to speak in church." And yet in each case, enlightened people have moved on from the world view such passages express…. And if science now teaches us that being gay may be a "natural" state, how can a reading of the Bible, including Saint Paul's condemnation of same-sex interaction in Romans [1:26–27], inarguably cast homosexuality in "unnatural" terms?

I discuss the other accusations against Paul later in this chapter, but as an introduction to him, what about that final one?

In his letter to the Romans, Paul definitely asserted that homosexuality between women or between men was wrong: "Their women exchanged natural intercourse for unnatural, and in the same way also the men, giving up natural intercourse with women, were consumed with passion for one another" (1:26–27). And not just wrong, you will notice, but "unnatural." That judgment is echoed, by the way, in all other Jewish writers who mentioned that same subject in Paul's time. Indeed, along with idolatry, it was a standard Jewish accusation against paganism.

The problem, however, is that the natural and the unnatural are open to social and cultural interpretation, so that what once was accepted as natural can later be judged as unnatural and vice versa. For example, Aristotle judged slavery to be natural, but Philo, as we saw in chapter 1, judged it unnatural. So also here, but in reverse. First-century Jewish writers considered homosexuality unnatural because they judged from organs and biology. Many of us today consider it natural because we judge from hormones and chemistry. Similarly, of course, we think war is natural, but if our species has a future, later generations will deem it unnatural. We can all agree not to do what is unnatural, but we still have to negotiate what is or is not unnatural. Is capital punishment, for example, natural or unnatural retribution?

Furthermore, in a section from 1 Corinthians to which I return in much greater detail later, Paul makes another judgment about what is natural and unnatural. "Does not nature itself teach you," he asks, "that if a man wears long hair, it is degrading to him, but if a woman has long hair, it is her glory? For her hair is given to her for a covering" (11:14–15). We would surely judge today that short male hair and long female hair are simply time-relative customs or place-relative habits at best, not irrevocable decrees of human nature. This is not to deny the existence of *natural* human rights or our ability to recognize and even legislate them, but nature neither commands hairstyle nor forbids homosexuality.

Before I begin this chapter's argument that Paul is an appealing apostle, I emphasize one fundamental set of presuppositions. They are not dogmatic ones of my own but rather historical ones from general biblical scholarship.

There are twenty-seven books in the New Testament. Of those, thirteen are letters *attributed* to Paul, and another one, Luke's Acts of the Apostles, is half about him. Paul takes up, therefore, exactly half the New Testament. But there is a massive scholarly consensus that only seven of those letters are *certainly* Pauline—Romans, 1 and 2 Corinthians, Galatians, Philippians, 1 Thessalonians, and Philemon. Of the remaining six letters, the general consensus is that three of them, 2 Thessalonians, Colossians, and Ephesians, are *probably not* from Paul and that the last three, 1 and 2 Timothy and Titus, are *certainly not* from Paul. The reason for those judgments is the difference in style, tone, vocabulary, and content between the latter six and the former seven letters. These six post-Pauline letters were written in his name by later tradition but are actually anti-Pauline on certain subjects, such as slavery and patriarchy. We are dealing, in other words, with a series of letters in which a *radical* Paul is transformed first into a *liberal* Paul and then into a *conservative or reactionary* Paul as we move from the seven *certainly* authentic letters through the three *probably not* authentic letters and finally into the three *certainly not* authentic letters.

The question of whether Paul was appealing or appalling therefore touches on half our present New Testament. This chapter is my proposal for a judgment of appealing. Here is another way to put it. Once, after a lecture, when I was autographing *In Search of Paul,* the purchaser asked me to write: "All we are asking is give Paul a chance." Exactly.

Recall from the start of the previous chapter that the geographical and historical matrix for Jesus as a homeland Jew was Antipas's program of Romanization by urbanization for commercialization in the 20s CE in lower Galilee. Similarly, I begin this chapter with the geographical and historical matrix for understanding Paul as a diaspora Jew in the great capital cities of the major provinces across the Roman Empire.

PAUL AND ROME

Our modern letters usually have some rather formulaic beginnings ("Hope you are well") and endings ("Best wishes"), and similar customs were applied to ancient ones. But one of the most striking aspects of Paul's letters is this absolutely consistent opening and only slightly varied ending:

> Grace to you and peace.... May the God of peace himself sanctify you entirely. (1 Thessalonians 1:1 and 5:23)
>
> Grace to you and peace....The God of peace will be with you. (Philippians 1:2 and 4:9)
>
> Grace to you and peace from God our Father and the Lord Jesus Christ. (Philemon 1:3)
>
> Grace to you and peace.... Send him on his way in peace. (1 Corinthians 1:3 and 16:11)
>
> Grace to you and peace.... Live in peace; and the God of love and peace will be with you. (2 Corinthians 1:2 and 13:11)
>
> Grace to you and peace.... Peace be upon them, and mercy. (Galatians 1:3 and 6:16)
>
> Grace to you and peace....The God of peace will shortly crush Satan under your feet. The grace of our Lord Jesus Christ be with you. (Romans 1:7 and 16:20)

Notice the consistency of "grace and peace" as the opening salutation and "peace" as the closing one (save for Philemon). But how exactly is the peace of God and Christ different from the peace of Rome and Augustus? What did Roman imperial peace look like?

The ancient city of Priene is located south of Ephesus off the midwestern coast of Turkey. It was built beneath a towering crag of the Samsun Dağlari, which turned the westward-flowing Meander River southward toward the Aegean Sea. It had—and its ruins still have—an absolutely spectacular view out over the Meander Valley.

Immediately after Actium, Paulus Fabius Maximus, governor of the rich Roman province of Asia, offered a golden crown for the best way to celebrate not just Octavian's victory but Octavian's very existence on this earth. It took about twenty years for the governor himself to win that award with this suggestion:

> [It is a question whether] the birthday of the most divine Caesar is more pleasant or more advantageous, the day which we might justly set on a par with the beginning of everything, in practical terms at least, in that he restored order when everything was disintegrating and falling into chaos and gave a new look to the whole world, a world which would have met destruction with the utmost pleasure if Caesar had not been born as a common blessing to all. For that reason one might justly take this to be the beginning of life and living, the end of regret at one's birth.... It is my view that all the communities should have one and the same New Year's Day, the birthday of the most divine Caesar, and that on that day, 23rd September, all should enter their term of office.

Notice the language. The birth of "the most divine Caesar" is a new creation for the world "in practical terms at least" since, without his intervention, that "whole world" was disintegrating "into chaos." In accepting the proconsul's proposal and awarding him the prize, the Asian League of Cities was even more fulsome in its praises:

> Since the providence that has divinely ordered our existence has applied her energy and zeal and has brought to life the most perfect good in Augustus, whom she filled with virtues for the benefit of mankind, bestowing him upon us and our descendants as a savior—he who put an end to war and will order peace, Caesar, who by his epiphany exceeded the hopes of those who prophesied good tidings [*euaggelia*], not only outdoing benefactors of the past, but also allowing no hope of greater benefactions in the future; and since the birthday of the god first brought to the world the good tidings [*euaggelia*] residing in him.... For that reason, with good fortune and safety, the Greeks of Asia have decided that the New Year in all the cities should begin on 23rd September, the birthday of Augustus ... and that the letter of the proconsul and the decree of Asia should be inscribed on a pillar of white marble, which is to be placed in the sacred precinct of Rome and Augustus.

Notice the language once again. Augustus is a "savior" whose "epiphany" brought "peace" to "mankind." He is the greatest benefactor of both past, present, and future, so that "the birthday of the god" is the ultimate "good tidings" for the world. Henceforth, throughout Asia, the new year would begin and all official magistracies would start on Caesar's birthday because the governor had "discovered a way to honor Augustus that was hitherto unknown among the Greeks, namely to reckon time from the date of his nativity." Augustus was now Lord of cosmic time as well as Lord of global place.

The imperial inscription's plural term, *euaggelia,* comes from the same root as our Christian singular term, *euaggelion,* meaning "gospel" or "good news." Each year at Christmas, then, the angels proclaim the "good news" of "peace on earth" because there "is born this day in the city of David a Savior, who is the Messiah, the Lord." Clearly, a different peace, a different gospel, and a different Lord are announced in the text of Luke 2:8–14 than the one proclaimed a few years earlier in the province of Asia. Clearly, Christian peace from a child in somebody else's stable is different from Caesarian peace from an emperor in somebody else's territory. But inaugurally, each was announced from heaven above.

There came from both Augustus and Paul a gospel of peace, but we know from chapter 1 that Augustus's was the normal imperial vision of peace through victory. Paul's was a vision of peace through justice, and we look now at how exactly that justice was enacted within his Christian communities.

PAUL AND LUKE

In the present sequence of the Christian New Testament, you read Luke's Acts of the Apostles, half of which is about Paul, before you read any of Paul's own letters. Since Luke is such a superb story-teller, it is hard, thereafter, not to see Paul through Lukan lenses, and hard not to understand Paul through Lukan interpretation. That Lukan interpretation raises this very specific question: if Paul opposed Christianity to Roman imperialism, did he also oppose it to his own native Judaism?

The Escape from Damascus

A paradigmatic example of the divergence between the Paul of Luke's Acts and the Paul of his own epistles appears in their twin accounts of the escape from Damascus. This is a classic instance because both Luke and Paul recount the incident but the difference is striking and illustrative:

Paul's Version
(2 Corinthians 11:32–33)

In Damascus, the governor under King Aretas guarded the city of Damascus in order to seize me, but I was let down in a basket through a window in the wall, and escaped from his hands.

Luke's Version
(Acts 9:23–25)

After some time had passed, the Jews plotted to kill him, but their plot became known to Saul. They were watching the gates day and night so that they might kill him; but his disciples took him by night and let him down through an opening in the wall, lowering him in a basket.

The *information* is the same concerning Paul's window-in-the-wall escape, but the *interpretation* is irreconcilably different. I take Paul's version first and then Luke's.

The Nabatean monarch, Aretas IV, who controlled Damascus between 37 and 39 CE, had his governor guarding the city gates to apprehend Paul. That fits very well with other items of Pauline biography. After a revelation from Christ called Paul to be an apostle to the pagans, his first mission was to Nabatean Arabia, whose capital city was at Petra. Or as he himself put it in his letter to the Galatians, "[I did not] go up to Jerusalem to those who were already apostles before me, but I went away at once into Arabia, and afterwards I returned to Damascus" (1:17). It was not, however, a good time for a Jewish missionary to operate among Arab pagans, since the Arab ruler Aretas had gone to war with the Jewish ruler Herod Antipas for divorcing his daughter. Once Aretas got control of Damascus, Paul was in lethal danger.

In Luke's version, however, there is no mention of that political situation. It is "the Jews" alone who are guarding the gates of Damascus. And the kindest comment on that is: *not possible!* The Jews had no such power in Arab cities. Now you can see the problem very clearly. First, it is not that Luke has no information about

Paul and is simply writing a Pauline novel. He has very good information, but he interprets it within his own vision for a later Christian time. Second, this excerpt gives us a pointed warning about how Luke handles "the Jews" in his Acts of the Apostles. He explains any opposition to Paul as simple jealousy from his fellow Jews because of his success among the pagans. In Acts 13:45, "when the Jews saw the crowds, they were filled with jealousy; and blaspheming, they contradicted what was spoken by Paul." And in Acts 17:5, "the Jews became jealous, and with the help of some ruffians in the marketplaces they formed a mob and set the city in an uproar." We meet here a major Lukan theme in the Acts: *it is Jewish jealousy, not Pauline teaching, that constantly creates trouble.*

Why would his fellow Jews care what Paul did or said among the pagans? Jealousy is a little too simple as an explanation, an idea I return to later. Paul's own explanation for why his fellow Jews were refusing to accept Jesus as their Messiah was not human jealousy but divine mystery. In his letter to the Romans, he warned his pagan converts: "So that you may not claim to be wiser than you are, brothers and sisters, I want you to understand this mystery: a hardening has come upon part of Israel, until the full number of the Gentiles has come in" (11:25). In the light of the divergence between Paul and Luke about his Damascus escape, I propose three principles for correlating Luke-on-Paul with Paul-on-Paul and for integrating data in Luke's Acts and Paul's letters.

The first principle is both easy and obvious: when Luke and Paul agree that he was a Jew, a Pharisee, and a persecutor of the early Christian community, I fully accept that common data.

The second principle is equally obvious but more controversial. What happens when Luke and Paul disagree? In that case, I follow Paul rather than Luke. For instance, Luke affirms, but Paul does not, that Paul was a freeborn citizen of Rome and raised in Jerusalem as a student of Gamaliel II. On this point, I follow Paul, not Acts—but would not argue about it too strongly. Here is a much more important disagreement. When Paul affirms and Luke denies that Paul was an apostle called by God through Christ and equal in authority to the Twelve Apostles, I follow Paul, not Luke—and would argue about it very, very strongly, as would Paul himself.

The third principle is the hardest of the three to use—and maybe even to understand. What about Lukan data that neither agree nor disagree with Pauline data? What if it is simply new information? When Luke has information that is neither *in* Paul's own data nor *against* Paul's data, I accept it *if* it can be correlated with Pauline rather than Lukan themes. A simple example is Luke's assertion in Acts 9:11, 21:39, and 22:3 that Paul came from Tarsus. Paul never confirms that explicitly, but Tarsus was the capital of the Roman province of Cilicia, and it may well be that Paul's strategic focus on Roman provincial capitals—Antioch for Syria, Thessalonica for Macedonia, Corinth for Achaia, Ephesus for Asia, and maybe even Ancyra for Galatia—implicitly confirms Luke's information. Paul is a man of capitals. In any case, what follows is a much more significant example, one that is basic and constitutive for my interpretation of Paul.

The Importance of the God-Worshipers

As with the paradigmatic Damascus incident, Luke first disagrees with Paul in this case, but then goes beyond him with information that does not come from Luke's own thematic emphases and in fact seems even to contradict them.

Luke elevates his own theological sequence of "first Jews, then Gentiles" into a historical pattern for Paul. He announces that principle in the Book of Acts: "It was necessary that the word of God should be spoken first to you [Jews]. Since you reject it and judge yourselves to be unworthy of eternal life, we are now turning to the Gentiles" (13:46). Then, in city after city, Luke sends Paul into the synagogue to preach Jesus on the Sabbath Day to his fellow Jews. That happens at Pisidian Antioch in 13:14, Iconium in 14:1, Thessalonica in 17:1, Beroea in 17:10, Athens in 17:17, Corinth in 18:4, and Ephesus in 18:19 and 19:8. But the claim that Paul always preached first to his fellow Jews raises intractable problems, as it contradicts him on two very important points.

Paul always insisted that he was called by God as an apostle to the Gentiles—that is, the pagans. "God," he told the Galatians, "was pleased to reveal his Son to me, so that I might proclaim him among the Gentiles" (1:15–16). Furthermore, once again in Galatians, Paul had accepted a separation of missionary focus at Jerusalem. God, "who worked through Peter making him an apostle to the circumcised also worked through me in sending me to the Gentiles," and all agreed that "we should go to the Gentiles and they to the circumcised" (2:8–9). Paul could not, as Acts claims, have gone to the synagogue to convert his fellow Jews against both his mandate from God and his agreement at Jerusalem. But in that very same context, Luke introduces another group that does not fit into his "first Jews, then Gentiles" dichotomy. Enter the God-fearers or God-worshipers. Who are they?

God-worshipers were neither those born Jewish nor those who converted from paganism to Judaism. They were pagans who, while remaining part of the pagan world, had accepted Jewish monotheism, Jewish morality, and Jewish synagogue attendance. They might have observed some kosher rules at home, for instance, but males would not have become circumcised. Think of them as a third group in between Jews and pagans. Louis H. Feldman, Professor of Classics at New York's Yeshiva University, describes them in his 1993 study *Jew and Gentile in the Ancient World:*

> The term G-d-fearers or sympathizers apparently refers to an "umbrella group," embracing many different levels of interest in and commitment to Judaism, ranging from people who supported synagogues financially (perhaps to get the political support of the Jews) to people who accepted the Jewish view of G-d in pure or modified form to people who observed certain distinctively Jewish practices, notably the Sabbath. For some this was an end in itself; for others it was a step leading ultimately to full conversion to Judaism. (p. 344)

In Acts

Throughout Acts, Luke speaks not only of "Jews" and "pagan Gentiles" but also of this third group—this in-between group that is "both/and" rather than "either/or"—and he uses two different Greek verbs to describe these pagan Jewish sympathizers. The phrases using the first verb, *phobeō,* translate as "the God-fearers" or "those fearing God." Here is the Lukan data from Acts for this term:

> [Cornelius] was a devout man who *feared God* with all his household; he gave alms generously to the people and prayed constantly to God. (10:2)
>
> Cornelius, a centurion, an upright and *God-fearing* man, who is well spoken of by the whole Jewish nation ... (10:22)
>
> In every nation anyone who *fears God* and does what is right is acceptable to God. (10:35)
>
> Paul stood up and with a gesture began to speak: "You Israelites, and others who *fear God,* listen." (13:16)
>
> My brothers, you descendants of Abraham's family, and others who *fear God,* to us the message of this salvation has been sent. (13:26)

The second verb used in describing this group, *sebomai,* translates as "the God-worshipers," or "those who are devout before God." (Rather ironically, *sebomai* is the word from which the title *Sebastos,* the Greek word for Augustus, is derived; *Sebastos,* however, does not mean "the Worshiping One" but "the Worshipful One," or "the One to Be Worshiped.") Here is the Lukan data from Acts for this second verb:

> When the meeting of the synagogue broke up, many Jews and *devout* converts to Judaism followed Paul and Barnabas, who spoke to them and urged them to continue in the grace of God. (13:43)

But the Jews incited the *devout* women of high standing and
the leading men of the city, and stirred up persecution
against Paul and Barnabas, and drove them out of their
region. (13:50)

A certain woman named Lydia, a *worshiper* of God, was listening to us; she was from the city of Thyatira and a dealer in
purple cloth. The Lord opened her heart to listen eagerly to
what was said by Paul. (16:14)

Some of them were persuaded and joined Paul and Silas, as did
a great many of the *devout* Greeks and not a few of the leading women. (17:4)

[Paul] argued in the synagogue with the Jews and the *devout*
persons, and also in the marketplace every day with those
who happened to be there. (17:17)

A certain Ananias, who was a *devout* man according to the law
and well spoken of by all the Jews living there ... (22:12)

Luke also calls them "converts" in 13:43, but that is not strictly
correct—they were something like semi-converts.

These twin verbs, divided sequentially and almost equally between (literally) "those fearing God" and "those worshiping God,"
should not be taken as absolute technical terms but rather as typical Jewish terms for pagan sympathizers. For example, neither expression is used to describe the "Ethiopian eunuch, a court official
of the Candace, queen of the Ethiopians, in charge of her entire
treasury," who, according to Acts 8:27, "had come to Jerusalem to
worship," but Luke probably saw him as a pagan sympathizer.

Notice that, in these quotations, Luke clearly distinguishes these
religious sympathizers from full Jews in 13:16, 43, and 50 and in
17:1–4, 17. Also, when Luke has Paul speaking in synagogues to his
fellow Jews, he also consistently has "God-fearers" or "God-
worshipers" in the audience. Furthermore, Acts often notes that
these pagan sympathizers were of high standing in their communities—Pisidian Antioch in 13:50, Philippi in 16:14, Thessalonica in

17:4, and Beroea in 17:12—and that they were both male and female. Indeed, with circumcision not applicable one way or the other, there might well have been more women than men among these God-fearers or God-worshipers.

At Aphrodisias

Hold on to this Lukan information as I turn to an inscription from the early 200s CE concerning the God-worshipers at the entrance to a Jewish building in Aphrodisias—eastward down the Meander Valley from Ephesus in western Turkey. That inscription, discovered in 1976, is locked in open-air storage at Aphrodisias, and although I was allowed to see it in late September 2004, it was not yet on public display in the site's archaeological museum when I was last there in March 2006—even though its footprint is only about a foot square and it could easily be tucked into a corner.

Imagine two square marble columns on either side of a building's doorway. (Only the right-hand one has been found so far.) There are lists of names on two of its three visible faces; these are records of the donors who sponsored the construction of the building, which might be the synagogue itself. One face lists nineteen names as members of the "decany," or the leadership of the project. Of that leadership group, fourteen are Jewish names, three are called "proselytes," or converts, and two are called "god-worshipers" (*theoseb[ēs]*). The other face has a top list of fifty-five names divided spatially from a bottom list of fifty-two names. The top group lists Jewish names, the bottom group pagan names. And most significantly, the bottom group is prefaced with the phrase: "and such as are god-worshipers" (*kai hosoi theosebis*). This is the longest Jewish inscription from antiquity and indicates close cooperation between Jews, pagan converts, and pagan sympathizers. Here, more clearly and certainly than anywhere else, are those enigmatic "God-worshipers" from Luke's Acts of the Apostles carved in stone.

Two important footnotes. First, the only woman mentioned in the entire list is Jael, the first cited in the leadership group on the first face; she is named as patron or protector. Second, the first nine names on the other face's list of fifty-two God-worshipers are noted as members of the council, the *boutē,* or governing body of the city.

Consider these statistics for one final moment. Before 1966, we did not know that there were any Jews or any Jewish buildings in Aphrodisias. We now have this information about the donors to that Jewish building: out of one hundred and twenty-six names, 55 percent (sixty-nine) were Jews, 2 percent (three) were converts, and 43 percent (fifty-four) were God-worshipers. And of the fifty-four God-worshipers listed on the column, 17 percent (nine) were council members.

These are rather extraordinary proportions, and even though generalizing from this one random-discovery case is surely precarious, how can we not do so? Was Aphrodisias an absolute exception or a standard example of the numerical proportions of Jews and God-fearers across the cities of the Roman Empire?

In Paul

My proposal is that Paul's pagan or Gentile mission focused primarily not on full Jews or pure pagans but on those in-betweens known as God-fearers or God-worshipers. He went to Jewish synagogues, as Acts says, but to convert God-worshiping pagans, not faithful Jews. I also insist that Paul never mentions a word about any such God-fearers or God-worshipers. Unlike Luke, he would have considered them worse than pagans in that they were lost between worlds. He would never have accepted a form that was both semi-Judaic and semi-pagan. For him, God-worshipers were not pagans-plus but pagans-minus. He understood faith and unfaith, but would never have understood semi-faith. As he told the Romans, "Whatever does not proceed from faith is sin" (14:23). For Paul, it was these neither-one-thing-nor-the-other people, these neither-Jews-nor-Gentiles, who most needed God's help, Christ's program, and his ministry. This Pauline focus on God-worshipers explains huge areas of his life and work.

First, it explains how his pagan readers could understand the intense Jewishness of his letters—they were God-worshipers already well versed in Judaism before they ever heard from Paul.

Second, it explains the virulence of both Jewish and pagan opposition to Paul. His poaching of their God-worshiping supporters must have infuriated his fellow Jews and may well have split the God-worshipers themselves for and against him.

Third, it is no longer necessary to imagine an anti-Pauline mission following him around the Roman Empire: converted God-worshipers would have been constantly pulled back locally toward their original synagogue loyalty—for example, in Galatia.

Fourth, it explains Paul's attack on *works without faith*—that is exactly how he would have characterized the God-worshipers and any Jews who found them acceptable.

Fifth, it explains how Paul could have moved so fast across the eastern Roman Empire and considered his work there finished by the mid–50s, as he wrote in Romans 15:23: he was focusing, as discussed earlier, on Roman provincial capitals rather than on ordinary Roman cities, and on God-worshipers rather than on pure pagans living in those capitals. The Pauline missionary express moved on God-worshiper rails and never had to slow down and lay track.

PAUL AND EQUALITY

It is well to remember that we moderns were not the first to imagine equality as an inalienable human right and that it is not a crude retrojection of contemporary democracy to speak of equality as justice at the time of Jesus and Paul. Reread, for example, this chapter's epigraph on equality-as-justice or justice-as-equality from Paul's contemporary fellow Jew, the philosopher Philo of Alexandria. That concept arose, of course, not from democratic values but from family values! "In Christ Jesus," says Paul in Galatians 3:26, "you are all *children of God* through faith." Equality under God as divine Father was modeled and understood to be like that in the family under a human father. Equality did not mean everyone getting the exact same amount, but rather everyone getting what they needed—everyone getting enough. It meant no child left behind in all the global family of God.

There is another rather fascinating example of equality-thinking in the earlier-seen *Sibylline Oracles,* a Jewish text that, like the quotation from Philo, was contemporary with Jesus and Paul. It imagined, as you will recall from chapter 2, the establishment of God's justice on earth with this description:

> The earth will belong equally to all, undivided by walls or
> fences. It will then bear more abundant fruits spontaneously.
> Lives will be in common and wealth will have no division.
> For there will be no poor man there, no rich, and no tyrant,
> no slave. Further, no one will be either great or small any-
> more. No kings, no leaders. All will be on a par together.
> (2.319–24)

But *if* one saw God's earthly kingdom as one of equality, and *if* one held that God's Kingdom was already here, then the position of a Jesus or a Paul was almost inevitable: equality now.

Looking next at Paul's vision of equality-as-justice or justice-as-equality in the *already-present* Kingdom of God here on earth, I begin with a general programmatic statement—probably a baptismal formula—from Paul's letter to the Galatians 3:27–29. Pay special attention to the frames about *Christ:*

> As many of you as were baptized into *Christ*
> have clothed yourselves with *Christ.*
>> There is no longer Jew or Greek,
>> there is no longer slave or free,
>> there is no longer male and female;

for all of you are one in *Christ* Jesus.
And if you belong to *Christ* ...

To understand Paul, the three central negations must never be read apart from the doubled frames that mention *into* Christ, *with* Christ, *in* Christ, and *to* Christ. Paul was speaking to those already Christian and saying that, whether they came into that community as Jew or Greek, slave or free, male or female, they were all equal inside the new community. Ethnic identity, social standing, and gender status do not establish any superiority among Christians—all are equal in Christ.

My Child Onesimus, My Own Heart

Sounds beautiful, even downright politically correct by our modern standards, but what did equality in Christ mean in ancient practice? For that I turn from general theory to specific example: the case of the slave Onesimus in Paul's letter to Onesimus's master, Philemon. Only twenty-five short verses, it is the only authentic Pauline letter addressed to an individual.

Paul's Situation

Paul was writing to Philemon from prison, most likely at Ephesus. He was obviously not in the worst mode of Roman imprisonment—alone in some forgotten dungeon and abandoned to hunger and rats. But neither was he in the best alternative—under simple house arrest. He was in between those extremes—chained to a soldier in the guardhouse, with his well-being depending on his jailer's capacity for human decency and susceptibility to normal bribery. Paul was helped and supported by his friends—otherwise he could not have dictated and sent a letter—but Ephesus was the capital of Roman Asia and he was in a proconsular jail, where he could have been condemned to death without any further warning.

Onesimus's Flight

Onesimus had fled to Paul from his owner Philemon. Roman law recognized two modes of such flight, and their distinction depended absolutely on the slave's intention.

One mode of slave-flight was *permanent*—fleeing with the intention of never returning but rather losing oneself in some big Roman city. For that, the penalties were as terrible as imperial terrorism could devise—branding or disfigurement of the body, condemnation to the mines, or very public execution by fire, arena, or cross. If that were Onesimus's intention, it would have been insane to approach the most dangerous place imaginable—a Roman jail—and the most dangerous person imaginable—a Roman prisoner. He would have endangered his own life and guaranteed Paul's execution.

The other mode of slave-flight was *temporary* rather than permanent and was deemed acceptable by Roman law. A slave under penalty of very severe punishment or even death could flee either to certain temples for *refuge* or to some friend of the owner for *intercession*. A temple or a friend might supply a cooling-off period for an irritated owner until it was safe for the slave to come home.

The classic example of temporary flight *ad amicum*—to the friend—is the story of an unnamed slave and his owner, Vedius Pollio, when he was host to the emperor Augustus. It is recorded by Seneca in his essay *On Anger* from the late 40s CE:

> One of the servants had broken a crystal cup. Vedius ordered him to be seized and executed in an unusual way—he was to be thrown to the giant lampreys which were kept in a pool (not for their owner's self-indulgence, as you might think, but to sate his savagery). The boy struggled free and fled to Caesar's feet, asking only for some other form of death, just not to be eaten. Shocked by the unprecedented cruelty, Caesar had him released, ordering all the crystal to be broken in front of him and the pool to be filled in. (3.40.2–4)

Notice that the slave's flight to the friend was a flight *upwards* from Pollio to Augustus. That was surely the situation with Onesimus. He was in some very serious trouble with his master Philemon and had fled to Paul for help and intercession.

There was, however, another complication. While they were together, Paul converted Onesimus to Christianity, so we now have a very clear problem between Philemon and Onesimus: could a Christian master have a Christian slave? It was not a question about *pagan* slavery in general, but a very precise application of that second negation ("no longer slave or free") from Galatians 3:28. Could the *Christian* master Philemon own the *Christian* slave Onesimus?

Before continuing, I would remind you about the distinction at the start of this chapter between the seven letters from the *radical* Paul, the first three from the *liberal* Paul, and the final three from the *conservative or reactionary* Paul.

The Solution from the Radical Paul

I ask you to read the full letter for yourself, because it is there that you can see most clearly two of the most fundamental aspects of Pauline theology.

The first aspect of Paul's theology represented in this letter is, as we have just seen, his insistence on equality within the Christian community. His reaction is this: You, Philemon, must free Onesimus, because a *Christian* master cannot have a *Christian* slave. You cannot be equal in Christ and unequal in Christ at the same time. Period.

The second aspect of Paul's theology emphasized in this letter is even more basic. Paul believed that, while faith *could* not exist without works, neither *should* works ever exist without faith. "Works," in fact, is precisely Paul's word for non-faith-based religious deeds. Apart from this second emphasis, the letter would have needed only six words: "Dear Philemon. Free Onesimus. Yours, Paul." But Paul did not want Philemon to free his slave because Paul commanded it—a liberation of Onesimus that came from external pressure rather than internal assent would have been *works without faith*.

The letter is longer than six words because Paul, dancing dangerously close to manipulation, *had to command Philemon to do it freely!* Freeing Onesimus had to be a work born of Philemon's faith, not a work born of Paul's command. On the one hand, Philemon had to free Onesimus *immediately* because Christians cannot be simultaneously equal and unequal to one another. On the other hand, Philemon had to free Onesimus *willingly*, "in order that your good deed might be voluntary and not something forced" (14). Not works operating without faith, but always faith operating through works. Here are some examples of Paul's persuasive (manipulative?) devices in this fascinating letter. It is only one chapter long, by the way, and quotations are usually cited by verse numbers alone.

First, the letter was not sent as a private note from Paul alone to Philemon alone. It was sent from both Paul and Timothy, "our brother," to "Philemon our dear friend and co-worker, to Apphia our sister, to Archippus our fellow soldier, and to the church in your house" (1–2), and it ends with: "Epaphras, my fellow prisoner in Christ Jesus, sends greetings to you, and so do Mark, Aristarchus, Demas, and Luke, my fellow workers" (23–24). In other words, dear Philemon, everyone is watching what you will do.

Second, Paul emphasizes his prisoner status four times. Twice he calls himself "a prisoner of Christ Jesus" (1, 9); twice he mentions his "imprisonment" (10, 13; actually the Greek is "in chains"); and he also refers to himself "as an old man" (9). Far from whining, however, Paul is simply making sure that Philemon cannot refuse him.

Third, note this startling sentence: "though I am bold enough in Christ to command you to do your duty, yet I would rather appeal to you on the basis of love" (8–9). Freeing Onesimus is a Christian obligation, but Philemon should do it from internal love, not external duty. Later Paul comes right out and says that, "confident of your obedience, I am writing to you, knowing that you will do even more than I say" (21).

Fourth, Paul calls Onesimus "my child" and "my own heart" (10, 12) and sends him back with the letter suggesting—delicately—that his presence with Paul in prison has been "of service to me in your place" (13). Otherwise put, where have *you* been, Philemon, when I needed you?

Fifth, read this one a few times. "Perhaps this is the reason he was separated from you for a while, so that you might have him back forever, no longer as a slave but more than a slave, a beloved brother—especially to me but how much more to you, both *in the flesh and in the Lord*" (15–16). Paul did not want Philemon to accept Onesimus as still his slave but rather as a brother in the Lord—and so he had to be a brother in the flesh as well. No inner and spiritual equality would suffice—equality had to be external and physical as well.

One footnote to that second aspect of this letter concerning Paul's belief about faith and works. It was from this same prison at Ephesus that Paul wrote his letter to the Philippians. He told them to "*work* out your own salvation with fear and trembling; for it is God who is at *work* in you, enabling you both to will and to *work* for his good pleasure" (2:12b–13). But if God does all the willing and working, why should we fear and tremble? Not because the radicality of God will punish us if we fail, but because the normalcy of civilization will punish us if we succeed.

The Solution from the Liberal Paul

The advice to Christian slaves and Christian masters is quite clear in both Colossians 3:22–4:1 and Ephesians 6:5–9. In both passages, slaves get first and most attention while masters get second and least attention—in each case, four verses are addressed to slaves and one is addressed to masters. Both passages begin with the same phrase: "Slaves, obey your earthly masters."

And in his letter to the Colossians, Paul ends by commanding masters to "treat your slaves justly and fairly," while he tells the Ephesians to "stop threatening them"—because, in both cases, slaves and masters alike "have the same Master in heaven." If, therefore, Paul had in fact written these two letters, we would expect him to tell the slave Onesimus to go back home and obey his master Philemon while giving Philemon a note telling him to forgive Onesimus. I call the writer of these two letters "the liberal Paul" because at least he demands mutuality and reciprocity of obligation between Christian slave (full obedience) and Christian master (fair treatment). And, maybe more significantly, he addresses both groups directly.

The Solution from the Conservative Paul

In Titus 2:9–10, pseudo-Paul speaks only about slaves—though, unlike Colossians and Ephesians, not directly ("*Tell* slaves ...")—and says nothing to their masters: "Tell slaves to be submissive to their masters and to give satisfaction in every respect; they are not to talk back, not to pilfer, but to show complete and perfect fidelity, so that in everything they may be an ornament to the doctrine of God our Savior." There is no mutuality or reciprocity of obligation in this one-sided admonition.

Finally, the historical Paul of the authentic letter to Philemon is not speaking about general slavery outside the Christian community. He is not speaking about pagan owners with pagan slaves. He is not talking about Christian owners with pagan slaves, or about pagan masters with Christian slaves. In that last case, he advises Christian slaves (in 1 Corinthians 7:21) that, if liberation is forthcoming, they should use their newfound freedom for Christ's advantage. Nevertheless, despite Paul's very specific focus on *Christian* owners and *Christian* slaves, his belief that all people should be Christian would inevitably have included the belief that all should be free and equal.

The Eucharist at Corinth

Villa and Shop

Imagine yourself standing before the south front of an elegant villa in Pompeii—not because Paul ever visited there, but because there are places he never went that are crucial for understanding where he did go. The villa takes up a full *insula,* or block, with small alleys to the east and west and a slightly wider street to the north. It has two large, open courtyards surrounded on all four sides by covered, cloister-like walks. There was once, on the floor of a room between these courtyards, a magnificent fresco of the victory of Alexander of Macedon over Darius III of Persia; its million-plus tiny tiles have now been relocated to a wall of the National Archaeological Museum in Naples. At around thirty-one thousand square feet, you are looking at the most magnificent villa buried and preserved under Vesuvian lava in 79 CE.

In front of you, along the villa's main-street frontage, are six doors. They are, from left to right, first shop, primary villa entrance, second shop, third shop, secondary villa entrance, and fourth shop. In other words, wider shop doors flank each of the villa's taller entrance doors. Furthermore, the first and second shops have a back entrance into the open-air atrium of the villa itself. That combination of shops and villas on main-street frontage was typical all over ancient Pompeii and Herculaneum, as is very evident from the color-coded maps available on-site. No matter how elegant the villa, the owner never wasted main-street frontage but used it for shops, which could be staffed by either slaves or freed persons. If rented out, the renters were considered clients. All of these persons would then be part of the extended family of a Roman dwelling, its various classes separated not so much spatially as hierarchically.

What you can still see clearly in Herculaneum or Pompeii was equally normal across the Roman Empire, including Corinth. There, the presence of some powerful patrons raised special problems for Paul's vision of Christian egalitarianism and threatened to pull that equality back into the normalcy of Roman hierarchical society. Like slavery and patriarchy, patronage was a specific mode of the normalcy of civilization's violence clothed in a Roman toga. But how did Paul ever get in contact with such elites at Corinth? I would argue that he did so through that osmotic relationship between shop and villa.

Inequality in the Christian Community

It was at Corinth that Paul first met Priscilla—Prisca for short—and her husband Aquila: "There he [Paul] found a Jew named Aquila, a native of Pontus, who had recently come from Italy with his wife Priscilla, because Claudius had ordered all Jews to leave Rome. Paul went to see them, and, because he was of the same trade, he stayed with them, and they worked together—by trade they were tentmakers" (Acts 18:2). Later, in Acts 18:18–19, the couple moved to Ephesus: "After staying there [at Corinth] for a considerable time, Paul said farewell to the believers and sailed for Syria, accompanied by Priscilla and Aquila.... When they reached Ephesus, he left them there." And so, when Paul wrote to Corinth from Ephesus, he added that "the churches of Asia send greetings. Aquila and Prisca, together with the church in their *house,* greet you warmly in the Lord" (1 Corinthians 16:19). Finally, the couple moved back to Rome, presumably after the death of Claudius and the accession of Nero in 54 CE. Paul mentions them there in Romans 16:3–5: "Greet Prisca and Aquila, who work with me in Christ Jesus, and who risked their necks for my life, to whom not only I give thanks, but also all the churches of the Gentiles. Greet also the church in their *house.*"

They were an artisan couple, and Priscilla may well have been the wealthier one. Paul stayed and worked with them, that is, under their patronage and in their house-church. Those earliest *house*-churches are probably more accurately described as *shop*-churches than as *apartment*-churches or *villa*-churches. As just mentioned, shops on prime street frontage were usually run by slaves, freed women and men, or renters, all of whom were clients of the villa owner.

Thus, Paul could easily have been—would necessarily have been—in contact with more elite members of society in Corinth than the artisans he had encountered at, say, Philippi and Thessalonica. That is why he spends all of 1 Corinthians 1–4 trying to put them in their place—not under him but under God.

First, he reminds them that "not many of you were wise by human standards, not many were powerful, not many were of noble birth" (1:26). But of course, "not many" means that *some* at least were of relatively more elite status than others.

Next, in a rhythm of soaring paradoxes, he repeats relentlessly that the wisdom and power of the world are foolishness and weakness for God and that the wisdom and power of God are foolishness and weakness for the world (1:27–29). Furthermore, he equates "the world" with "the flesh": "You are still of the *flesh*. For as long as there is jealousy and quarreling among you, are you not of the *flesh*?" (3:3).

Finally, Paul equates "the world" and "the flesh" with "this age": "Yet among the mature we do speak wisdom, though it is not a wisdom of *this age* or of the rulers of *this age,* who are doomed to perish. But we speak God's wisdom, secret and hidden, which God decreed before the ages for our glory. None of the rulers of *this age* understood this; for if they had, they would not have crucified the Lord of glory" (2:6–8). The "rulers of this age" are those transcendental forces (such as imperialism) that undergird human powers (such as emperors). By executing Jesus, says Paul, they have doomed themselves.

In this context, by the way, we should not confuse "the world" with the created earth, nor "the flesh" with the human body. "The world," "the flesh," and "this age" are Paul's words for what I term civilization's dominational and imperial normalcy. It is the age-old normalcy of civilization's *violent injustice* that is weakness and foolishness with God, and it is God's *nonviolent justice* that is weakness and foolishness for civilization's violent normalcy. In other words, 1 Corinthians 1-4 is the finest commentary ever written on that scene between Jesus and Pilate included at the end of this book's prologue. It may even be necessary to render that expression used by both Jesus and Paul as one word—"this-world"—to emphasize that it designates what we have done with God's creation and not that creation itself.

Inequality at the Christian Eucharist

What happened, then, at Corinth when a villa owner gave a feast for friends, clients, freed slaves, and maybe even some very special and privileged slaves? Such a feast might well have been conducted according to a strict hierarchy, not only with regard to place and seating but also when it came to food and wine. A feast could be and often was a ritual of social discrimination and overt humiliation. At the end of the first century CE, the Spanish poet Martial complained bitterly in his *Epigrams* about such calculated social humiliation at Roman feasts. "While the throng of invited guests looks on, you, Caecilianus, alone devour the mushrooms" (1, 20). Again: "Why do I dine without you although, Ponticus, I am dining with you ... let us eat the same fare" (3.60).

One of Martial's patrons was Pliny the Younger, who found such feast discrimination morally repugnant; here is how he describes two options in one of his *Letters:*

Some very elegant dishes were served up to [the host] and few more of the company; while those which were placed before the rest were cheap and paltry. He had apportioned in small flagons three different sorts of wine.... One was for himself and me; the next for his friends of a lower order;... and the third for his own freed-men and mine. One who sat next to me took notice of this, and asked me if I approved of it. "Not at all," I told him. "Pray, then," said he, "what is your method on such occasions?" "Mine," I returned, "is to give all my company the same fare; for when I make an invitation, it is to sup, not to be censoring. Every man whom I have placed on an equality with myself by admitting him to my table, I treat as an equal in all particulars." "Even freed-men?" he asked. "Even them," I said; "for on these occasions I regard them not as freed-men, but boon companions." "This must put you to great expense," says he. I assured him not at all; and on his asking how that could be, I said, "Why you must know my freed-men don't drink the same wine I do—but *I* drink what *they* do." (2.6)

Instead of patronal discrimination, Pliny preferred patronal slumming. He never even imagined, however, the third option: all guests receiving not only the same food and drink, but the best.

In writing to the Romans from Corinth, Paul adds that "Gaius, who is host to me and to the whole church, greets you" (16:23). Imagine, therefore, a patronal meal hosted by Gaius, or someone like him, as the matrix for what Paul writes in 1 Corinthians 11:17–34. Recall, of course, that those earliest Eucharistic meals were not our present morsel-and-sip ritual but a true meal, called the Lord's Supper because it was the style of share-meal created by Jesus as a meal-symbol of equality within a community that believed in God's ownership of food as the material basis of life itself. The radicality of God's egalitarian Christian meal opposed the normalcy of Rome's hierarchically patronal meal. So how did the more elite Corinthians create that contradiction in terms—a hierarchical Eucharist?

Imagine that Gaius, or someone like him, invites all the Corinthian assemblies to a common celebration of the Lord's Supper. His peers, who do not work manually, arrive well before those who do, and they bring or are served their own better-class food and drink. "When the time comes to eat," accuses Paul, "each of you goes ahead with your own supper, and one goes hungry and another becomes drunk" (11:21). "Do you," he asks, "show contempt for the church of God and humiliate those who have nothing?" (11:22).

Paul's solution is actually a compromise that may remind you too much of Pliny's aristocratic moral complacency. Paul could have insisted that each member bring the best food and drink they could, but instead, he makes two suggestions. On the one hand, the *haves* should eat their better food at home before attending the Eucharist: "What! Do you not have homes to eat and drink in?" (11:22), and again, "If you are hungry, eat at home, so that when you come together, it will not be for your condemnation" (11:34). On the other hand, the order of the Lord's Supper must be in this traditional—and Paul insists that it is traditional—sequence:

1. The invocation and *breaking* of the bread (11:23–24)
2. The supper itself (11:25a)
3. The invocation and *passing* of the cup (11:25b–26)

First, the twin frames in this list emphasize commonality, with the emphasis not just on the bread and wine but on the *breaking* of the bread and the *passing* of the wine cup. Next, the supper itself takes place totally in between them and not in any way before them. It must be, therefore, a common share-meal, like its frames. Furthermore, and unfortunately, that was maybe the best that Paul could get. The *haves* could still bring cheaper food for all to eat, but at least everyone had to eat together at the same place and the same time, from the same food and the same drink. Finally, the Eucharist or Lord's Supper, the central symbolism of Christianity's divine responsibility for a shared earth, was fractured badly at Corinth. The equality for which Christ died—bread and wine as separated body and blood—had become a source of tension at best and a symbol of inequality at worst. Paul knew how serious the situation was. His terminal warnings about illness and death, judgment and condemnation in 11:27–34 indicate very clearly that much more was at stake than common courtesy and public politeness.

PAUL AND GENDER

Recall what I said at the start of this chapter about the seven letters written by Paul and the other six ones written in his name. Recall also that I asked whether those non-Pauline letters were not just post-Pauline but anti-Pauline—at least with regard to equality within the Christian community. We have already seen how Colossians 3:22–4:1 and Ephesians 6:5–9 contradict Philemon on the subject of Christian owners and their Christian slaves. We now see a similar but even more complicated situation with regard to patriarchy. In all of this—be it slavery, patronage, or patriarchy—you will recognize the drag of Roman normalcy pulling hard against the vision of intra-Christian equality. Watch, then, how the radical Paul is once again changed before our eyes, first into the liberal Paul, and then into the conservative or, better, reactionary Paul.

The Radical Paul

The best place to see Paul's view on female-male equality within Christianity is in the list of names in Romans 16:1–15. He greets twenty-seven Christians, some of whom he knows personally, some only by name, in that huge metropolis that gathered in people from all over the eastern provinces. The first detail to get clear in your mind is who is female and who is male in that list. That done, you find the following differences with regard to gender.

First and above all, it is a woman who carries Paul's letter from Corinth's eastern port to the Christian groups at Rome. "I commend to you our sister Phoebe, a deacon of the church at Cenchreae, so that you may welcome her in the Lord as is fitting for the saints, and help her in whatever she may require from you, for she has been a benefactor (*prostatis*) of many and of myself as well" (16:1–2). A

Pauline letter carrier would also have had to circulate, read, and explain the letter among the Christian communities at Rome.

Second, two couples (presumably married) are singled out for extraordinary praise: "Greet Prisca and Aquila, who work with me in Christ Jesus, and who risked their necks for my life, to whom not only I give thanks, but also all the churches of the Gentiles" (16:3–4); and "Greet Andronicus and Junia, my relatives [fellow Jews] who were in prison with me; they are prominent among the apostles, and they were in Christ before I was" (16:7). Notice that Prisca (Priscilla) is mentioned first in that designation. For Paul, Priscilla and Aquila were probably the premier Christian-pagan (God-worshiper?) missionary couple, while Andronicus and Junia were probably the premier Christian-Jewish missionary couple.

Third, of the twenty-seven individual Christians on the list, ten are women (Phoebe, Priscilla, Mary, Junia, Tryphaena, Tryphosa, Persis, an unnamed mother, Julia, and an unnamed sister), and the other seventeen are men (Aquila, Epaenatus, Andronicus, Ampliatus, Urbanus, Stachys, Apelles, Herodion, Rufus, Asyncritus, Phlegon, Hermes, Patrobas, Hermas, Philologus, Nereus, and Olympas). Conversely, however, five women (Mary, Tryphaena, Tryphosa, Persis, and the unnamed mother) and six men (Epaenatus, Ampliatus, Urbanus, Stachys, Apelles, and Rufus) are singled out for special praise.

Fourth, Paul's word for dedicated apostolic activity is *kopiaō,* meaning "to work hard." He uses it of himself twice, in Galatians 4:11 and 1 Corinthians 15:10, but four times in Romans, and exclusively for women (Mary, Tryphaedna, Tryphosa, and Persis).

Finally, back to Junia in 16:7, a case that would be funny to ridiculous if it were not sad to tragic. For the first 1,200 years of Christianity, commentators had no trouble identifying her name as female and presuming that she was the wife of Andronicus, just as Prisca was Aquila's wife. Then, however, Junia was made male by the allegation that her name was short for Junianus. Unfortunately, there are over 250 known cases of a female Junia in antiquity and not a single one ever discovered for such an abbreviation of the male name Junianus. The problem, of course, was with Paul's supreme accolade for both members of that married couple and specifically for the female Junia. The only reason for suggesting that Junia is a masculine abbreviation was to avoid recognizing Junia as a major *female apostle*. But that problem was not Paul's. For him, women as well as men could be called by God to be apostles of Christ—equality was not only in the community but in the apostolate.

The Liberal Paul

The household codes or family values for married couples in Colossians 3:18–19 and Ephesians 5:22–33 represent a first step in sanitizing Pauline Christian equality back toward Roman patriarchal hierarchy. To be fair and accurate, they are not a complete capitulation to that normalcy; they are more like a Christian compromise with it, or even a definite improvement over it. That is why I call them liberal—less than the radical and original Paul would have envisioned, but not yet what the conservative and reactionary pseudo-Paul would assert.

A Roman *paterfamilias,* for example, would probably have been willing to accept the instructions for wives, but not those for husbands—even absent the Christian language. But of course, these instructions from the liberal Paul, directed specifically at Christian couples, are very much couched in Christian language.

Colossians 3:18–19	*Ephesians 5:22–33*
Wives, be subject to your husbands, as is fitting in the Lord.	*Wives,* be subject to your husbands as you are to the Lord. For the husband is the head of the wife just as Christ is the head of the church, the body of which he is the Savior. Just as the church is subject to Christ, so also wives ought to be, in everything, to their husbands.

Husbands, love your wives and never treat them harshly.	*Husbands,* love your wives, just as Christ loved the church and gave himself up for her, in order to make her holy by cleansing her with the washing of water by the word, so as to present the church to himself in splendor, without a spot or wrinkle or anything of the kind—yes, so that she may be holy and without blemish. In the same way, husbands should love their wives as they do their own bodies. He who loves his wife loves himself. For no one ever hates his own body, but he nourishes and tenderly cares for it, just as Christ does for the church, because we are members of his body. "For this reason a man will leave his father and mother and be joined to his wife, and the two will become one flesh." This is a great mystery, and I am applying it to Christ and the church. Each of you, however, should love his wife as himself, and a wife should respect her husband.

I have placed these texts in parallel columns to emphasize that wives and husbands get one verse each in Colossians but three and nine verses, respectively, in Ephesians. The latter text seems much more worried about husbands than about wives. And it also lays upon them a far heavier burden. For wives to obey their husbands just as the Church obeys Christ is surely easier than for husbands to sacrifice themselves for their wives just as Christ sacrificed himself for the Church. What, in fact, does that latter injunction mean? Maybe that, in a persecution, a father might have to die in order to save his family?

What is most striking about these instructions—even granted that they are less radical than Pauline equality—is their mutuality and reciprocity. We seem to have spent much more Christian time debating the details of wifely obedience than discussing the details of husbandly self-sacrifice, but in fact there are obligations on both sides. It is surely terribly and sadly ironic that Christian tradition demanded subjection from wives and then, rather than demanding self-sacrifice from husbands, transferred that obligation to wives as well.

The Conservative Paul

"Reactionary" is probably more accurate than "conservative" for this next pseudo-Pauline text. Timothy and Titus are imagined as left by Paul in charge of Ephesus and Crete, respectively. The subject of female leadership within the Christian assembly arises in the post-Pauline first letter to Timothy and also as an insertion in the Pauline first letter to the Corinthians.

1 Timothy 2:8–15

In this text, female leadership is absolutely forbidden by the pseudo-Pauline Paul. Women are also not allowed to teach or instruct men.

> I desire, then, that in every place the men should pray, lifting up holy hands without anger or argument; also that the women should dress themselves modestly and decently in suitable clothing, not with their hair braided, or with gold, pearls, or expensive clothes, but with good works, as is proper for women who profess reverence for God. Let a woman learn in silence with full submission. I permit no woman to teach or to have authority over a man; she is to keep silent. For Adam was formed first, then Eve; and Adam was not deceived, but the woman was deceived and became a transgressor. Yet she will be saved through childbearing, provided they continue in faith and love and holiness, with modesty.

Clearly, of course, pseudo-Paul would not bother to forbid what never happened. That prohibition therefore tells us that women were praying and teaching within the community's catechetical practice and liturgical worship. But this text dismisses women from those functions and relegates them to home, silence, and childbearing.

1 Corinthians 14:33b–36

The problem here is not with an inauthentic Pauline letter, like 1 and 2 Timothy or Titus, but with an insertion from that later tradition inside an original, earlier authentic letter of Paul. In the New Revised Standard Version of the Bible, this insertion appears as a bracketed paragraph:

> (As in all the churches of the saints, women should be silent in the churches. For they are not permitted to speak, but should be subordinate, as the law also says. If there is anything they desire to know, let them ask their husbands at home. For it is shameful for a woman to speak in church. Or did the word of God originate with you? Or are you the only ones it has reached?)

These details emphasize manuscript problems in the earliest textual transmission. First, 1 Corinthians 14:34–35 is not at that location but at the end of the chapter in some manuscripts. Second, these verses are given as a separate paragraph in all Greek manuscripts. Third, this section was deemed problematic very early, and this is the most important argument for its later insertion into Paul's original text. It was probably inserted by a copyist who approved strongly of 1 Timothy 2:8–15 and included it first in the margin of 1 Corinthians 14, whence it was later copied, by another scribe into the text itself.

On a Frescoed Wall at Ephesus

Ancient Ephesus was built along a narrow east-west valley between and up the slopes of two hills to the north and south. High

on the southern hill—Bülbül Dağ in Turkish, or Mount Nighten-
gale in English—a long narrow cave was discovered in 1906 and
first excavated in 1955. In the 1998 season, the Austrian Archaeological Institute found that there were three layers of paintings
under the whitewash on this so-called Cave or Grotto of St. Paul.
My present focus is on a central-layer fresco that dates to the fifth
century and is located on the west wall just inside the shaft-cave's
entrance.

In the summers of 2002 and 2003, when Jonathan Reed and I
were writing our 2004 book *In Search of Paul,* we both tried, sepa-
rately but unsuccessfully, to gain permission to enter the cave,
which, with excavation, restoration, and preservation still in process, had to be kept securely locked. We had first learned of the
fresco in an article on "St. Paul at Ephesus" by the archaeological
reporter Özgen Acar from Ankara in *Archaeology* magazine's
"Online News" for January 17, 2002. Acar's photograph of a two-
figure fresco was the same photograph sent us by the Austrian archaeologists to use in our book.

In late September 2004, I finally got official permission to enter
the cave. I saw immediately that the fresco was actually a three-
figure image of, from the viewer's left to right, Thekla, Paul, and
Theoklia—the mother of Thekla—with all three individuals
clearly named. You can see the full three-figure scene, by the way,
in my article "A Woman Equal to Paul: Who Is She?" in the
summer 2005 issue of the magazine *Bible Review.*

What remains of primary interest to me is how Paul and
Theoklia represent *in image* the same movement *in text* from Paul's
radical gender equality in Galatians and Romans to anti-Paul's reactionary gender inequality in Timothy and Titus. As you stand in
front of the full three-figure image, you see a seated man named
"Paul" in the center, and to your right you see a standing woman
named "Theoklia." Both have their right hands raised and their
fingers separated as two and three digits in the official Christian
teaching gesture for the two natures in Christ and the three persons in the Trinity.

Initially, therefore, Paul and Theoklia were both authoritative apostolic preachers, with her raised right arm and divided fingers a mirror image of his. But here is the point. While the male Paul's eyes and hand are untouched, the female Theoklia's eyes have been rubbed out and her hand burned off. If the eyes of both figures had been obliterated, we might have presumed standard minimal iconoclasm—destroy the eyes, the image loses its power, and further eradication is not necessary. But it is Theoklia's eyes, not Paul's, that have been destroyed, and it is her authoritative teaching hand that has been semi-destroyed. That two-stage process by which a female teaching authoritatively was transformed into a female silenced and defaced is a perfect symbol for what happened to women apostles as the radical Paul was deformed into the reactionary Paul.

THE UNVEILED WOMEN AT CORINTH

We lingered that evening before the fresco of Thekla-Paul-Theoklia high above the ruins of an Ephesus now almost totally emptied of the morning's thronging visitors. I recognized immediately that the wall images we had seen in *Archaeology*'s "Online News" in 2002 and received from the Austrians in 2003 were quite inadequate. The fresco was a three-figure not a two-figure scene. It was, in fact, the opening scene from *The Acts of Thekla,* included at the start of the late-second-century *Acts of Paul,* one of the five major Acts not included with Luke's canonical Acts of the Apostles in the New Testament—the four others are the *Acts of Peter, of Thomas, of Andrew,* and *of John.* But what struck me for the first time as we stood within the Ephesian shaft-cave was that it might shed light on the interpretation of Paul's tortured discussion of those unveiled women at Corinth in 1 Corinthians 11:2–16.

The clue to that new interpretation is the fact that Thekla, as a nubile but virginal young woman, has her hair unveiled but Theoklia, as mother and matron, has her hair veiled. In that society, and granted menstrual status, unveiled was to veiled as virginal-marriageable was to matronal-married. That is confirmed from a contemporary Jewish novel, *Joseph and Aseneth,* whose female protagonist is a nubile young virgin:

> [Aseneth] took an unused and elegant linen veil and covered her head. And she went to the angel into her outer room and stood before him. And the angel said to her, "Remove the veil from your head, and why did you do this? For you are a chaste virgin today, and your head is like that of a young man." And Aseneth removed the veil from her head. (14:1–15:1, 2)

Later, when she is to be married, "with a veil she covered her head like a bride, and she took a scepter in her hand" (18:6). But how do these observations about Thekla in fresco and Aseneth in story help the interpretation of the Corinthian problem and its Pauline solution in 11:2–16?

There is absolutely no consensus in scholarship about either the problem involved at Corinth or the solution offered by Paul, and we had almost given up on it in writing *In Search of Paul.* In Paul's letter, as in any correspondence, if you do not know the problem, it is rather difficult to understand the solution. I begin, therefore, with a reconstruction of the problem of veils at Corinth, but working closely and explicitly with the general context of 1 Corinthians.

The Context from 1 Corinthians 7

First, I think that Paul was an ascetic celibate, presumably a virginal one, and I find it likely that his ascetic commitment derived from the pre-Christian Jewish tradition that stretched from Egyptian Mareotis through Judean Qumran to Syrian Damascus (see also chapter 1), since he never cites Jesus as source or example for that commitment. Be that as it may, he was such an ascetic by the time he wrote to the Corinthians.

Then, in 1 Corinthians 7, Paul *advises* but—unlike the pseudo-Paul of *The Acts of Thekla*—never *demands* that all Christians practice (virginal) celibate asceticism. And of course, his advice applies to males and females alike, and to just interested, already betrothed, or actually married couples.

Next, a problem arose at Corinth, and it is the first one discussed by Paul in 1 Corinthians 7. Granted the Christian equality of wife and husband, what if one wants to practice celibate asceticism and the other does not? How exactly does equality work in such a case? What about the sexual mutuality of the marriage contract? Here is what Paul writes in answer to that first problem in 7:1–7:

> Now concerning the matters about which you wrote: "It is well for a man not to touch a woman." But because of cases of sexual immorality, each man should have his own wife and each woman her own husband. The husband should give to his wife her conjugal rights, and likewise the wife to her husband. For the wife does not have authority over her own body, but the husband does; likewise the husband does not have authority over his own body, but the wife does. Do not deprive one another except perhaps by agreement for a set time, to devote yourselves to prayer, and then come together again, so that Satan may not tempt you because of your lack of self-control. This I say by way of concession, not of command. I wish that all were as I myself am. But each has a particular gift from God, one having one kind and another a different kind.

He gives that advice because "the appointed time has grown short; from now on, let even those who have wives be as though they had none ... and those who deal with the world as though they had no dealings with it. For the present form of this world is passing away" (7:29–31). That is not, by the way, the most profound reason for Christian ascetic celibacy, and one wonders if it would have impressed Priscilla and Aquila or Andronicus and Junia.

In any case, in 7:1–7, it was the wife who was asserting her right to celibacy and the husband who was refusing it. That problem was not yet causing external social repercussions but was already causing internal moral problems. The rejected husbands were turning to slaves and/or prostitutes. With gender equality and marriage mutuality, that is a real and serious problem, and the only alternative to Paul's advice would have been those divorces he was trying to prevent.

The Problem in 1 Corinthians 11

I would emphasize here that the radical-historical Paul, as distinct from the later, conservative-reactionary pseudo-Paul, took it for granted that women and men ministered equally in the liturgy of the Corinthian community: "Any man who prays or prophesies with something on his head disgraces his head, but any woman who prays or prophesies with her head unveiled disgraces her head" (11:4–5). The problem was not about female capacities and power, but about female heads and veils. What was happening at Corinth, in my proposed interpretation, was that *those wives who had rejected marital intercourse were publicly proclaiming their new "virginal" status by abandoning the veils of their matronly status.* That was causing conflict in the community from noncelibate husbands and possibly other noncelibate wives as well. I take that interpretation by putting together 1 Corinthians 7 and 1 Corinthians 11, as well as the stories about Thekla and Aseneth.

Paul uses several arguments against the practice of unveiled hair as a symbol of female marital celibacy. With all due respect, each is dumber than the next, and Paul himself seems to recognize their vacuity.

First, he argues from the order of *creation* that "man was not made from woman, but woman from man" (11:8), but then qualifies that statement by adding, "Just as woman came from man, so man comes through woman; but all things come from God" (11:12).

Second, he argues from *nature,* but again, he searches for an equality of obligation: "a woman ... should wear a veil," but "a man ought not to have his head veiled" (11:6–7).

Third, after giving these seemingly unanswerable arguments from divine creation and human nature, Paul concludes with this one: "If anyone is disposed to be contentious—we have no such custom, nor do the churches of God" (11:16). But this final argument destroys the preceding ones. If nonveiled matrons are against *divine creation* and *human nature,* it is profoundly weak to climax the argument by saying they are against *church custom.*

In summary, therefore, there is a serious problem within the Christian equality of husband and wife if one demands and the other rejects celibacy. In those cases, there are two basic alternatives: either 1 Corinthians 7:1–7 or divorce/annulment. Later on, the Christian church opted often for the second alternative.

PAUL AND RESURRECTION

Three historical questions guide this section. What did pre-Christian Jews mean by the general bodily resurrection? What did Christian Jews mean by Jesus's bodily resurrection? And how did any Jew ever come up with so anti-intuitive a concept as bodily resurrection? In what follows, the term "resurrection" always means "bodily resurrection."

Why Bodily Resurrection?

Until the very end of the Old Testament, there was no belief in an afterlife among those who created the majesty of the Law, the challenge of the prophets, the splendor of the Psalms, and the wisdom of the sages. It was certainly not that the idea of immortality or life after death had never occurred to the Israelites or ancient Jews. That would have been impossible for a people living next door to Egypt. But they never discussed any types or possibilities of afterlife, so we must infer (and it can only be an inference) that they considered an afterlife just one more pagan usurpation of rights and privileges that belonged exclusively to God. It was, in other words, an act of faith *not* to believe in life after death.

One could, of course, "live on" in one's extended family and in one's good reputation, and since the people of God lived on, one was always part of that sacred community. But after death, all individuals, good and bad alike, went down to Sheol, which was, quite simply, the Grave writ large, the End with emphasis. It was neither hell nor heaven; it was simply never-no-more.

Recall, for example, the various terms used in parallel with the word "Sheol" in the Old Testament. In Psalm 16:10, it is "Sheol/Pit": "For you do not give me up to Sheol, or let your faithful one see the Pit." In 2 Samuel 22:6, it is "Sheol/Death": "The cords of Sheol entangled me, the snares of Death confronted me." In Job 17:16, it is "Sheol/Dust": "Will it go down to the bars of Sheol? Shall we descend together into the Dust?" These parallels emphasize that Sheol is simply the Grave itself. What happened, then, to change that insistence that there is no afterlife, that, as Psalm 6:5 says to God, "in death there is no remembrance of you; in Sheol who can give you praise?" What happened and when?

In the 160s BCE, Antiochus IV Epiphanes launched a program to integrate Jerusalem and the Jewish homeland politically and economically into his Greco-Syrian Empire. Finding that opposition to his plans by some Jews was founded on and fueled by their faith, he turned to religious persecution and decreed that those who refused to deny God and negate Torah by eating pork would die under torture, while those who did so would be spared. Even though military resistance by the Maccabees had defeated Antiochus and led to the founding of the Jewish dynasty of the Hasmoneas, the question of those martyrs still haunted the religious faith of many Jews.

Where, some Jewish writers asked, was God's justice when martyrs were being brutalized, tortured, and murdered? It was not possible to invoke the Deuteronomic answer (see chapter 2) and claim that death was a divine punishment and life a divine reward. How could anyone say that a martyr was being punished by God with death and an apostate was being rewarded by God with life? There would have to be, some Jewish writers answered, a day of global reckoning, a tribunal of cosmic justice, a general *bodily* resurrection in which those who had suffered in the flesh could be openly, publicly, officially vindicated by the just God for whom they had died. In other words, the general bodily resurrection was not about the survival of the individual but about the justice of God. The chant was this: God will overcome someday. And soon!

Recall (also from chapter 2) the Jewish expectation of the Great Divine Cleanup of the world. Those who thought about the Maccabean martyrs proposed bodily resurrection as the first act of that long-awaited transformation of the earth here below. How could one accept God's justice for the future unless it was accompanied by God's justice for the past? The Great Divine Cleanup would have to start with that great backlog of injustice. And martyrdom happened to bodies, not just to souls. Therefore, there would have to be a *bodily* resurrection as the first order of divine business at the eschatological transfiguration of the earth. Here is the classic example of that claim.

In 2 Maccabees—a book in the Roman Catholic but not the Protestant Old Testament—as the martyrs are dying, they insist that their tortured bodies will be returned to them by God's future justice:

> And when he was at his last breath, he said, "You accursed wretch, you dismiss us from this present life, but the King of the universe will raise us up to an everlasting renewal of life, because we have died for his laws."... [The third victim] quickly put out his tongue and courageously stretched forth his hands, and said nobly, "I got these from Heaven, and because of his laws I disdain them, and from him I hope to get them back again." (7:9–11)

Furthermore, "a certain Razis, one of the elders of Jerusalem" (14:37), manages to outdo even the Roman Cato's noble and suicidal death by falling on his sword: "With his blood now completely drained from him, he tore out his entrails, took them in both hands and hurled them at the crowd, calling upon the Lord of life and spirit to give them back to him again" (14:46). Biologically crude, but theologically clear.

For popular first-century Pharisaic Judaism, therefore, a this-world-now of divine justice and righteousness demanded at its inception a general bodily resurrection in which the just, especially the martyrs, would be vindicated and the unjust, especially the persecutors, would be punished. Cosmic transformation, yes, but bodily resurrection also—and at the very beginning of the Great Divine Cleanup of God's world. It was a matter of divine justice.

If, before Jesus and Paul were born, a liberal Pharisee argued with a conservative Sadducee about "the resurrection," the debate was about whether there would be a general bodily resurrection as the first act of God's transformation of this world from a place of injustice and violence to one of justice and peace. For how could God establish global justice for the future and ignore global injustice in the past? What about the backlog of all those who had lived for justice or died from injustice? What about—they even had a special title—"them that sleep"?

The Bodily Resurrection Has Begun

Those who proclaimed Jesus's resurrection were not simply proclaiming his *exaltation* to the right hand of God. That would have been a stunning enough climax to Jesus's destiny as Messiah, Son of God, and Lord, based, for example, on Psalm 110. Going much further than that, however, *they proclaimed that the general bodily resurrection had already begun with Jesus's bodily resurrection,* and that of course was why "resurrection" was the only proper and adequate word for what had happened to Jesus. Not assumption, not exaltation, but precisely resurrection. That meant that Jesus's resurrection was not just an individual privilege but a communal process—and a communal process for past, present, and future, with Jesus's resurrection as the heart of that process. Similarly, the general bodily resurrection was not a future and instantaneous flash of divine time, but an event with a past beginning, a present continuation, and a future consummation in human time. Of course, they thought that future conclusion was still rather imminent. Note, however, that it was an imminent end and not an imminent start that they were now expecting.

Furthermore, and therefore, the present was an in-between period in which Christian believers were called to a resurrected life with, in, and through the resurrected Jesus. It was not as if there is a start (the Christ resurrection), a yawning gap, and then an end (the general resurrection)—like two bookends but with no books in between. We Christians *are* the books in between. The challenge for Christian believers was and is to live lives of bodily resurrection in that in-between period—which at first, by the way, was thought to be but a very short period of time.

For Paul, such lives could only be lived *in the Body of Christ* or *in the Spirit of Christ,* expressions we should take as organically and corporately as possible. In Galatians 6:15, Paul claims that "a new creation is everything." In 2 Corinthians 5:17, he claims that, "if anyone is in Christ, there is a new creation: everything old has passed away; see, everything has become new!" In 2 Corinthians 3:17–18, he claims that "the Lord is the Spirit, and where the Spirit of the Lord is, there is freedom. And all of us, with unveiled faces, seeing the glory of the Lord as though reflected in a mirror, are being transformed into the same image from one degree of glory to another; for this comes from the Lord, the Spirit." To understand Paul's theology, we must never take these sentences as rhetorical hyperbole but as precise description.

THE CHALLENGE OF "ALREADY"

Recall from chapter 3 that the terms "Kingdom of God" and "Son of Man" represent different theological expressions for the same reality. They are divergent ways of asserting that the Great Divine Cleanup is no longer imminent but has already begun here below upon this earth with Jesus and that in Christ God is calling all to the miracle of a collaborative eschaton. Here, in conclusion, are the three ways seen in chapters 3 and 4, along with a final one:

For the historical Jesus, the Kingdom of God is *already* here.
For the Pauline tradition, the general resurrection is *already* begun.
For the Synoptic Gospels, the Son of Man is *already* present.
For John's gospel, the Logos of God is *already* incarnate.

The *Logos,* or Word, means God's inaugural vision for the world at the dawn of creation. It is not as if God came up with a new idea or a new program at the time of Christ. The divine vision of freedom and justice, of nonviolence and peace, and of an earth in which all have a fair and equitable share was there from creation itself. Recall the discussion of the Sabbath from Genesis 1 in chapter 2: it was not a vision invented for or by Jesus; it was simply incarnated through and in him. It was as if the mighty stream of divine nonviolent radicality had been pushing steadily against the logjam of civilization's violent normalcy until it finally broke through. "And the Logos became flesh," according to John 1:14, "and lived among us." Already.

Paul would have agreed with that vision of a mystery hidden in the mind of God from all eternity. He put it this way in Romans 8:19–23:

For the *creation* waits with eager longing for the revealing of the children of God; for the *creation* was subjected to futility, not of its own will but by the will of the one who subjected it; in hope that the *creation* itself will be set free from its bondage to decay and will obtain the freedom of the glory of the children of God. We know that the whole *creation* has been groaning in labor pains until now; and not only the *creation,* but we ourselves, who have the first fruits of the Spirit, groan inwardly while we wait for adoption, the redemption of our bodies.

Paul repeats "creation" five times in as many verses, and you will notice how the cosmic and the personal, the global and the individual, intertwine in this magnificent peroration. Paul's vision is never just about Christianity but always about creation. It is always about this: to whom does the earth belong?

JUSTICE AS LOVE

I have been speaking in the preceding chapters about the radicality of divine distributive (not retributive) *justice,* and you may have objected to yourself that God is not *justice* but *love.* You could cite 1 John 4:8 ("Whoever does not love does not know God, for God is love") or 1 John 4:16 ("God is love, and those who abide in love abide in God, and God abides in them"). You could quote, especially in this chapter on Paul, what he himself announced in 1 Corinthians 13:1–3:

> If I speak in the tongues of mortals and of angels, but do not have *love,* I am a noisy gong or a clanging cymbal. And if I have prophetic powers, and understand all mysteries and all knowledge, and if I have all faith, so as to remove mountains, but do not have *love,* I am nothing. If I give away all my possessions, and if I hand over my body so that I may boast, but do not have *love,* I gain nothing.

Or as Paul says famously at the end of that section, in 13:13, "And now faith, hope, and love abide, these three; and the greatest of these is *love.*" How, then, does the biblical tradition in general, and the Pauline tradition in particular, hold together justice and love?

My proposal is that justice and love are a dialectic—like two sides of a coin that can be distinguished but not separated. We think of ourselves as composed of body *and* soul, or flesh *and* spirit. When they are separated, we have a physical corpse. Similarly with distributive justice and communal love. Justice is the body of love, love the soul of justice. Justice is the flesh of love, love is the spirit of justice. When they are separated, we have a moral corpse. Justice without love is brutality. Love without justice is banality.

APOCALYPSE AND THE PORNOGRAPHY OF VIOLENCE

We had fed the heart on fantasies,
The heart's grown brutal from the fare.
—WILLIAM BUTLER YEATS,
"THE STARE'S NEST BY MY
WINDOW" (1922)

On the thirtieth of January in 1948, we got a fleeting hint of what was to come. Maybe it is only now that we recognize it clearly for what it was—an early warning about the distant future. On the evening of that Friday, faith-based violence met faith-based nonviolence as Ram Nathuram Godse waited for Mohandas Karamchand Gandhi among the gardens of Birla House in New Delhi.

The assassin's hands were joined in conventional greeting, but hidden between them was a small pistol whose three bullets ended the life of the Great Soul of India. "Gandhi crumpled instantly, putting his hand to his forehead in the Hindu gesture of forgiveness to his assassin," James Michaels reported immediately over the United Press International wire from the Indian capital.

Godse then turned the gun on himself, but failing at suicide, he was later tried and hung by the Indian government. It was an act that Gandhi would have considered a greater crime than his own murder. Gandhi, after a life of nonviolent resistance to the British

Empire, was killed, not by a British imperialist but by a Hindi fundamentalist, by a violent religious extremist who planned his own suicide rather than his own escape.

THE ULTIMATE HYMN TO A SAVAGE GOD

Gandhi's assassination was not just a faith-based act against a faith-based figure. It was, I repeat, faith-based violence against faith-based nonviolence. Furthermore, it was not yet faith-based terrorism: Godse did not hurl a bomb into a random crowd of Hindus or Muslims. Finally, it was not yet directly but only indirectly suicidal. Godse did not use a grenade intended to kill Gandhi and himself at the same time, but a gun that he fired successfully at Gandhi and then unsuccessfully at himself. Still and all, it was a small cloud that heralded a coming storm when all of those aspects would be developed into *suicidal religious terrorism* as the ultimate hymn to a savage God.

I have relied on Mark Juergensmeyer's 2000 book, *Terror in the Mind of God: The Global Rise of Religious Violence,* for this chapter's general background on religious violence. In 1980 the U.S. State Department recorded "scarcely a single" faith-based example among those on its list of terrorist groups, but by 1998 it "listed thirty of the world's most dangerous groups" and "over half were religious" (p. 6). Of course, not all violent extremism is religious, not all religious violence is terrorist, and not all religious terrorism is suicidal. Like Juergensmeyer, I am considering religious violence here in its ideological theory rather than its lethal practice, particularly within American Christianity's Bible-based faith in Rapture, Tribulation, and Armageddon.

The database for Juergensmeyer's analysis includes five major religions. Beginning with Christianity, he considers the Army of God's anti-abortion and Christian Identity's antigovernment violence in this country. Judaism is next: he discusses the assassination of Yitzhak Rabin in Tel Aviv and the massacre of Muslims by Baruch Goldstein in Hebron. On Islam, the book emphasizes what we call suicide bombings but what "one of the founders of the Hamas movement, Dr. Abdul Aziz Rantisi," calls by the Arabic word *istishhadi,* which he translates as "self-chosen martyrdom" (p. 72). Rantisi himself was killed by the Israeli military on April 19, 2004. For Sikhism, Juergensmeyer describes the murders of the Indian prime minister Indira Gandhi in 1984, by an assassin who was immediately killed, and the Punjabi chief minister Beant Singh Sikh in 1995, by an assassin who acted as a suicide bomber. Finally, Buddhism is represented by the Japanese group Aum Shinrikyo, which released sarin gas in the Tokyo subway system in 1995. Clearly, then, any of the world's major religions can inspire actions along the whole range from violent extremism to suicidal terrorism, and no religion has an absolute monopoly on such activities.

Two opposite reactions to this inventory are possible. One is to reject religion as a lethal addiction. Logically, however, such a rejection would also require that we reject the nuclear family, the nation-state, and in fact just about any group we can imagine. The other reaction is my present concern, and it is to claim that all of Juergensmeyer's case studies are not faith-based or grounded in religion but in fact are perversions of religion; they are anti-religion, in this claim, or nonreligion. From this reaction it follows that truly religious people do not need to search their own communities, traditions, scriptures, and consciences in the light of these violent events.

In response to the second reaction, I look at just one example that shows that *any* given religion can generate horrible violence and that it is up to each religion's adherents to preempt extremism in theory and proscribe fanaticism in practice—unless, of course, they agree with it.

In an article for the January 17, 2002, issue of the *New York Review of Books,* Hassan Mneimneh and Kanan Makiya reported that

three handwritten copies of a five-page Arabic document were found by the FBI after the September 11 attack.... From everything in it, the author seems to have been an organizer of the attacks.... One of its underlying assumptions is that all its intended readers were going to die. It seems clearly intended for the eyes of the hijackers and no one else, and reads as if it were written to stiffen their resolve. One would expect each person to have studied his copy very carefully beforehand, reading it over many times before the mission.

Presumably all the hijackers had a copy of this text that was intended to prepare them for their mission. While there were some suggestions for practical preparation—"inspect your weapon before you leave"—most of the instructions were for spiritual preparation. In fact, unless you recognized that the Arabic *M* is used for *matar* (airport) and *T* for *ta'irah* (plane), you might think this was just general religious advice, at least for the most part. The document is deeply and repeatedly grounded in Islam's earliest history and calls on the hijackers to "remember the battle of the Prophet ... against the infidels, as he went on building the Islamic state," because, "as the Prophet said: 'A raid ... on the path of God is better than this World and what is in it.'" After that introduction, the text has three sections.

On the eve: On the last night a ceremony of preparation purifies body and soul as a living unity. After a "'mutual pledge to die' ... a ritual washing should take place;... excess hair should be shaved from the body, and perfume applied to it. The night is to be spent in prayer, going over the details of the plan, reciting selected chapters of the Koran." The hijackers are to "forget and force yourself to forget that thing which is called World."

To the airport: On the final morning, they are repeatedly to remind themselves of God. They are to "smile and feel secure, God is with the believers, and the angels are guarding you without you feeling them." They are not to fear their enemies, because "all their [the enemy's] equipment, and all their gates, and all their technology do not do benefit or harm, except with the permission of God." Do not fear them, but "fear Me, if you are Believers."

On the plane: They are to continue silent and repeated invocations of God until "the hour of the encounter between the two camps." They are not in a plane of the twenty-first century but in the desert of the seventh century: "Clench your teeth, as did [your] predecessors, God rest their souls, before engaging in battle." Then comes the most terribly religious and religiously terrible injunction in the entire document: "If God grants [*manna*] any one of you a slaughter [*dhabaha*], you should perform it as an offering on behalf of your father and mother, for they are owed by you." *Manna* is a gift from God, like the manna from heaven during the Exodus, and *dhabaha* is how one slits an animal's throat for sacrifice.

When I first read the entire document—now also available in Bruce Lincoln's 2003 book *Holy Terrors: Thinking About Religion After September 11*—I was plunged back over fifty years to my year as a novice monk in 1950–51. There was nothing, of course, about violence or slaughter in that training. But the instructions for staying in close contact with God and the methods for remaining in the presence of God were identical in Islamic document and Christian novitiate. There were also special injunctions for traveling outside the monastery—as I did when I sailed on the *Queen Mary* from Southampton to New York after my novitiate was complete in October 1951—and even an *Itinerarium* to pray in that process.

My point in making this comparison is very specific. It is not—positively not—to confuse spiritual preparations for Christian monasticism and Islamic terrorism. My point is that those three copies represent a deeply religious document; it is not possible to claim it is anti-religious or nonreligious. Neither can anyone claim that only Islam could produce such a document or such an attack. The interviews Juergensmeyer conducted for his chilling book indicate that *any* religion could have produced it. I would claim that adherents of *any* given religion are called in conscience to state where they stand on faith-based violence before it happens, when it happens, and after it happens and that they should do so both within their own religion and within every other one as well.

There is, of course, a great difference between ideologically violent rhetoric and physically violent action within faith-based religious extremism. It is surely better to speak ideological rhetoric than to wreak terrorist destruction. The former action, however, often prepares for the latter, and in fact the latter cannot occur without the former. That is why I focus in this chapter on ideological rhetoric rather than on terrorist action, and on American Christianity in particular rather than on religion in general.

This chapter is on violence that is *religious* not just secular, *terrorist* not just military, and *suicidal* not just homicidal. I believe that *suicidal religious terrorism* is the most dangerous force in the world today because it alone could blissfully move from homicide through genocide to *cosmicide*—the destruction of the world—in the serene confidence that a better world awaits elsewhere. Only that form of violent religious extremism would risk cosmicide as a religious duty, as a compelling vocation, and as a divine mandate. No doubt, cosmicide could be considered, intended, or planned without being faith-based, but that possibility is not my present concern. I look here at Christian fundamentalism in America and its ideological lust for imminent human slaughter and cosmic catastrophe. I look, in other words, at its apocalyptic vision of a violent God and, above all else, at the biblical roots it claims for that vision of a terrible future consummation.

Here is one way to ask this chapter's main question: do you think that the scenario of the Jenkins-LaHaye's Left Behind series could be derived as easily from the Jesus of the Sermon on the Mount as from the Jesus in the Revelation of John? Here is another way to put it: do you think, in the terms introduced in chapter 2, that a violent apocalypse would be the climax of God's radicality or the climax of civilization's normalcy? Here is a final way to think about it: do you think that American Christian fundamentalism is a dangerous and fanatical delusion and, if yes, is that fanatical delusion inside or outside the Bible itself?

A TIME FOR DISBELIEF, NOT UNCONCERN

In late October 1999, I discussed "A Future for Christian Faith?" at the Westar Institute's Jesus Seminar in Santa Rosa, California, and it was published the following year in a book entitled, like the conference itself, *The Once and Future Jesus*. My main proposal was that, since the Age of Enlightenment has been replaced by the Age of Entertainment, the future clash would not be between science and religion but between both of them and fantasy. While noting that "the gains and losses of the Enlightenment Era are already clear and set, although, of course, there will still be legal disputes well into the next century," I explained that "what I am trying to imagine is what Christianity must do clearly and honestly to distinguish itself from fantasy. If it does not do that, it will certainly survive but as an important and even lucrative sub-division of world-wide entertainment and global illusion" (p. 114).

In 1999 I never imagined, even as prophetic nightmare, the speed with which faith-based thinking would morph into fantasy-based dreaming to infiltrate medicine, education, domestic program, foreign policy, and even news reporting (which would become so separated from reality that a network's boast of "We report, you decide," could be more accurately rephrased as "We distort, you deride"). "Faith is," according to Hebrews 11:1, "the assurance of things hoped for, the conviction of things not seen," but you should not go to war on the faith-based existence of mass destruction weapons or the faith-based conviction of terrorist collusion documents. Those are, for some people, things still hoped for, still not seen.

In this Age of Entertainment, then, I find it necessary to make a crucial distinction in my mind between two possible responses to certain data—as if my computer had two separate trash bins, one marked "Bin of Unconcern" and the other "Bin of Disbelief." Huge swaths of contemporary culture go into the former—everything from magical powers to conspiracy theories to alien abductions. But my Bin of Disbelief is too precious and valuable, too desperately needed, to waste on matters like those. I need the Bin of Disbelief to say relentlessly what I oppose and what I reject: discrimination and oppression, homophobia and patriarchy, injustice and violence, force and empire.

Into which of those bins do I put faith claims of future rapture, global tribulation, apocalyptic vision, divine violence, and the entire Left Behind scenario? Should I consider them simply as religious escapism, transcendental snake oil, or the latest view from Cloud-Cuckoo-Land so that I can deposit them speedily into the Bin of Unconcern? Is seriously opposing them akin to machine-gunning butterflies? My answer is emphatically negative. For all of that program I need Disbelief. I need, in fact, faith-based, Bible-based, and Christianity-based rejection, disbelief, and anti-belief. Here's why.

The Late Great Prophet Lindsey

In the late 1940s, with the invention of the atomic bomb and the creation of the Israeli state, fantasy-based Christian religion merged steadily and relentlessly with faith-based American foreign policy. By now, our homegrown fundamentalist violence—even if it is only in imagination—has become for me a matter for positive disbelief and not just negative unconcern.

In his magisterial 1992 book, *When Time Shall Be No More,* Paul Boyer discusses, as his subtitle promises, *Prophecy Belief in Modern American Culture.* He describes how, in the multimillion-copy bestseller *The Late Great Planet Earth,* "for page after mind-numbing page, [Hal] Lindsey systematically went through the apocalyptic scriptures, mechanically transcribing every phrase and image into the vocabulary of Pentagon strategists" (p. 127).

Boyer then gives the following soul-searing set of similar beliefs from the mid-1960s through the mid-1980s as other apocalypticists happily contemplated the coming cosmicide after their own prior removal from our doomed earth (pp. 135–37, 150):

- Thank God, I will get a view of the Battle of Armageddon from the grand stand seats of the heavens. All who are born again will see the battle of Armageddon, but it will be from the skies (Carl McIntire, 1965).
- What then should be the believer's attitude to the destruction of the world by fire? First of all, he should welcome it and pray for its nearness (Robert Gromacki, 1970).
- The world has one great war yet to endure.... The slaughter that will take place is too frightening to imagine. Just be thankful that you're not going to be around (Chuck Smith, 1977).
- The Tribulation will result in such bloodshed and destruction that any war up to that time will seem insignificant (Jerry Falwell, 1983).
- Some day we may blow ourselves up with all the bombs.... But I still believe God's going to be in control.... If He chooses to use nuclear war, then who am I to argue with that? (Charles Jones, 1986).

Jesus departed this earth issuing a series of "fear nots," but these Christians have replaced them with a series of "fear lots."

If anyone thought that "prophecy beliefs" were material for unconcern, they should have known better and thought again. Boyer cites Hal Lindsey's own claim that "when he spoke at the American Air War College 'virtually the entire school turned out, including many officers accompanied by their wives, and that, at the Pentagon, 'hundreds ... jam[med] the room' with more crowding outside" (p. 141). During the Reagan administration, Defense Secretary Caspar Weinberger said, "I have read the Book of

Revelation and yes, I believe the world is going to end—by an act
of God, I hope—but every day I think the time is running out,"
and Interior Secretary James Watt said, "I do not know how many
future generations we can count on before the Lord returns"
(p. 141). How exactly then, in the early 1980s, would those beliefs
have influenced the administration's external military policies and
internal conservation practices?

Armageddon as Spectator Sport

Barbara Rossing's 2004 book, *The Rapture Exposed,* is a powerful
indictment of American Christian fundamentalism's lust for divine
ethnic cleansing and transcendental cosmicide. As a professor of
the New Testament at Chicago's Lutheran School of Theology, she
can expertly judge the anti-scriptural excesses of "the destructive
racket of rapture" (pp. 1–18). That "rapture racket" has existed only
since around 1830 and is based on the presupposition that the
Second Coming of Christ will be a double advent—once for the
Rapture and again, seven years later, for Armageddon. Rossing
outlines that complete final scenario for our world like this (p. 56;
italicized additions of numbers and titles are mine):

1. *Israel:* The rebirth of the nation of Israel.
2. *The Rapture:* The removal of born-again Christians off the
   earth by Christ.
3. *The Tribulation:* The emergence of an evil Antichrist (and his
   one-world currency), probably in Europe. The Antichrist
   signs a seven-year peace treaty with Israel, setting in motion
   the seven years of tribulation—but the Antichrist will break
   the treaty after three and one half years.
4. *The Temple:* The rebuilding of the temple in Jerusalem and
   the resumption of animal sacrifices there. The desecration of
   the temple by the evil Antichrist, followed by the second
   half of the seven years of tribulation.

5. *Armageddon:* Jesus' return in the "Glorious Appearing" exactly seven years after the Rapture, beginning with his
   touch-down on the Mount of Olives, which will split the
   mountain into two.
6. *The Millennium:* After Jesus wins the battle of Armageddon
   he will then set up his millennial kingdom from the throne
   of David in Jerusalem and will reign for one thousand years
   over a kingdom repopulated by converted Jews and un-
   Raptured people left behind on earth.
7. *Judgment:* After that comes the last judgment.
8. *Eternity:* [The last judgment will be] followed by eternity
   itself—"God's New Jerusalem."

Reading this summary, you can see clearly why the full Rapture
program cannot be readily dismissed as simple religious fantasy
arising from faith's freewheeling imagination. For those who
accept its vision, there are very specific connections to American
foreign policy relations in the volatile Middle East. For example,
how can there ever be both a Palestinian and an Israeli state between the Mediterranean and the Jordan if it is against God's end-
time plans for Jesus's return?

A first example. "The Bible is my Road Map," declares an Inter-
net petition circulated by Robertson, Falwell, and LaHaye in opposition to a negotiated solution to the Israeli-Palestinian conflict.
"Peace and peace plans in the Middle East are a bad thing, in the
view of fundamentalist Christians, because they delay the count-
down to Christ's return" (p. 46). How does that opinion influence
our administration's policy toward the Palestinians and Israelis? Is
that why it has a map and a road but no progress and no traffic?

A second example. Here are five questions that Rossing records
from the Left Behind Prophecy Club's website: "Have events in
Iraq launched an unstoppable chain that leads to Armageddon?
Could the Antichrist be alive now? Is the UN a precursor of One
World government prophesied in the Bible? Are ATMs and other

revolutions in banking foretelling the Mark of the Beast? Is SARS a fulfillment of Jesus' prophecy about plagues in the End Times?" (p. 43). Answers from myself: no, no, no, no, and no. But how would positive answers from a major constituency directly and indirectly influence an administration's foreign policy?

In chapter 1, we saw three kinds of witnesses——martyrs, pacifists, and, especially, monks—to *another world* here below upon this earth who proclaim that the normalcy of civilization's brutality is not the inevitability of humanity's destiny. On the one hand, therefore, any fiction that opens one's mind—especially at an early age—to imagine a world other than our own is surely magnificently therapeutic. On the other hand, any alternative universe that presumes the normalcy of violence is not *other* at all. It is simply our own world transferred beyond the skies or beneath the seas, our own world but with animals, aliens, or robots acting just like ourselves.

My point here is extremely specific. It is *not* that violence and war should never be portrayed in books or drama; they are a part of our reality that needs to be portrayed, although we might want to think more about their current ubiquity. The point is *not* that our children are being introduced too early and too easily to that reality's portrayed normalcy, although we might also want to think more about that aspect. The point is that our other worlds and alternative universes are neither *other* nor *alternative* except in the most superficial ways. The truly other world would be one without injustice, and the truly alternative universe would be one without violence.

"Mankind," said T. S. Eliot, "cannot bear too much reality." W. B. Yeats warns us in this chapter's epigraph that those who grow up on fantasy grow old on brutality. If we cannot bear too much reality, we might at least avoid too much fantasy. In the rest of this chapter, therefore, and against the preceding discussion of fantasy-based religious violence and faith-based foreign policy, I turn to consider the Rapture, the apocalypse, and the return of Jesus Christ.

RAPTURE TO HEAVEN *BUT* RETURN TO EARTH

It has often been noted that the word "rapture" never appears any-where in the Christian Bible. But it is even more important to note that neither does the idea, the theme, or the concept as inter-preted by contemporary fundamentalist Christians. "The Rapture" is the basis for the ten-point end-time fantasy outlined earlier, but it is quite simply a mistake, a misunderstanding of what Paul speaks about in 1 Thessalonians 4:15–17 (key Greek words are in brackets):

> For this we declare to you by the word of the Lord, that we who are alive, who are left until the coming [*parousian*] of the Lord, will by no means precede those who have died. For the Lord himself, with a cry of command, with the archangel's call and with the sound of God's trumpet, will descend from heaven, and the dead in Christ will rise first. Then we who are alive, who are left, will be caught up in the clouds to-gether with them to meet [*eis apantēsin*] the Lord in the air; and so we will be with the Lord forever.

What is wrong with translating "caught up" as "raptured"? Surely they are but different words for the same event? They are, and that is not the problem—you can translate "caught up" as "raptured" if you wish. The problem is that Paul is trying to tell us something quite different that demands *our* acceptance of *his* meaning rather than the imposition of an alien concept on his text. To get back to Paul, I will speak about one image, two words, and three cities.

One Image

The ancient healing city of Hierapolis is at the eastern end of the Meander Valley inland from Ephesus on the Aegean coast of Turkey. If you enter the excavated ruins along the city's northern road, you find yourself walking through a cemetery with broken tombstones, fractured sarcophagi, and shattered mausoleums on all sides. If you can imagine a monstrous giant taking an equally monstrous sledgehammer to the aboveground cemeteries in New Orleans, you can envisage the destruction of the thousand-plus tombs that once lined the approach road to Hierapolis.

From that northern necropolis you often see photos of the restored mausoleum of the merchant Flavius Zeuxis from the late first century. It announces above the door that he had "sailed on seventy-two voyages beyond Cape Maleus toward Italy." That many times around the southern tip of Greece's Peloponnesus—the Cape Horn of the Mediterranean—was certainly pushing his maritime luck. If you have seen photos of only that one famous tomb, you can hardly imagine the absolutely chaotic destruction all around it throughout the city's northern necropolis.

In any case, for what follows, remember that anyone approaching an ancient city on any of its main roads would pass first through the common graves and especially the elegant tombs of its citizens. You would be met, in other words, by the city's dead beyond the gate before you encountered the city's living inside the gate. I ask you to keep that *image* of approaching Hierapolis—or any other Roman city—in your imagination as I discuss the two key words used by Paul in 1 Thessalonians 4:15–17.

Two Words

I concentrate next on the two Greek words italicized in the extract from Paul's letter to the Thessalonians, *parousia* and *eis apantēsin*. They are both ordinary, everyday terms but also, in certain contexts, technical expressions for a very specific event. In its special, technical usage, *parousia* means the arrival at a city of a conquering general, an important official, an imperial emissary, or, above all, the emperor himself. The proper response—especially under the Pax Romana—would have been for the leading citizens to go outside their opened city gates, make the appropriate welcome, and escort the arriving dignitary back inside with them (*eis apantēsin*). Here is an example from long before that peaceful era.

In November of 333 BCE, Alexander the Great defeated and humiliated Darius of Persia at Issus in northwestern Syria and then marched inexorably southward toward Egypt. The Jewish high-priest Jaddus remained unwisely loyal to Darius and repulsed Alexander's initial demand for submission, according to Josephus's *Jewish Antiquities* (11.327–28). After devastating sieges at Tyre and Gaza, Alexander finally turned against Jerusalem. Jaddus was afraid, "not knowing how he could meet [*apantēsai*] the Macedonians," so he sacrificed for deliverance, and "God spoke oracularly to him in his sleep, telling him to take courage and adorn the city with wreaths and open the gates and go out to meet them [literally, make the *hypantēsin*], and that the people should be in white garments.... And, after doing all the things that he had been told to do, [he] awaited the coming [*parousian*] of the king." Notice the twin technical terms for an official *arrival* and its appropriate *reception*.

In times of war, *parousia* was, of course, a threatening advent, as in this story, but under the Pax Romana an imperial visitation would usually be a happy occasion for a city and quite possibly a once-in-a-lifetime event. It demanded tremendous preparation for civic sacrifice, aristocratic festivity, popular celebration, and, especially, a formal greeting by elites and people at the submissively opened gates of the city.

My point is that in the Greco-Roman world, the reception, or *apantēsis,* always involved individuals *going out* to meet somebody and *escorting* that somebody back into their place of residence. It never meant meeting an arriving person and returning with him whence he came. That would be simple nonsense. Notice, therefore, Paul's use of these technical terms for *visitation* and *reception* in 1 Thessalonians. He uses *parousia* for "our Lord Jesus at his *coming*" in 2:19, "the *coming* of our Lord Jesus with all his saints" in 3:13, "the *coming* of the Lord" in 4:15, and "the *coming* of our Lord Jesus Christ" in 5:23. He uses *apantēsis* for Thessalonian Christians "*meeting* the Lord in the air" at his *parousia* in 4:17. That metaphor controls the entire discussion. But what does the discussion concern?

Three Cities

Hold on to that *one image* and those *two words* as I turn to Paul's situation in terms of *three cities*—Thessalonica, Athens, and Corinth. In the early 50s CE, Paul finally crossed the northern Aegean—Homer's "wine-dark sea" and Yeats's "dolphin-torn and gong-tormented sea"—from Asia to Europe. He stopped at Philippi before moving on to Thessalonica, capital of the Roman province of Macedonia. He would write in 1 Thessalonians 2:2, "Though we had already suffered and been shamefully mistreated at Philippi, as you know, we had courage in our God to declare to you the gospel of God in spite of great opposition."

In Philippi, according to Luke's Acts of the Apostles, the accusation was that Paul and Silas were "advocating customs that are not lawful for us as Romans to adopt or observe" (16:21), and in Thessalonica they were accused of "acting contrary to the decrees of the emperor, saying that there is another king named Jesus" (Acts 17:7). Eventually Paul had to flee Macedonia for the adjacent Roman province of Achaia, but he was so worried about leaving the Thessalonians under persecution that, as he tells them in the first letter, "when we could bear it no longer, we decided to be left alone in Athens; and we sent Timothy, our brother and co-worker for God in proclaiming the gospel of Christ, to strengthen and encourage you for the sake of your faith, so that no one would be shaken by these persecutions" (3:1–3).

As he awaited Timothy's return, Paul moved on to his new base at Corinth, capital of the Roman province of Achaia, and from there he wrote to the Thessalonians that "Timothy has just now come to us from you, and has brought us the good news of your faith and love. He has told us also that you always remember us kindly and long to see us—just as we long to see you" (3:6). But

Timothy also brought back from them one very important question for Paul.

Some of the Thessalonians had died under persecution after Paul himself escaped to Athens and Corinth. It was probably those martyrdoms that Paul had in mind when he told them that "you became an example to all the believers in Macedonia and in Achaia. For the word of the Lord has sounded forth from you not only in Macedonia and Achaia, but in every place your faith in God has become known, so that we have no need to speak about it" (1:7–8). But those deaths had worried the Thessalonians. If Jesus, as Paul had told them, was supposed to return within their own lifetime, would those dead Christians be at some disadvantage compared with those still alive?

It was both a theological and a pastoral question, and Paul responded to both those aspects. But notice one point. The obvious and easy answer would have been that living and dead Christians would all go to meet Christ simultaneously and together. But that was not pastorally compassionate enough for Paul. The Thessalonians worried that the living would precede the dead, so Paul reversed their fear and assured them the dead would precede the living: "We who are alive ... will by no means precede those who have died. For ... the dead in Christ will rise first. Then we who are alive, who are left, will be caught up in the clouds together with them" (4:15–17).

Paul's Vision

I now bring together all these elements into one emphatic conclusion. Paul—like Jesus before him—believed that God's Great Cosmic Cleanup had already begun. He also believed—quite incorrectly—that it would be consummated within his own generation. But just as a visiting emperor is greeted first by the dead and only then by the living as his entourage approaches an imperial city, and just as the citizens go out to meet him and escort him *back into* their city for festivity and celebration, so also will it be with Christ on his return. First the dead Christians and then the living Christians will be taken up ("raptured"—if you like) to meet Christ not "in heaven" but "in the clouds" or "in the air." And they will meet Christ to return to an earth totally transformed, utterly transfigured, and fully completed in nonviolence and holiness, justice, and peace. That is Paul's vision, and it is confirmed both by the general expectation for eschatological consummation *here below upon this earth* and by the specific meaning of his *parousia* and *apantēsis* metaphor.

Finally, it is indeed ironic that, when Paul himself spoke of "we who are alive, who are left" (*hoi perileipomenoi*)—that is, of those *left behind*—he meant those living Christians who would have to wait for the dead Christians to meet Christ first. Then all would return to our re-created earth to be "with the Lord forever." What the Left Behind series has actually left behind is Jesus's faith in the Kingdom of God, Paul's hope for the Lordship of Christ, and God's love for the future of the earth.

A TWO-STEP RETURN OF JESUS

In the general Jewish tradition, there was an expectation of *a single coming of a single Messiah* as the agent of God's Great Divine Cleanup of the earth. But those Qumran Essenes who produced the Dead Sea Scrolls mutated that expectation into *a single coming of a double Messiah*. One would be priestly and the other royal to emphasize the invalidity of the Hasmonean or Maccabean monarchy, which had made the same ruler both king and priest for about one hundred years before the arrival of the Romans in the 60s BCE.

It was therefore yet another but a different religious mutation when some Jewish Christians announced *a double coming of a single Messiah*. Jesus was that Messiah/Christ, and as we saw in chapter 3, believers were called to cooperate with God in this new era between the twin advents—the past one of incarnation and the future one of consummation—of this Messiah/Christ. By the way, unlike Jesus and Paul, some Christians were not sure whether that future or second coming was to *create* the Kingdom that we had failed to co-establish with God here below or to *celebrate* the Kingdom we had succeeded in co-instituting with God on our transfigured earth.

Only in the last two hundred years has a new submutation appeared, and only within Christian fundamentalist faith. There will be, it claims, *a double stage for that second advent,* and there will also be a period in between those twin stages (recall that basic structure from the ten-point scenario outlined earlier by Barbara Rossing). But of course, there is absolutely no such idea anywhere in the New Testament. Nobody there ever imagined a double-stage Second Coming of Christ. It is simply wrong, and as we have just seen, it is based on a misunderstanding of Paul's vision in 1 Thessalonians 4:15–17. That Pauline scenario was one of many ways in which New Testament authors imagined the *single-stage* Second Coming of Jesus. Paul had simply adapted his description to the specific worries of a community that had lost loved ones in a local persecution.

THE LITTLE APOCALYPSE OF MARK

I focus on Mark because it is, by a broad consensus of scholarship, the first of the four gospels in our present New Testament. Moreover, it is certainly the major source for Matthew and Luke and possibly also for John. I understand Mark's gospel within the historical situation of the early 70s, when the great rebellion of 66–74 CE had already left Israel devastated, Jerusalem destroyed, and the Temple demolished. I locate its composition among "the villages of Caesarea Philippi" (8:27), those small towns around the capital city of the tetrarchy of Herod Philip near the headwaters of the Jordan River. In the early 70s, therefore, his territories were a relatively safe place for refugees fleeing to the far north from Jerusalem and Judea.

Many of those refugees had lost loved ones to death or slavery and their homes and possessions to looting and destruction. They had also lost, or almost lost, something else as well. Where was Jesus in the horror from which they had escaped? If he was supposed to return, why had he not come to save them from the Roman revenge? Such questions would have been asked by members of Mark's own community. Where was Jesus as the Temple burned to the ground?

Here is a parallel case that may help us to understand those questions. Even as the Temple was being destroyed by the Roman siege, its Jewish defenders expected the Messiah to come and save them at the last moment. Josephus's *Jewish War* tells how six thousand "of the poor women and children of the populace" took refuge on the one remaining portico of the outer court; when the soldiers fired the portico from below, "some were killed plunging out of the flames, others perished amidst them, and out of all that multitude not a soul escaped."

> They owed their destruction to a false prophet, who had on that day proclaimed to the people in the city that God had commanded them to go up to the temple court, to receive there the tokens of their deliverance. Numerous prophets, indeed, were at this period suborned by the tyrants to delude the people, by bidding them await help from God.... Thus it was that the wretched people were deluded at that time by charlatans and pretended messengers of the deity. (6:283–88)

Later, in 6.312–13, Josephus gives this even more stunning interpretation of imminent Messianic expectation even as the Temple burned and was being destroyed in 70 CE:

> What more than all else incited them [the rebels] to the war was an ambiguous oracle, likewise found in their sacred scriptures, to the effect that at that time one from their coun-

try would become ruler of the world. This they understood to mean someone of their own race, and many of their wise men went astray in their interpretation of it. The oracle, however, in reality signified the sovereignty of Vespasian who was proclaimed Emperor in Jewish soil.

Amid the climactic horrors of the Roman revenge, some non-Christian Jews expected the first and only coming of their Messiah, and some Christian Jews expected the second and final coming of their Messiah. Both groups were sadly and terribly disappointed.

You can read all of Mark as a text of explanatory consolation for those Christians whose lives had been spared but whose faith had been shaken during the Great Revolt of 66–74 CE. That is why, for example, Mark has Jesus die in agony and abandonment, in betrayal, denial, and mockery. That is precisely how their fellow Christians had died during the Great Revolt. That is also why Mark's story ends at 16:8 *not* with apparitions of the risen Jesus but with an empty tomb and promises about the future. Their fellow Christians had not been saved from martyrdom in the Great Revolt by any visionary interventions of the resurrected Jesus. It is, above all else, those experiences during the Great Revolt that explain the function and meaning of the Little Apocalypse in Mark 13.

Here are the purposes behind Mark 13. First, to separate the destruction of Jerusalem from the return of Jesus by showing that Jesus himself had warned beforehand against that very confusion. Second, to maintain that the return of Jesus, although consequent to that destruction, was imminent thereafter and required constant vigilance. Third, to insist that the exact time was known only to God. The Little Apocalypse begins with this deliberately doubled question and deliberately separated location in 13:1–4:

[1] As he came out of the temple, one of his disciples said to him, "Look, Teacher, what large stones and what large

buildings!" Then Jesus asked him, "Do you see these great buildings? Not one stone will be left here upon another; all will be thrown down."

[2] When he was sitting on the Mount of Olives opposite the temple, Peter, James, John, and Andrew asked him privately, "Tell us, when will this be, and what will be the sign that all these things are about to be accomplished?"

The first and public question is about the Temple; in answer, Jesus foretells its destruction. The second and private question presumes that such a destruction will entail the consummation of all things. In answer, Jesus distinguishes these two events by speaking first of the Temple's fate in 13:5–23 and only then ("after that suffering") of his own return in 13:24–27.

The Destruction of the Temple

The war of 66–74 CE—especially the destruction of the Temple—begins in Mark 13:5–6 and ends in 13:21–23 with double warnings against false claims for his own presence in connection with that destruction:

[1] Then Jesus began to say to them, "Beware that no one leads you astray. Many will come in my name and say, 'I am he!' and they will lead many astray."

[2] "And if anyone says to you at that time, 'Look! Here is the Messiah!' or 'Look! There he is!'—do not believe it. False messiahs and false prophets will appear and produce signs and omens, to lead astray, if possible, the elect. But be alert; I have already told you everything."

Within those frames, with their emphatic warnings against being led astray by anyone claiming that Titus's Roman siege meant

Jesus's Messianic return, Mark describes three special aspects of the revolt.

First, in 13:7–8: "When you hear of wars and rumors of wars, do not be alarmed; this must take place, but the end is still to come. For nation will rise against nation, and kingdom against kingdom; there will be earthquakes in various places; there will be famines. This is but the beginning of the birthpangs." Imagine, for example, the rumors reaching Jerusalem about Vespasian's initial 67 CE campaigns in Galilee.

Next, in 13:9–13, Mark foretells the particular sufferings of Christian Jews, who would have been considered disloyal to the rebellion, and how that persecution would split families so that, like Judas Iscariot with Jesus, "brother will betray brother to death, and a father his child, and children will rise against parents and have them put to death" (13:12).

Finally, there is that most significant and enigmatic statement in 13:14: "But when you see the desolating sacrilege set up where it ought not to be (let the reader understand), then those in Judea must flee to the mountains." Only here does the writer step out from authorial anonymity and directly address the reader. This is also—if the reader understands—the clearest indication that Mark is speaking now of the desecration of the Temple in 70 CE. It is clearest for two reasons.

The first reason is that phrase "the desolating sacrilege," which, in Greek, is literally "the abomination of desolation," or "the abomination that makes desolate." The point is that, however our English translations diverge, the Greek originals are identical, and the phrase in Mark 13:14 is the exact same expression used in the Greek translation of Daniel for the desecration of the Temple by Antiochus IV Epiphanes in the 160s BCE. Here are examples in Daniel:

[1] Forces sent by him shall occupy and profane the temple and fortress. They shall abolish the regular burnt offering and set up the abomination that makes desolate. (11:31)

[2] From the time that the regular burnt offering is taken away and the abomination that desolates is set up, there shall be one thousand two hundred ninety days. (12:11)

It is quite certain, therefore, that Mark 13:14 refers to the desecration of Jerusalem's Temple by Titus's legions in 70 CE, and that verse serves as the securest index to the subject throughout 13:5–23.

The second reason is that Luke was a very early "reader" of Mark 13:14, and he was well able to understand its meaning. In copying all of Mark 13, he deliberately rephrased 13:14 and added in another verse lest his readers not understand its meaning. Compare Luke's two explanatory changes framing his Markan source:

Mark 13:14, 17–19	*Luke 21:20–21a, 23–24*
When you see *the desolating sacrilege* set up where it ought not to be (let the reader understand), then those in Judea must flee to the mountains....	When you see *Jerusalem surrounded by armies,* then know that its desolation has come near. Then those in Judea must flee to the mountains....
Woe to those who are pregnant and to those who are nursing infants in those days! Pray that it may not be in winter. For in those days there will be suffering, such as has not been from the beginning of the creation that God created until now, no, and never will be.	Woe to those who are pregnant and to those who are nursing infants in those days! For there will be great distress on the earth and wrath against this people; they will fall by the edge of the sword and be taken away as captives among all nations; *and Jerusalem will be trampled on by the Gentiles, until the times of the Gentiles are fulfilled.*

Luke makes it emphatically clear that Mark 13:14 is about Jerusalem besieged and fallen to Gentile violence. Thus, in Mark 13:5–
23, it is especially the frames in 13:5–6 and 13:21–23, with their
doubled warnings against the deceptive illusion that Jerusalem's
destruction and Jesus's return will be concomitant, that are most
important.

The Return of Christ

Only after his allusion to the destruction to the Temple is clearly
and emphatically established does Mark speak about the actual
return of Jesus in 13:24–27. The two events are separated by these
ending and opening phrases:

> *Jerusalem's destruction:* "in those days there will be suffering"
> (13:19)
> *Jesus's Second Coming:* "in those days, after that suffering"
> (13:24)

With that separation established, Mark describes Jesus's eventual
return in standard apocalyptic language for a world turned upside
down and changed absolutely:

> In those days, after that suffering, the sun will be darkened,
> and the moon will not give its light, and the stars will be fall-
> ing from heaven, and the powers in the heavens will be
> shaken. Then they will see "the Son of Man coming in
> clouds" with great power and glory. Then he will send out
> the angels, and gather his elect from the four winds, from the
> ends of the earth to the ends of heaven. (13:24–27)

Those cosmic phenomena reflect the visions of Israelite prophets
like Isaiah ("For the stars of the heavens and their constellations will
not give their light; the sun will be dark at its rising, and the moon

will not shed its light" [13:10]) and Joel ("The earth quakes before them, the heavens tremble. The sun and the moon are darkened, and the stars withdraw their shining" [2:10] and "The sun and the moon are darkened, and the stars withdraw their shining" [3:15]).

No doubt there is an implicit threat behind the "*they* will see" phrase, but there is a striking absence of threatened punishments in that scenario. It is primarily about the promise of consolation for the elect as they are gathered into a single community.

The Question of When

The final section in 13:28–37 concerns the separate timing of these two discrete events, and it is not always easy to tell which is which. The problem is that, while Mark clearly separates Jerusalem's destruction from Jesus's return, he also believes that the latter will occur *very soon* after the former and that both will occur within the lifetime of his audience. That has already been mentioned in 9:1: "Truly I tell you, there are some standing here who will not taste death until they see that the kingdom of God has come with power."

Tentatively, therefore, I think that Jerusalem's destruction is timed in 13:28–31 and Jesus's return is timed in 13:32–37. That division refers back to the double question of the four disciples in 13:4a (about Jerusalem's destruction) and 13:4b (about Jesus's return). And each gets its own parable: first the burgeoning fig tree and then the returning master. Mark also brings these two times together by asserting that, when the former occurs, the latter will be close—indeed, at the very gates. They are separate, says Mark, but so close that one will almost be prelude to the other.

Mark—like Paul before him—was wrong on the timing of the latter event—off by two thousand years and still counting. But he was wise enough to say this: "About that day or hour no one knows, neither the angels in heaven, nor the Son, but only the Father" (13:32). And this: "Beware, keep alert; for you do not know when the time will come" (13:33). And this: "Therefore, keep awake—for you do not know when the master of the house will come" (13:35). And this: "And what I say to you I say to all: Keep awake" (13:37).

Finally, here is the main point I would emphasize before continuing. The Little Apocalypse insists that the horrors of war come *before* the return of Jesus and that those who equate war and return are false and deceiving. Therefore, of course, one could never speak of the returning Jesus conducting or promoting that warfare. A paroxysm of final violence or an orgy of ultimate destruction is a fairly standard prelude to a world transfigured into nonviolence, justice, and peace. But that is very different from suggesting that God—or Jesus—effects both those events at the same time. It is, says Mark 13, a very serious mistake to confuse Vespasian and Titus with God and Jesus: "Beware that no one leads you astray" (13:6) and "do not believe it" (13:21). But what if some Christians ignored those warnings by combining imperial war with Jesus's return and, worse still, asserted that Jesus's return would be by an imperial war?

THE GREAT APOCALYPSE OF JOHN

On the one hand, the Book of Revelation is but another example of the biblical ambiguity seen throughout chapter 2—that constant dialectic between the radicality of nonviolent justice pressed upon us by God and the normalcy of violent injustice pressed upon God by us. Recall my argument that Christians are called to choose between the nonviolent God and the violent God by believing one or the other was incarnate in Jesus. On the other hand, we now have a First and Second Coming of Jesus, so which is normative for Christians? Is our criterion the incarnational Jesus or the apocalyptic Jesus? Or more precisely, is it the nonviolent Jesus of Mark's Little Apocalypse or the violent Jesus of John's Great Apocalypse?

My basic criticism of the Christian Bible's final and climactic book is this: It is one thing to announce, as in Mark's Little

Apocalypse, that there will be a spasmic paroxysm of *human* violence *before* the returning Christ. It is another thing to announce,
as in John's Great Apocalypse, that there will be a spasmic paroxysm of *divine* violence *by* the returning Christ. The First Coming
has Jesus on a donkey making a nonviolent demonstration. The
Second Coming has Jesus on a war horse leading a violent attack.
We Christians still have to choose.

I am quite aware that the Lamb is the central symbol for Christ
in the Book of Revelation. It is introduced by emphasizing that
"the Lion of the tribe of Judah, the Root of David, has conquered" and that it is "a Lamb standing as if it had been slaughtered" (5:5–6). This is the Jesus who has already conquered by
death-and-resurrection, so that he is again "the Lamb that was
slaughtered" in 5:12 and 13:8. But that is just the First Coming of
the Lamb. In the Lamb's Second Coming, in 6:15–17,

> the kings of the earth and the magnates and the generals
> and the rich and the powerful, and everyone, slave and free,
> hid in the caves and among the rocks of the mountains, call-
> ing to the mountains and rocks, "Fall on us and hide us from
> the face of the one seated on the throne and from the wrath
> of the Lamb; for the great day of their wrath has come, and
> who is able to stand?"

Opponents "will make war on the Lamb, and the Lamb will conquer them, for he is Lord of lords and King of kings, and those
with him are called and chosen and faithful" (17:14). The Slaughtered becomes the Slaughterer.

Rome in the Great Apocalypse

The Book of Revelation, the Great Apocalypse from John of
Patmos (1:9), is, first of all, a linked and interwoven attack on the
empire of Rome, the city of Rome, and the emperor of Rome—
or, in my language, on Roman imperial theology. Rome's empire

and its capital city are repeatedly called "Babylon" because, just as the Babylonian Empire had destroyed Jerusalem's First Temple in 596 BCE, so also had the Roman Empire destroyed its Second Temple in 70 CE. The imminent destruction of "Babylon" intends the *imminent* destruction of Rome, from 14:8 through 16:19 to 18:2, 10, and 21, and that event is signaled through the use of two kinds of language.

Beast-Language

As we saw in chapter 3, Daniel (7:1–7) uses beast-language to describe imperial opponents of God's world: he *"saw ... four great beasts* [come] *up out of the sea,"* and they were "like a *lion ...* like a *bear ...* like a *leopard ...* [and] had *ten horns."* The four great empires of the Babylonians, Medes, Persians, and Greeks thus envisioned in Daniel are all combined for the Book of Revelation in the empire of Rome: "I *saw* a *beast* rising out of the *sea* having *ten horns* and seven heads.... And the beast that I saw was like a *leopard,* its feet were like a *bear's,* and its mouth was like a *lion's* mouth" (13:1–2).

The attack on Rome as both empire and city is—at least symbolically—quite clear. But the attack on the emperor is much more convoluted. The Rome-beast, as just seen, had seven heads, but as John relates:

> The angel said to me ... *"This calls for a mind that has wisdom:* the seven heads are seven mountains on which the woman is seated; also, they are seven kings, of whom five have fallen, one is living, and the other has not yet come; and when he comes, he must remain only a little while. As for the beast that was and is not, it is an eighth but it belongs to the seven, and it goes to destruction." (17:7, 9–11, emphasis mine)

That opening phrase, "this calls for a mind that has wisdom," is an address to the reader or hearer similar to that in Mark 13:14, "let the reader understand." They both warn us that very special symbolism is coming up and that we must pay careful attention to understand its meaning.

We are certainly talking about Roman emperors—but which ones? I think the best identification is that of Adela Yarbro Collins in her 1986 book *Crisis and Catharsis: The Power of the Apocalypse.* The fallen five are "emperors who were especially feared and hated ... Caligula, Claudius, Nero, Vespasian, and Titus. Domitian would be the 'one [who] is.' A seventh was expected, to fill out the traditional number seven" (p. 64). The even more enigmatic "eighth [who] belongs to the seven" is Nero because of this widespread belief:

> Shortly after Nero committed suicide in 68, the rumor began to spread that he had not really died, but had escaped to the East. The common people in Rome and many in the East whom he had benefited hoped that he would return with the Parthians (successors of the Persians) as his allies and regain power in Rome. (p. 59)

That expectation of Nero's return appeared earlier in the Book of Revelation: "One of its heads seemed to have received a death-blow, but its mortal wound had been healed" (13:3). And Nero is the one to whom another enigmatic allusion was made in 13:18, again with that same opening appeal for special understanding: "*This calls for wisdom:* let anyone with understanding calculate the number of the beast, for it is the number of a person. Its number is six hundred sixty-six." In languages that use letters for numerals, like Hebrew and Greek, the name CAESAR NERO(N) comes out to 666. The theme of Nero's return is also found, by the way, in Jewish texts written against Roman imperialism in that same period.

Whore-Language

In the Old Testament, whore-language is traditional for those who commit the fornication or adultery of abandoning God for pagan idols. Faithless Israel plays the whore, as it were, by betraying her divine spouse. Whore-language and beast-language come together for Rome in the Great Apocalypse at 17:1–2:

> Then one of the seven angels who had the seven bowls came and said to me, "Come, I will show you the judgment of the great whore who is seated on many waters, with whom the kings of the earth have committed fornication, and with the wine of whose fornication the inhabitants of the earth have become drunk."

In 17:5, "Babylon the great" is the "mother of whores and of earth's abominations." All the wealth and luxury in Rome, all the travel to and from Rome, are but the signs of a highly successful whorehouse. Rome, the city on the "seven mountains" in 17:9, is "the great whore who corrupted the earth with her fornication" in 19:2. But when we compare Revelation with similar apocalypses within contemporary Judaism, the question arises: why is its attack on Rome so savagely sexual and so excessively violent?

John could have gone to Asia Minor as a refugee from the Roman destruction of his Jewish homeland in 66–74 CE. That might explain the venomous fury with which he announces the *imminent* destruction of the Roman Empire. But that would be pure conjecture.

The text itself might make you think that Domitian, under whom it was written in the 90s CE, was a major persecutor of Christians, at least in Asia Minor. For example, in 6:9–11:

> When he opened the fifth seal, I saw under the altar the souls of those who had been slaughtered for the word of God and for the testimony they had given; they cried out with a loud voice, "Sovereign Lord, holy and true, how long will it be before you judge and avenge our blood on the inhabitants of the earth?" They were each given a white robe and told to rest a little longer, until the number would be complete both

of their fellow servants and of their brothers and sisters, who were soon to be killed as they themselves had been killed.

And yet we only hear of two named individuals who have actually suffered persecution. One is "I, John, your brother who share[s] with you in Jesus the persecution and the kingdom and the patient endurance [and] was on the island called Patmos because of the word of God and the testimony of Jesus" (1:9), but he was exiled, not martyred. The other is "Antipas my witness, my faithful one, who was killed among you, where Satan lives" in Pergamum (2:13). There is actually no evidence whatsoever of any major persecution in Roman Asia under Domitian.

The best explanation comes from the two opening chapters of the book, in which the exiled John addresses the seven Christian communities at Ephesus in 2:1–7, Smyrna in 2:8–11, Pergamum in 2:12–17, Thyatira in 2:18–29, Sardis in 3:1–6, Philadelphia in 3:7–13, and Laodicea in 3:14–22. It is they who receive first and emphatic attention. The Apocalypse, which in fact is written to them about Rome, *is not consolation for their persecution by Rome but admonition against their acculturation to Rome.*

The venom of the book's anti-Roman rhetoric is especially for internal rather than external effect. It intends to preclude any Christian cooperation with the Roman Empire, although John believes that collusion is already happening. "Come out of her, my people," is his mantra (18:4). This deliberately "no compromise" attack is behind John's criticism of the Nicolaitans (2:6, 2:15), those "who hold to the teaching of Balaam" (2:14), and those who "tolerate that woman Jezebel" (2:20) and learn "the deep things of Satan" (2:24). Furthermore, not only are some of the urban Asian Christians finding Romanism attractive, but they are also finding Judaism attractive, and John's seven inaugural letters attack that compromise as well. He speaks against "those who say that they are Jews and are not, but are a synagogue of Satan" (2:9) and "those of the synagogue of Satan who say that they are Jews and are not, but are lying" (3:9), and later he calls Jerusalem "the great city that is prophetically called Sodom and Egypt, where also their Lord was crucified" (11:8).

Finally, John describes the "new song" in heaven of "the one hundred forty-four thousand who have been redeemed from the earth" (14:3), whom he characterizes as those "who have not defiled themselves with women, for they are virgins; these follow the Lamb wherever he goes. They have been redeemed from humankind as first fruits for God and the Lamb" (14:4). John is advocating virginal celibate asceticism as the Christian ideal, and his whore-language may reflect the misogynistic vision of one who is male rather than the celibate vision of one who is free.

Christ in the Great Apocalypse

Recall the Little Apocalypse of Mark 13 one final time. First, Jesus insists there that the terrible events at the Roman destruction of Jerusalem were to come before the Second Coming and were not to be confused with the latter event. Certainly, one could fill out those verses with the horrible scenes of the city's fall from Josephus's *Jewish War*. That historical event was as bad as anything imagined in the Great Apocalypse's most frightening scenes. Second, one might say (but I would not) that those horrors were the will of God, since the Bible often attributes to God anything—good or bad—that happens on earth. Third, one might say, as Matthew does (but I would emphatically not), that those events were a divine punishment of Jerusalem for the crucifixion of Jesus.

To say that those events were conducted by Jesus or were in any way part of his Second Coming is a deception against which the Markan Jesus warns his people. That, however, is exactly what the Great Apocalypse does in imagining the destruction of Rome as part of the Second Coming of Christ. Indeed, the destruction of Rome will be conducted precisely *in* and *by* the Second Coming of Christ. It is thus a double negation of Mark's warning not to confuse imperial violence *with* or *by* Christ's return.

To turn the nonviolent resistance of the slaughtered Jesus into the violent warfare of the slaughtering Jesus is, for me as a Christian, to libel the body of Jesus and to blaspheme the soul of Christ. That is my indictment against the Great Apocalypse, and here is my evidence against it, with a focus on two scenes that frame it.

The first scene occurs early in the Great Apocalypse. In a scene set in heaven, God holds "a scroll written on the inside and on the back, sealed with seven seals" (5:1). This is the scroll of judgment on the world, and it is reminiscent of a similar scene in Daniel 7:10 when God's "court sat in judgment, and the books were opened" (recall the scene from chapter 3). The Great Apocalypse continues in 5:2–7:

I saw a mighty angel proclaiming with a loud voice, "Who is worthy to open the scroll and break its seals?" And no one in heaven or on earth or under the earth was able to open the scroll or to look into it. And I began to weep bitterly because no one was found worthy to open the scroll or to look into it. Then one of the elders said to me, "Do not weep. See, the Lion of the tribe of Judah, the Root of David, has conquered, so that he can open the scroll and its seven seals." Then I saw between the throne and the four living creatures and among the elders a Lamb standing as if it had been slaughtered, having seven horns and seven eyes, which are the seven spirits of God sent out into all the earth. He went and took the scroll from the right hand of the one who was seated on the throne.

It is Jesus, the dead-and-risen Lion-Lamb, who opens the scroll and unleashes its contents on the earth. The first four seals opened by Jesus release on the world the infamous Four Horsemen of the Apocalypse (6:2–8):

- *The First Seal—The White Horse of Empire:* "A white horse! Its rider had a bow; a crown was given to him, and he came out conquering and to conquer."

- *The Second Seal—The Red Horse of War:* "Another horse, bright red; its rider was permitted to take peace from the earth, so that people would slaughter one another; and he was given a great sword."
- *The Third Seal—The Black Horse of Famine:* "A black horse! Its rider held a pair of scales in his hand, and I heard what seemed to be a voice in the midst of the four living creatures saying, 'A quart of wheat for a day's pay, and three quarts of barley for a day's pay, but do not damage the olive oil and the wine!'"
- *The Fourth Seal—The Green Horse of Pestilence:* "A pale green horse! Its rider's name was Death, and Hades followed with him; they were given authority over a fourth of the earth, to kill with sword, famine, and pestilence, and by the wild animals of the earth."

The Four Horsemen are sometimes interpreted differently, but the *sequence* of Conquest, War, Famine, and Pestilence as the bringers of Death and fillers of Hades will suffice here because my point is that it is Jesus Christ, the Lamb-Lion, who unleashes them on the world, according to 5:2–7. They do not simply happen as the last spasmic violence of civilization before the final transformation of the world. They are part of that transformation, and they are conducted by Christ.

The second scene occurs toward the end of the Great Apocalypse, in Revelation 19:11–21, and once again, it concerns Jesus. I do not know whether anything is deliberately intended in the repetition from that preceding scene to this one—with a more literal translation of the Greek:

I saw, and behold a white horse, and the one riding on it. (6:2)

I saw ... and behold a white horse, and the one riding on it. (19:11)

That might be pure coincidence, but even if that is all it is, I find it a most unfortunate one. Be that as it may, the conquering Christ is described in 19:11–21. It is a long citation, but I cannot excise any part of it:

> Then I saw heaven opened, and there was a white horse! Its rider is called Faithful and True, and in righteousness he judges and makes war. His eyes are like a flame of fire, and on his head are many diadems; and he has a name inscribed that no one knows but himself. He is clothed in a robe dipped in blood, and his name is called The Word of God. And the armies of heaven, wearing fine linen, white and pure, were following him on white horses. *From his mouth comes a sharp sword with which to strike down the nations, and he will rule them with a rod of iron;* he will tread the winepress of the fury of the wrath of God the Almighty. On his robe and on his thigh he has a name inscribed, *"King of kings and Lord of lords."*
>
> Then I saw an angel standing in the sun, and with a loud voice he called to all the birds that fly in midheaven, "Come, gather for the great supper of God, to eat the flesh of kings, the flesh of captains, the flesh of the mighty, the flesh of horses and their riders—flesh of all, both free and slave, both small and great." Then I saw the beast and the kings of the earth with their armies gathered to make war against the rider on the horse and against his army. And the beast was captured, and with it the false prophet who had performed in its presence the signs by which he deceived those who had received the mark of the beast and those who worshiped its image. These two were thrown alive into the lake of fire that burns with sulfur. And the rest were killed by the sword of the rider on the horse, the sword that came from his mouth; and all the birds were gorged with their flesh.

This Divine Warrior is the Lamb-Lion Jesus Christ, as is shown by earlier examples of the phrases I italicized in this citation: "from

[Jesus's] mouth came a sharp, two-edged sword" (1:16); he is the "son, a male child, who is to rule all the nations with a rod of iron" (12:5); and the imperial powers of Rome are going to "make war on the Lamb, and the Lamb will conquer them, for he is Lord of Lords and King of kings" (17:14). You will also recognize the source for the lines "Mine eyes have seen the glory of the coming of the Lord, He is trampling out the vintage where the grapes of wrath are stored"—from "The Battle Hymn of the Republic"—in the statement that Christ "will tread the winepress of the fury of the wrath of God the Almighty."

But above all else, you will recall from chapter 2 that magnificent vision of God's consummation of the earth's transformation into a world of nonviolence, justice, and peace in Isaiah 25:6–8. It was to be "a feast of rich food, a feast of well-aged wines, of rich food filled with marrow, of well-aged wines strained clear." But in the Great Apocalypse, God's eschatological feast, "the great supper of God," would be a feast for the vultures from the bodies of the slain.

You do not have to like and accept present human violence to dislike and refuse even more this vision of future divine violence. There are, as I have insisted before and now do once again, human consequences for our acts—personal, national, and global—but no divine punishments. In the last century alone, we humans have done worse things to one another on this earth and to the earth itself than anything imagined even in that terrible vision of the Warrior Christ or in any of the other visions of the Great Apocalypse. And we may yet destroy our species or our earth. But how do we dare say that God plans and wants it or that Jesus leads and effects it? For me as a Christian, that seems to be *the* crime against divinity, *the* sin against the Holy Spirit.

Earth in the Great Apocalypse

We saw already, in chapters 3 and 4, how Jesus and Paul announced that the Kingdom of God was *already* present and how they challenged believers to accept it, enter it, and live it as fully as they themselves were doing. God's Kingdom, in other words, was already freely available as a divine gift for anyone with the faith and courage to embody it. It was present here below upon this earth—whatever one thought about any future consummation. They probably also imagined a plan or model, as it were, for that perfect earthly world hidden in the Architect's Office in heaven. But, I repeat, it had already started here below with and in Jesus of Nazareth as the radicality of God's justice climactically opposing the normalcy of civilization's injustice.

The Book of Revelation agrees that the Kingdom of God is already present—*but in heaven up above rather than upon earth here below.* Here is earth: "The great dragon was thrown down, that ancient serpent, who is called the Devil and Satan, the deceiver of the whole world—he was thrown down to the earth, and his angels were thrown down with him" (12:9). Here is heaven: "The kingdom of the world has become the kingdom of our Lord and of his Messiah, and he will reign forever and ever" (11:15).

Christ has called Christians "to be a kingdom, priests serving his God and Father" (1:6), and John himself is "your brother who [shares] with you in Jesus the persecution and the kingdom and the patient endurance" (1:9). But actual martyrdom, or at least potential martyrdom, is how one enters that heavenly Kingdom, as we saw in 6:9–11, where the "slaughtered" martyrs cry out for vengeance. Furthermore, before martyrdom—or even instead of it—Christians should enter God's heavenly Kingdom by celibate asceticism:

> Then I looked, and there was the Lamb, standing on Mount Zion! And with him were one hundred forty-four thousand ... who have been redeemed from the earth. It is these who have not defiled themselves with women, for they are virgins; these follow the Lamb wherever he goes. They have been redeemed from humankind as first fruits for God and the Lamb, and in their mouth no lie was found; they are blameless. (14:1, 3–5)

Rome has taken over the earth, and you can read what the angels will do to the imperial world—as *imperial* and as *world*—in 8:7–10:7 and 16:1–21. John's message about the earth is for virgins and martyrs: "Come out of her, my people" (18:4). They are to "come out" not by incarnating God's Kingdom in and against the world but by abandoning the earth to its fate and leaving it for heaven. At the start of the Great Apocalypse, John announces that earth's final destruction is "what must soon take place ... for the time is near" (1:1, 3), and at the end he repeats, "what must soon take place ... for the time is near" (22:6, 10).

Those virgins and martyrs "who have come out of the great ordeal" have left this doomed earth and are already in the heavenly Kingdom, where "they will hunger no more, and thirst no more; the sun will not strike them, nor any scorching heat; for the Lamb at the center of the throne will be their shepherd, and he will guide them to springs of the water of life, and God will wipe away every tear from their eyes" (7:14, 16–17). That prepares us for this final consummation:

Then I saw a new heaven and a new earth; for the first heaven and the first earth had passed away, and the sea was no more. And I saw the holy city, the new Jerusalem, coming down out of heaven from God, prepared as a bride adorned for her husband. And I heard a loud voice from the throne saying, "See, the home of God is among mortals. He will dwell with them as their God; they will be his peoples, and God himself will be with them; he will wipe every tear from their eyes. Death will be no more; mourning and crying and pain will be no more, for the first things have passed away." And the one who was seated on the throne said, "See, I am making all things new." (21:1–5)

It is hard to imagine a more magnificent consummation, but it will all be done by God and only after that terribly violent ethnic cleansing in the preceding chapters, with its climactic vulture-feast

at Armageddon in 19:11–21. In conclusion, therefore, the Book of
Revelation is the Christian Bible's last and thus far most successful
attempt to subsume the radicality of God's nonviolence into the
normalcy of civilization's violence. That is the vision of John of
Patmos. "In the spirit he carried me away to a great, high mountain and showed me the holy city Jerusalem coming down out of
heaven from God" (21:10). Heaven *to earth,* certainly, but as replacement for an earth destroyed rather than as reformation for an
earth transfigured.

On March 31, 1968—a week before he was assassinated—the
Reverend Martin Luther King Jr. chose that apocalyptic vision to
conclude his sermon "Remaining Awake Through a Great Revolution," delivered at the National Cathedral in Washington, D.C.:

> Thank God for John, who centuries ago out on a lonely, ob-
> scure island called Patmos caught vision of a new Jerusalem
> descending out of heaven from God, who heard a voice
> saying, "Behold, I make all things new; former things are
> passed away." God grant that we will be participants in this
> newness and this magnificent development. If we will but do
> it, we will bring about a new day of justice and brotherhood
> and peace. And that day the morning stars will sing together
> and the sons of God will shout for joy.

But you can see that King interpreted that vision by the First rather
than the Second Coming of Jesus. As we saw earlier for Jesus of
Nazareth and Paul of Tarsus—but not for John of Patmos—that all-
new world depends on our becoming "participants" with God so
that, together, "if we will but do it, we will bring about a new day of
justice and brotherhood and peace." But as Christianity follows John
in emphasizing the Second over the First Coming, and apocalypse
over incarnation, it finds itself waiting for God to act violently while
God is waiting for us to act nonviolently.

That leaves me with these conclusions. The Second Coming of
Christ is not an event that we should expect to happen *soon*. The

Second Coming of Christ is not an event that we should expect to happen *violently*. The Second Coming of Christ is not an event that we should expect to happen *literally*. The Second Coming of Christ is what will happen when we Christians finally accept that the First Coming was the Only Coming and start to cooperate with its divine presence.

LAMB AND WHORE, LION AND WITCH

On December 9, 2005, the film version of the 1950 book *The Lion, the Witch, and the Wardrobe,* the second book of C. S. Lewis's seven-book Chronicles of Narnia series, was released, with a PG rating for its "battle sequences and frightening moments."

The book begins like this: "Once there were four children whose names were Peter, Susan, Edmund, and Lucy. This story is about something that happened to them when they were sent away from London during the war because of the air-raids." The film begins with German voices and bombers, British search-lights and anti-aircraft tracers. After that, the film is very faithful to the book but with some exceptions, such as Santa Claus bringing armor and not only weapons for the boys and the White Witch having polar bears for her war-chariot. In any case, when a verbal medium becomes visual, violence is necessarily heightened and intensified. In both book and film, the four siblings, displaced from London to the countryside, pass through a wardrobe into "some other world," or "another world," or "the other world" of Narnia.

The film's publicity strove mightily to have it both ways by asserting, in different contexts, that the story *was* and/or *was not* an allegory for Christianity. It could therefore attract the audience of *The Passion of the Christ* as well as the audience of *The Lord of the Rings.* It is, of course, an allegory, and indeed a super-allegory, of Christianity. It ranges beyond Christianity itself to show how many other (false) religious myths find their fulfillment in the (true) Christian one.

Alan Jacobs's 2005 biography of C. S. Lewis, *The Narnian: The Life and Imagination of C. S. Lewis,* records this letter of Lewis's from October 1931:

> Now the story of Christ is simply a true myth: a myth work-
> ing on us in the same way as the others, but with tremendous
> difference that it *really happened:* and one must be content to
> accept it in the same way, remembering that it is God's myth
> where the others are men's myths: i.e. the Pagan stories are
> God expressing himself through the minds of poets, using
> such images as He found there, while Christianity is God ex-
> pressing himself through "real things." (p. 149)

In this Christian super-allegory, good versus evil appears as the lion Aslan versus the White Witch. The book—and even more so the film—gets its triumphant divine violence from the Apocalypse of John, which has fed alike both the allegory in the Chronicles of Narnia and the fantasy in the Left Behind series. Here are the three major allegorical features connecting Aslan and Jesus, the Lion and the Christ, the fictional "son of the great Emperor-beyond-the-Sea" (p. 79) and the biblical Son of God.

First, in a Gethsemane Garden scene, Aslan's "tail and his head hung low and he walked slowly as if he were very, very tired." He tells Susan and Lucy, "You may come, if you will promise to stop when I tell you, and after that leave me to go on alone." Then "he stumbled and gave a low moan," and declared himself to be "sad and lonely." He finally told them to stay behind as he "walked out on to the top of the hill" (pp. 149–50).

Next, Aslan/Christ gives his own life to save that of the traitor Edmund and dies "instead of him ... surrounded by the whole crowd of creatures kicking him, hitting him, spitting on him, jeering at him" (p. 154). He dies, under the White Witch's knife, "instead of" Edmund (p. 155).

Then Aslan resurrects as the Stone Table/Stone Tomb splits in two. "The Stone Table was broken into two pieces by a great crack that ran down it from end to end; and there was no Aslan" (p. 161). He then appears first to the young women, Lucy and Susan: "'Aren't you dead then, dear Aslan?' said Lucy. 'Not now,' said Aslan. 'You're not—not a —?' asked Susan in a shaky voice. She couldn't bring herself to say the word ghost" (p. 162).

Finally, before his death and the final war, Aslan "went on to outline two plans of battle—one for fighting the Witch and her people in the wood and another for assaulting her castle" (p. 146). Then, after his resurrection and during that final battle,

> with a roar that shook all Narnia from the western lamp-post to the shores of the eastern sea the great beast [Aslan] flung himself upon the White Witch. Lucy saw her face lifted toward him for one second with an expression of terror and amazement. Then Lion and Witch had rolled over together but with the Witch underneath.... Most of the enemy had been killed in the first charge of Aslan and his companions; and when those who were still living saw that the Witch was dead they either gave themselves up or took to flight. (pp. 177–78)

The brutal sexism of Romans against Amazons has returned via Revelation's Lamb against Whore to reappear in Narnia's Lion against Witch.

There is, as Lewis said, a magic deeper and older than that of the White Witch. That Emperor's Magic was established in "the stillness and the darkness before Time dawned," and it proclaimed "that when a willing victim who had committed no treachery was killed in a traitor's stead, the table would crack and Death would start working backward" (p. 163). And then the nonviolent Victim returns as the violent Avenger?

I myself believe every bit as deeply as Jack Lewis did in that primordial magic, but it was revealed for me in the First and not the Second Coming of Christ. It was revealed by Jesus of the gospel, riding on a docile donkey, and not by Jesus of the apocalypse, riding on a battle stallion. To turn Jesus into a divine warrior allows once again—but now terminally in the last book of the Bible—the normalcy of human civilization's violent injustice to subsume the radicality of God's nonviolent justice.

My point about *The Lion, the Witch, and the Wardrobe* is not, emphatically not, to equate the Narnia series with the Left Behind series. They are utterly different in tone, style, and grace, in basic theology, in simple decency, and in common humanity. The Left Behind series is based on a two-hundred-year-old idiosyncratic belief in a two-stage Second Coming of Christ. The Narnia series is based on a two-thousand-year-old traditional belief in the Double Coming of Christ—a First Coming that ends in sacrificial death and bodily resurrection and a Second Coming that ends in the climactic battle of good and evil. Also, Lewis, unlike Jenkins-LaHaye, never falls into absolutely unconscious self-parody, such as can be found in the final volume of the Left Behind series, entitled *Glorious Appearing: The End of Days.*

For example, an incident that takes place at the Damascus Gate of Jerusalem features Montgomery Cleburn "Mac" McCullum, who is a "former pilot for Global Community [GC] Supreme Potentate Nicolae Carpathia" and has now converted to become the "chief Tribulation Force pilot on assignment at Petra" (p. ix). "'Lord, forgive me,' he breathed, spraying his Uzi and dropping at least a dozen GC from behind. He felt no remorse. *All's fair.*... It was only fitting, he decided, that the devil's crew were dressed in black. *Live by the sword, die by the sword*" (p. 27). Mac destroys his opponents with no sense of remorse—and no sense of irony either.

In another example, Mac is in conversation with another Tribulation Force pilot named Abdullah Smith. Their location is the plain of Jezreel or Esraelon or Megiddo—whence our name Armageddon. "'Isn't Jesus' hometown up there somewhere? Nazareth?' Mac asked Abdullah. 'On the northern side of the valley,' Abdullah said. 'Imagine how it will feel for Him to fight an entire army that close to home'" (p. 235). You can almost imagine the TV interviewer asking, *How does it feel, Jesus …*

Once all of these quite significant differences between the Narnia and Left Behind series are properly and fairly emphasized, this must still be said, and this is my point. Each series climaxes with the last book of the Bible, the Great Apocalypse in the Book of Revelation. The climactic battles in each are won by a violent, warlike Christ. Indeed both the Narnia and Left Behind series go beyond the biblical Book of Revelation. There is no suggestion in that latter text that Christians will participate in any way in the divine violence of the returning Christ. But each of the series presumes and describes—in its own way, to be sure—both that and how apocalyptic violence involves not only God and Christ but faithful Christians as well. That is, of course, the logical conclusion from combining collaborative eschatology and divine violence. Once again, as always, the fundamental question is whether we Christians imagine our God as violent or nonviolent.

"Put your sword back into its place," says Jesus to Peter in the Gospel of Matthew, "for all who take the sword will perish by the sword" (26:52).

"You have forgotten to clean your sword," says Aslan to Peter in *The Lion, the Witch, and the Wardrobe.* "Whatever happens, never forget to wipe your sword" (pp. 132–33).

EPILOGUE

The 10,000-year experiment of the settled life will stand or
fall by what we do, and don't do, now.
                              —RONALD WRIGHT,
                              A Short History of Progress (2004)

I have spent the last thirty-five years thinking about earliest Christianity—from the historical Jesus, through the birth of Christianity,
and on to the apostle Paul—and attempting to live within its visionary program for our world. Earliest Christianity arose within
the *Old* Roman Empire, and America, we are told, is the *New*
Roman Empire. Three questions are then obvious for anyone who
is both Christian and American today:

How is it possible to be a faithful Christian in the American Empire?
But then another question appears beneath that one:

*How is it possible to be a nonviolent Christian within a violent Chris-
tianity based on a violent Christian Bible?*
Chapter 5 brought those two questions together into a third
question:

*How is it possible to be a faithful Christian in an American Empire
facilitated by a violent Christian Bible?*
In this book, I have attempted to answer that last question on the
deepest level possible—on the level where the radicality of God's
nonviolence constantly challenges the normalcy of civilization's violence and where the normalcy of civilization consistently negates
the radicality of God. The story of that struggle is the integrity of

the Christian Bible for itself, its authority for Christians, and its value for anyone. It is the radicality of God's justice and not the normalcy of civilization's injustice that, as a Christian, I find incarnate in Jesus of Nazareth. Thereafter, within the Christian Bible's New Testament, first Paul of Tarsus lives and proclaims that same radical God until his vision is deradicalized by the pseudo-Pauline letters, and finally, John of Patmos deradicalizes the nonviolent Jesus on the donkey by transforming him into the violent Jesus on the battle stallion. In conclusion, I leave you with three images for the struggle—ever-ancient and ever-new—emphasized by those three questions.

The first image is from an article posted on WSJ.com's *Opinion-Journal* from *The Wall Street Journal* Editorial Page on October 27, 2005. Peggy Noonan argues there that some (but not all) of America's elite professional leadership—"the ones who are supposed to dig us out and lead us"—have made "a separate peace" with imminent disaster. They recognize that "in some deep and fundamental way things have broken down and can't be fixed, or won't be fixed any time soon," and "they consciously, or unconsciously, [take] grim comfort in this thought: I got mine. Which is what the separate peace comes down to, 'I got mine, you get yours.'"

Although Noonan once coined phrases of spectacular inaccuracy in speeches for the elder President Bush—think, for example, of "a thousand points of light" or "a kinder, gentler nation" or, especially, "read my lips: no new taxes"—she may well be right about "a separate peace." My present focus, however, is on the metaphor repeated throughout her article. Here it is as a medley:

> The wheels are coming off the trolley and the trolley off the tracks.... Off the tracks and hurtling forward, toward an unknown destination.... The wheels are coming off the trolley.... Trolley thoughts are out there.... The wheels are off the trolley and the trolley's off the tracks.... There are a lot of people... trying to... get the trolley back on the tracks.... There are two groups. One has made a separate peace, and

one is trying ...[but] wonder[s] if they'll go... into bad territory with the trolley.

The metaphor is for me an image of the decline and fall of
empire, a symbol of what has happened to every empire that has
ever existed: eventually the wheels come off the trolley and the
trolley comes off the tracks. But I read it here not just as a metaphor but as an allegory of imperial destiny with the wheels as violence, the trolley as empire, and the tracks as civilization. There
have been enough imperial crashes throughout history to question
not only about the wheels of violence and the trolley of empire
but especially about the tracks of civilization itself. And that question was already raised long, long ago by Jesus to Pilate and by
Paul to Corinth when they used "this-world" for the violent normalcy of civilization. So there remain these three: the Trolley, the
Wheels, and the Tracks, but the greatest of them is the Tracks.

The second image is from the biblical tradition. The metaphori-
cal geography of that great tradition was composed of three territories. To the west and the setting sun was the Sea, which was
imagined as wild and chaotic, beating always against the Land, and
seeking to destroy it. You will recall from chapter 5 that the Babylonian, Medean, Persian, and Macedonian Empires of Daniel and
the Roman Empire of Revelation were like fierce beasts that rose
from out of the chaos of the Sea.

In the center was the Land, which was granted to God's people
to be maintained in justice and holiness. It was God's staging area
for the justification of the entire earth. The Torah relentlessly attempted to establish that realm of divine justice, and as the prophets
bore eloquent witness, the normalcy of life worked steadily to
defeat it.

To the east and the rising sun was the Desert. Everything came
from there, and to it everything returned to be renewed and
started over again. It was the geographical witness that the normalcy of human civilization was not the inevitability of human
nature. That, of course, was why both Jewish and Christian monks

chose to live there. It was only after God's people had spent time
in the Desert that they entered the Land. It was only after spend-
ing forty days in the Desert that Jesus was ready to return to the
Land. And above all else, it was in the Desert that Satan promised
Jesus world dominion (Matthew 4:8–10 and Luke 4:5–8)—he
could enter the Land and the whole world as its demonic ruler.
Jesus was offered and refused the redundancy of demonic imperialism. So there remain these three: the Sea, the Land, and the
Desert, but the greatest of them is the Desert.

The third image is my own way of rephrasing the biblical tradition from microcosm to macrocosm. Imagine, on the model of
plate tectonics beneath our geological earth, the metaphor of plate
tectonics beneath our historical world.

Deep below the surface of history is a giant tectonic plate that
some have called Macroparasitism, Kleptocracy, the Cage, or the
Trap but that I call Civilization itself. The normalcy or even the
cutting edge of human civilization in all its imperial inevitability
has as its chant "First victory, then peace," or "Peace by victory."

On one side, another plate grinds relentlessly against that great
central one. Some call it Idealism, Utopia, Eschatology, or Apocalypse, but I call it Post-Civilization, and its chant is "First justice,
then peace," or "Peace by justice."

On the other side of Civilization's great central plate, a third
one also grinds relentlessly against it. Some call it Nihilism, Genocide, Totalitarianism, or Terrorism, but I call it Anti-Civilization,
and its chant is "First death, then peace," or "Peace by death."

The plate tectonics of human history curve around, as does our
globe, so that the two smaller plates of Anti-Civilization and Post-
Civilization grind not only against Civilization but also against
each other. In the first century, however, and indeed for most of
the next two thousand years, Post-Civilization's nonviolent alternative seemed to many of us a sweetly romantic, politically irrelevant, and idealistically unreal dream. Or else, of course, it was safely
transferred from earth to heaven, from present to future, from the

external to the internal life, or from an enfleshed spirit to a disembodied soul.

Now, at the start of the twenty-first century, Post-Civilization's message seems more like a terrible warning two millennia ahead of its time. "If you live by the sword you will die by it" no longer applies minimally to Israel or maximally to Rome, but minimally to the world and maximally to the earth. So, then, there remain these three: Anti-Civilization, Civilization, and Post-Civilization, but the greatest of these is Post-Civilization.

I make no presumption that my own Christianity is the first, best, last, or only vision for global peace on our distracted earth. But I have talked primarily about Christianity, the Bible, and America in this book because I have spent all of my life as a Christian, half of my life as a biblical scholar, and the end of my life as an American citizen. This book is therefore less an exercise in historical reconstruction than a witness in religious responsibility.

My conclusion is that there is both good news and bad news. The bad news is that our problem is as deep as human civilization itself. Jesus described that problem to Pilate as the violence of "this-world," a term it is necessary to hyphenate lest we confuse it with "the-world" or "the-earth," which means creation as belonging to God. Jesus's "this-world" means what we have done with "the-world," and the best commentary on the escalatory violence of our desecration is from Paul in 1 Corinthians 1–4. He told the Corinthians, for example, that "the wisdom of this-world is foolishness with God" (3:19), that "the present form of this-world is passing away" (7:31), that (changing the phrase to an equivalent) "the rulers of this-age ... are doomed to perish" (2:6), and that "the rulers of this-age ... crucified the Lord of glory" (2:8).

The good news, as just seen from Jesus and Paul, is that the violent normalcy of human civilization is not the inevitable destiny of human nature. Christian faith and human evolution agree on that point. Since we *invented* civilization some six thousand years ago along the irrigated floodplains of great rivers, we can also *un-invent* it—we can create its alternative. In the challenge of Christian faith, we are called to cooperate in establishing the Kingdom of God in a transformed earth. In the challenge of human evolution, we are called to Post-Civilization, to imagine it, to create it, and to enjoy it on a transfigured earth.

INDEX